Daily Hope

WITH

Lady Rhoda Obiri Yeboah

PUBLISHED BY
KRATOS PUBLISHER

Daily Hope with Lady Rhoda Obiri Yeboah
Copyright © 2024 Lady Rhoda Obiri Yeboah
Published by: Kratos Publisher

All rights reserved under international copyright law. No part of this book may be reproduced without permission in writing from the copyright owner, except by a reviewer, who may quote brief passages in review.

Scripture quotations are from:

Amplified Bible (AMP)

Copyright © 2015 by The Lockman Foundation, La Habra, CA 90631. All rights reserved.

Amplified Bible, Classic Edition (AMPC)

Copyright © 1954, 1958, 1962, 1964, 1965, 1987 by The Lockman Foundation

Berean Study Bible (BSB) Public Domain

BRG Bible (BRG)

Blue Red and Gold Letter Edition™ Copyright © 2012 BRG Bible Ministries. Used by Permission. All rights reserved. BRG Bible is a Registered Trademark in U.S. Patent and Trademark Office #4145648

Contemporary English Version (CEV)

Copyright © 1995 by American Bible Society For more information about CEV, visit www.bibles.com and www.cev.bible.

Easy-to-Read Version (ERV)

Copyright © 2006 by Bible League International

EasyEnglish Bible (EASY)

EasyEnglish Bible Copyright © MissionAssist 2019 - Charitable Incorporated Organisation 1162807. Used by permission. All rights reserved.

English Standard Version (ESV)

The Holy Bible, English Standard Version. ESV® Text Edition: 2016. Copyright © 2001 by Crossway Bibles, a publishing ministry of Good News Publishers.

GOD'S WORD Translation (GW)

Copyright © 1995, 2003, 2013, 2014, 2019, 2020 by God's Word to the Nations Mission Society. All rights reserved.

Good News Translation (GNT)

Good News Translation® (Today's English Version, Second Edition) © 1992 American Bible Society. All rights reserved. For more information about GNT, visit www.bibles.com and www.gnt.bible.

King James Version (KJV) Public Domain

King James Version, American Edition (KJVAAE)

King James Version 1611, spelling, punctuation and text formatting modernized by ABS in 1962; typesetting © 2010 American Bible Society.

The Message (MSG)

Copyright © 1993, 2002, 2018 by Eugene H. Peterson

New Century Version (NCV)

The Holy Bible, New Century Version®. Copyright © 2005 by Thomas Nelson, Inc.

New International Version (NIV)

Holy Bible, New International Version®, NIV® Copyright ©1973, 1978, 1984, 2011 by Biblica, Inc.® Used by permission. All rights reserved worldwide.

New International Reader's Version (NIRV)

Copyright © 1995, 1996, 1998, 2014 by Biblica, Inc.®. Used by permission. All rights reserved worldwide.

New Living Translation (NLT)

Copyright © 1996, 2004, 2015 by Tyndale House Foundation. All rights reserved.

New Revised Standard Version, Anglicised (NRSVA)

New Revised Standard Version Bible: Anglicised Edition, copyright © 1989, 1995 the Division of Christian Education of the National Council of the Churches of Christ in the United States of America. Used by permission. All rights reserved.

Revised Standard Version (RSV)

Revised Standard Version of the Bible, copyright © 1946, 1952, and 1971 the Division of Christian Education of the National Council of the Churches of Christ in the United States of America. Used by permission. All rights reserved.

The Living Bible (TLB)

Copyright © 1971 by Tyndale House Foundation. All rights reserved.

Tree of Life Version (TLV)

Tree of Life (TLV) Translation of the Bible. Copyright © 2015 by The Messianic Jewish Family Bible Society.

The Passion Translation® (TPT)

Copyright © 2017, 2018, 2020 by Passion & Fire Ministries, Inc. Used by permission. All rights reserved. ThePassionTranslation.com

The Weymouth New Testament Public Domain

Young's Literal Translation (YLT) Public Domain

DEDICATION

To my dad Rev. Yaw Obiri Yeboah, I have seen the work of God through your life. A testament that who He loves, He keeps. Thank you for showing me the love and trust Christ has for His children. I love you.

CONTENTS

DEDICATION	i
INTRODUCTION	v
JANUARY	
Holy Spirit	6
Breath of God	20
The Gospel	26
Faith	33
Wisdom	35
FEBRUARY	
Free From Sin	42
Christian Life	45
Challenges	52
Commit to God	58
MARCH	
God's Promise to Abraham	74
His Promise	83
APRIL	
Christ Our Example	107
Paul Exhorts	113
Claim the Word	122
Repent	127
Our Strength	131
MAY	
Rejoice	142
His Mercies	149
Prayer and Praise	153
God of Justice	158
Hurt	161
Listening to God	166
JUNE	

Praise God	179
God's Love	181
Give Thanks	185
Our Help and Confidence	188
Speak the Work	192
Faithfulness	195
Names of God	197
JULY	
Victory	216
Peace and Blessing	219
God's Work	222
Great God	225
Praise the Lord	231
Safe in Christ	235
AUGUST	
Prayer	253
How to Pray	265
Pray for Others	271
Pray for Victory	278
SEPTEMBER	
God's Goodness	288
Bless the Lord	297
God is King	307
Trust God	315
OCTOBER	
Have Faith	322
New Life	337
NOVEMBER	
Pray Always	355
Worship God	380
DECEMBER	
God Remembers	387
Be Thankful	391

Seek God	408
Christ came	412
ABOUT THE AUTHOR	423

INTRODUCTION

In the beginning Scriptures reveal the voice of Elohim (God) walking in the garden of Eden to commune with Adam and Eve. The desire of Elohim is to relate with humans. Although Him being the Spirit, He chose to reveal Himself through our experiences with Him, in our everyday interactions, through creation, dreams, visions and many other ways.

This devotional purposes to help you develop your spiritual sight, insights, intellect, understanding, wisdom, knowledge and enhance your experience with the one who wants to be known.

As you read through the Scriptures and exaltations, the Holy Spirit is with you to reveal more to you according to your need. He is present with you and able to bring life through His Word to your everyday situations.

Trust Him through every page, He is with you. Talk to Him, ask questions, and trust the inner voice that will answer.

Be engulfed by the Spirit of the Word. Happy reading.

Lady Rhoda

JANUARY

Holy Spirit

JANUARY

Day 1

And behold, I send the promise of my Father upon you; but stay in the city, until you are clothed with power from on high.
Luke 24:49 RSV

The last words of a dying person are very important. But thanks be to God that Jesus is alive. Our Lord's last command to His disciples on the day of ascension was to wait for the promise of the Father.

The Holy Spirit is the most important personality on this earth. If you desire to live successfully in this life on earth and after, you need the Holy Spirit, the third person of the Trinity.

Through our earthly life, the Lord commands us to walk in the Supernatural. We can only do this with the help of His Spirit. The spirit life is an interesting one. Get ready to journey with the third person of the Trinity. Selah (Pause and meditate).

PRAYER

Father, thank you for your Spirit. I welcome Him into my life and ask that He teaches me your will and way through Christ our Lord Amen.

JANUARY

Day 2

And behold, I am sending the promise of my Father upon you. But stay in the city until you are clothed with power from on high. Then he led them out as far as Bethany, and lifting up his hands he blessed them.
Luke 24:49-50 RSV

The presence of God brings enlightenment. His presence lifts burdens and brings peace. The last words of Jesus our Lord promised that He will send the promise of the Father upon you which is the Holy Spirit. This Spirit, as we have learned, has everyone who has accepted Jesus as their Lord and Saviour. You are a carrier of the Holy Spirit. He lives in you, Amen.

He added specifically, wait not only for the Holy Spirit but also for Power from on high. There is a big difference between having the Holy Spirit and having the Power of the Spirit. Acts 10:38 says, *"How God anointed Jesus of Nazareth with the Holy Ghost and with power: who went about doing good, and healing all that were oppressed of the devil; for God was with him."* Don't just be content with the presence of the Holy Spirit, wait on God to anoint you with His power before you go about doing anything.

PRAYER

Holy Spirit, thank you for making me your dwelling. Teach me how to wait on you, grant me a discerning heart to know your power through Christ our Lord, Amen.

JANUARY

Day 3

How God anointed Jesus of Nazareth with the Holy Spirit with power that He went about everywhere doing acts of kindness; and curing all who were being continually oppressed by the Devil--for God was with Jesus.
Acts 10:38 Weymouth New Testament

Now that you know you have the Holy Spirit residing in you, you need to learn how to wait for His guidance and power. You will only be equipped for the *assignment* in which He will anoint you as you wait on Him. When God anointed Jesus with the Holy Ghost and Power, He was led to act in a particular way to the glory of God. Scriptures say that Jesus went about doing acts of kindness, healing diseases, and delivering the oppressed of the devil.

The Power God gives is for a purpose. Isaiah 61:1-3, and Luke 4:18 says, the Spirit of the Lord is on me to preach good tidings to the poor. You are empowered for a purpose. Be obedient to the will and counsel of the Almighty God. He always leads us in triumph. Selah. (Pause and Meditate)

PRAYER

Father God, thank you for the leadership of the Holy Spirit in my life. I submit to Him to lead me in all my ways in Jesus' name, Amen.

JANUARY

Day 4

In the beginning, God created the heavens and the earth. The earth was without form and void, and darkness was upon the face of the deep; and the Spirit of God was moving over the face of the waters.
Genesis 1:1-2 RSV

In the beginning, God brought into existence what already existed. He brought into being what was. Hebrews 11:3 of the Berean Study Bible says, "*By faith, we understand that the universe was formed at God's command, so that what is seen was not made out of what was visible.*"

The wisdom of God brought into our physical sphere what He wants you and me to see and know. Remember, the secret things belong to God, but what is revealed is for us and our children (Deuteronomy 29:29).

Amid His creation was a condition of darkness, but the presence of the Spirit of God brought light. It is important to know that everything created has a "spirit" that governs it.

Your victory as a child of God is to know whose you are and walk in the grace given you by faith. Jesus has already overcome. You have the Spirit of God (1 John 5:4). You are an overcomer in Jesus' name.

PRAYER

Heavenly Father, I thank you for the grace to do your will. Holy Spirit, you are welcome in my life. Amen.

JANUARY

Day 5

The Sovereign Lord has filled me with his Spirit. He has chosen me and sent me to bring good news to the poor, to heal the broken-hearted, to announce release to captives and freedom to those in prison.
Isaiah 61:1 GNT

Through the Word, we have established that the "Dunamis", or power/force of God, comes on a man for a purpose. Throughout the scriptures in the Old Testament, the Holy Spirit empowers or comes on someone for the assignment given to them. But in our dispensation the Holy Spirit through Christ lives in us.

Jesus in the synagogue in Luke 4:18 read this verse to fulfil what was written. As He fulfilled the scriptures concerning Himself, you are also called to proclaim the good news by His Spirit in you. Proclaim the gospel of our Lord Jesus Christ to the poor, heal the broken-hearted, reach out to those who have no hope, loosen the bonds of the captives, and bring freedom to those in prison by pain, fear and discouragement.

You are the one sent because you have the Holy Spirit. Take the message of the cross to the ends of the earth. The Sovereign Lord has filled you with His Spirit.

PRAYER

I am filled with God's spirit. I am empowered to preach the gospel, heal the sick, raise the dead and bring freedom to the captive. Holy Spirit, guide my steps and lead me to those I need to touch with your word today. Amen.

JANUARY

Day 6

It is clear that Christ himself wrote this letter and sent it by us. It is written, not with ink but with the Spirit of the living God, and not on stone tablets but on human hearts.
2 Corinthians 3:3 GNT

The Spirit of God is a master architect. Not only does He brood over the secrets of the Lord, Genesis 1:2, but He also inscribes the Word of God on our hearts.

Jeremiah 31:33: *"But this is the covenant I will make with the house of Israel after those days, declares the LORD. I will put My law in their minds and inscribe it on their hearts. And I will be their God, and they will be My people.*

God's covenant with you is such that He has put His words in you. You know the truth, and can discern right, and wrong and know what God's will is.

Your part is to be equipped in your inner man by the same Spirit of truth to walk by faith and not by sight. You can only do this by the Spirit's help. "We say this because we have confidence in God through Christ." 2 Corinthians 3:4 GNT. Selah.

Study the Word of the Lord to know His will and mind concerning how you should live. You are not alone.

PRAYER

Thank you, Spirit of God, for equipping me with all that I need to bring glory to your name on this day. Amen.

JANUARY

Day 7

There is nothing in us that allows us to claim that we are capable of doing this work. The capacity we have comes from God; it is he who made us capable of serving the new covenant, which consists not of a written law but of the Spirit. The written law brings death, but the Spirit gives life.
2 Corinthians 3:5-6 GNT

"But by the grace of God I am what I am, and His grace to me was not in vain. No, I worked harder than all of them— yet not I, but the grace of God that was with me."
1 Corinthians 15:10 TLV

Identity is a very important thing in our walk on earth. Your knowledge of yourself as a child of God will aid you in a victorious lifestyle on this earth. Our main verse echoes what Christ has accomplished for us.

The grace of God does it in our obedience. Our obedience to the Word and the Spirit of God makes the will of God complete in our lives on this earth.

Our union with the Word of God as priests, prophets, and kings solidifies who we are and our walk of faith. You are who God says you are: a royal priesthood, a holy nation, God's special possession (1 Peter 2:9). Selah. (pause and meditate)

PRAYER

Father God, thank you for making me like you. I believe that as you are, so I am on this earth. I live for the glory of your name through Christ our Lord Amen.

JANUARY

Day 8

The Law was carved in letters on stone tablets, and God's glory appeared when it was given. Even though the brightness on Moses' face was fading, it was so strong that the people of Israel could not keep their eyes fixed on him. If the Law, which brings death when it is in force, came with such glory, how much greater is the glory that belongs to the activity of the Spirit!
2 Corinthians 3:7-8 GNT

This kind of glory comes with an intimate relationship with the Holy Spirit. He rubs His splendour on you. His fragrance is smeared on you as you tarry on Him.

In the Old Testament, Moses had an encounter with the Lord where the glory of Elohim was smeared like oil on him. The children of Israel couldn't look at him, he had to cover his face. You too can have this kind of glory on you on this earth, through your intimacy with the Holy Spirit which will be evident for all to see (Exodus 34:35).

In the New Testament, the glory of the Spirit of God beautifully manifested on the day of Jesus's baptism. The scriptures say it descended like a dove (Luke 3:22). The disciples of Jesus were identified by the glory of the presence of the Holy Spirit (Acts 4:13). You are a carrier of the divine personality of God- the Holy Spirit. As you wait on Him, He will smear His presence on you. Selah

PRAYER

Holy Spirit my beautifier, as I tarry on you, glorify thou me with the glory of the Christ, Amen.

JANUARY
Day 9

The Law was carved in letters on stone tablets, and God's glory appeared when it was given. Even though the brightness on Moses' face was fading, it was so strong that the people of Israel could not keep their eyes fixed on him. If the Law, which brings death when it is in force, came with such glory, how much greater is the glory that belongs to the activity of the Spirit! The system which brings condemnation was glorious; how much more glorious is the activity which brings salvation!
2 Corinthians 3:7-9 GNT

Although the Word of God was on a tablet of stone, it came with the glory of God. How much more the Spirit of God who dwells in you?

The law or commandments of God was glorious because it was written by Himself. How much more so now that we are not under law but under grace? (Romans 6:14). Whereby God's laws are written on the tablets of our heart (Romans 2:15), which makes you a glorified temple. Hallelujah, praise God.

You are sanctified by truth, which is the Word (John 17:17). You are glorious in God's sight. No wonder He calls you a royal priesthood, a peculiar people, holy (1 Peter 2:9). You are not an ordinary temple. Selah.

PRAYER

Father God, thank you for choosing me to be the host of your presence. May your name be praised through Christ our Lord. Amen.

JANUARY

Day 10

Now, "the Lord" in this passage is the Spirit; and where the Spirit of the Lord is present, there is freedom. All of us, then, reflect the glory of the Lord with uncovered faces; and that same glory, coming from the Lord, who is the Spirit, transforms us into his likeness in an ever-greater degree of glory.
2 Corinthians 3:17-18 GNT

The Lord expressed in this study is the Spirit. Where the Spirit of the Lord is present, there is liberty. Freedom is the publicising of God's goodness. John 8:32: "Then you will know the truth, and the truth will set you free." Celebrate the truth of God by being free to express yourself in the liberty of your salvation.

Psalm 84:7 "They go from strength to strength, until each appears before God in Zion." You are set free, transformed into the likeness of God in greater glory. You are living in that glorified life delights God and blesses His name.

John 17:22 "I have given them the glory You gave Me, so that they may be one as We are one." Your manifestation testifies to your oneness with God. Do not be afraid, child of God, to walk in this newness of life. Selah.

PRAYER

My Father, thank you for making me unique just like Jesus. I thank you for the grace to walk in this identity I have in you through Christ our Lord Amen.

JANUARY

Day 11

But thanks be to God! For in union with Christ we are always led by God as prisoners in Christ's victory procession. God uses us to make the knowledge about Christ spread everywhere like a sweet fragrance.
2 Corinthians 2:14 GNT

Romans 8:14 says, "For all who are being led by the Spirit of God, these are sons and daughters of God." Thanks be to God, you and I are led by the Spirit of God. As we decide to live in union with Christ and in obedience, the Holy Spirit will lead us.

You are led as a child of God and in Christ's victory procession. Hallelujah, praise God. What does that mean to you? It means as a prisoner of Christ, you are not of yourself. He leads you in the path of righteousness that will lead only to victory.

The victory has already been won in Christ. We need to trust the Holy Spirit to lead us. In His leading, He makes the knowledge of Christ known. Such wisdom is profound and only found in our union with Christ (2 Corinthians 4:7). You are earthen vessels, that the excellency will be of God a sweet fragrance. It is the work of the Spirit. Selah.

PRAYER

Spirit of the living God, I am your prisoner to lead and do as you will with my life. I humble myself to you. Lead my Lord, Amen.

JANUARY

Day 12

For we are like a sweet-smelling incense offered by Christ to God, [...] For those who are being lost, it is a deadly stench that kills; but for those who are being saved, it is a fragrance that brings life. Who, then, is capable for such a task?
2 Corinthians 2:15-16 GNT

After accepting Jesus as your Lord and Saviour, you have to make that decision in your heart and mind to submit to His Lordship and obey His commands. For all who allow themselves to be led by the Spirit of God are sons of God. Romans 8:14 AMP. This is a conscious decision you make daily. You need to be led by the Holy Spirit, for in yourself, you cannot be the sweet-smelling fragrance; it is the work of the Spirit.

Verse 15 of this scripture expresses that you become one with Christ, then you become a sweet-smelling incense offered by Christ to God. Remember that Christ's sacrifice was the atonement for sin, the only blood that purchased our redemption from sin and death.

In your union with Him, He presents you as a fragrant offering to God, and an aroma perceived by the lost and the saved. What a privilege! Let's learn to submit under the mighty hand of God through the leading of His Spirit, Amen. Selah.

PRAYER

Heavenly Father, thank you for giving me Jesus. Because of Him, I can become a sweet-smelling aroma to the praise of your name. Amen.

JANUARY

Day 13

The scripture says, "I spoke because I believed." In the same spirit of faith, we also speak because we believe. We know that God, who raised the Lord Jesus to life, will also raise us up with Jesus and take us, together with you, into his presence. All this is for your sake; and as God's grace reaches more and more people, they will offer to the glory of God more prayers of thanksgiving.
2 Corinthians 4:13-15 GNT

As a child of God, it is important to have your foundation firm by believing that God is true and faithful. The Holy Spirit helps us do and say things that align with the counsel of heaven. When we speak, faith is ignited, turning impossibilities to possibilities because faith empowers God's promises.

What do you believe? And what are you saying? The Spirit of faith speaks. The Spirit knows the mind of God; your Spirit receives this truth and releases it to your being. Your soul needs to declare this for the body to obey. Obedience to God brings manifestation of the word and glory to God's name. Be hopeful here on this earth and in the world to come.

PRAYER

I believe so I decree and declare... (your prayer), Amen.

JANUARY

Breath of God

JANUARY

Day 14

The spirit of God has made me, and the breath of the Almighty gives me life.
Job 33:4 RSV

The Spirit of God is the life-giving Spirit. He is the breath of God—the sustainer of all living things.

Genesis 2:7: *"Then the LORD God formed man from the dust of the ground and breathed the breath of life into his nostrils, and the man became a living being."* Here is an account of how the human being became a living being by the breath of God. God's Spirit sustains all creation. The "Ruach", in Hebrew, meaning the Spirit, wind, and life of God, is the sustainer of all creation.

Job 12:10: *"The life of every living thing is in His hand, as well as the breath of all mankind."* The book of Job shows us the life of everything is in the hands of God. He determines who and what to sustain the breath or take away its life. That is another reason one cannot take his own life; it is not yours to take.

As the Prophet exclaimed in Ezekiel 37, when asked if the dry bones can live, he answered, only you Sovereign Lord knows. He knows and upholds you by His breath. Rest in Him. Selah.

PRAYER

By the power of Christ, I rebuke every spirit of fear of death. I will live and fulfil my days as God sustains me. Amen.

JANUARY

Day 15

But it is the spirit in a man, the breath of the Almighty, that makes him understand. It is not the old that are wise, nor the aged that understand what is right.
Job 32:8-9 RSV

The breath of the Almighty, the Lord of Host, His Spirit resides in you. His very life is what gives you life and sustains all things. As a child of God, who has accepted Jesus as Lord over you, He gives you His salvation and assigns the Holy Spirit to come and have His abode in you. You are not ordinary! Hallelujah Amen.

The scriptures make you aware that you have the breath of God, which gives you an **understanding of all truth**. John 14:26 teaches us that when the Advocate comes, who is the Holy Spirit, He will teach us all truth. That is why no one is without excuse. Whether born again or not, you have the truth of God within you, His breath that shows you a level of understanding.

Understanding, then, involves the cognitive, the spiritual, and the moral. While human efforts are called for, the ability to understand comes from God. The final test of understanding is obedience to God.

PRAYER

Father, thank you for the spirit of understanding. I choose to humble myself under the counsel of the Holy Spirit through Christ our Lord, Amen.

JANUARY

Day 16

But it is the spirit in a man, the breath of the Almighty, that makes him understand. It is not the old that are wise, nor the aged that understand what is right.
Job 32:8-9 RSV

He that hath knowledge spareth his words: and a man of understanding is of an excellent spirit.
Proverbs 17:27 BRG

By the Word of God, we become aware that understanding comes from the Spirit of God. Having the mind of God (His Spirit) gives you information that becomes your knowledge, this is because the Spirit of God is all-knowing and convicts of sin and judgement.

Since you have this Spirit at work in you, you restrain your words and act wisely. A person with understanding has an excellent Spirit. You desire to do right and please the Lord. You act with compassion.

Proverbs 10:19 says, "*When words are many, sin is unavoidable, but he who restrains his lips is wise.*" Proverbs 14:29 also adds, "*A patient man has great understanding, but a quick-tempered man promotes folly.*" May you be conscious of the Spirit of God in you and His presence around you so that you become aware of what comes from you.

PRAYER

Holy Spirit, help me to be more aware of your presence.
Amen.

JANUARY

Day 17

As long as I live, while I have breath from God, my lips will speak no evil, and my tongue will speak no lies. I will never concede that you are right; I will defend my integrity until I die. For what hope do the godless have when God cuts them off and takes away their life? Will God listen to their cry when trouble comes upon them? Can they take delight in the Almighty? Can they call to God at any time?
Job 27:3-5, 8-10 NLT

The Spirit of God, which is also the breath of God, is the spirit of truth. It causes your lips not to speak evil and your tongue not to lie. <u>It is a defence for the upright.</u> Whatever God is, His Spirit in you gives you the capacity to become like Him. 1 John 3:9 says this; *Whoever has been begotten of God does not practice sin, because his seed abides in him, and he cannot sin, because he has been begotten of God.*

Because you are the seed of God, you cannot practice sin. Sin cannot remain in you. His Spirit is in you. You are His temple. Remember to live for Him alone. Selah.

PRAYER

I declare to my hearing I am the seed of God; I cannot practise sin. I live above the standard of this world with the help of the Holy Spirit through Christ our Lord, Amen.

JANUARY

Day 18

These all look to thee, to give them their food in due season. When thou givest to them, they gather it up; when thou openest thy hand, they are filled with good things. When thou hidest thy face, they are dismayed; when thou takest away their breath, they die and return to their dust. When thou sendest forth thy Spirit, they are created; and thou renewest the face of the ground.
Psalms 104:27-30 RSV

God takes care of all His creation. He is responsible for the work of His hands. For those who believe in His benevolence and look to Him for their sustenance, be rest assured He will provide in due season. He gives your daily bread and provides your needs according to His riches, but also according to the power at work in you, which I believe is faith. Ephesians 3:20, only have faith and believe.

The breath of God sustains all creation, when He takes His breath, the thing dies. But when He sends forth His breath, that is His Spirit, life comes. For every dead situation, you need the breath of God to breathe on it. Decree and declare the force, power, and breath of the Living God on that situation in Jesus' name. Amen. May you receive the breath of God that brings life. Amen.

PRAYER

God of all flesh, you always show us the way. In the name of Jesus, I speak life, declaring your breath in me right now. I declare it will not die because your life is in it
Amen.

JANUARY

The Gospel

JANUARY
Day 19

We are not like so many others, who handle God's message as if it were cheap merchandise; but because God has sent us, we speak with sincerity in his presence, as servants of Christ.
2 Corinthians 2:17 GNT

The Gospel of our Lord Jesus Christ is not cheap! If it cost God His only begotten Son to give you Salvation, by dying that shameful death on the cross, then you and I have the responsibility of holding and contending for this faith and the Gospel in all earnest.

We have been entrusted with this merchandise, the scriptures call it, to speak this truth which has the power to change, heal and deliver.

1 Peter 4:11: *"If anyone speaks, he should speak as one conveying the words of God. If anyone serves, he should serve with the strength God supplies, so that in all things God may be glorified through Jesus Christ, to whom be the glory and the power forever and ever."* Amen.

You are chosen to be a sweet aroma, a fragrance to both saved and unsaved. Selah.

PRAYER

Father, thank you for Jesus. Through the help of your spirit, I will declare your truth to all creation. Amen.

JANUARY

Day 20

Now, it's because of God's mercy that we have been entrusted with the privilege of this new covenant ministry. And we will not quit or faint with weariness. We reject every shameful cover-up and refuse to resort to cunning trickery or distorting the Word of God. Instead, we open up our souls to you by presenting the truth to everyone's conscience in the sight and presence of God.
2 Corinthians 4:1-2 TPT

It is a privilege to be called out among billions of people, an honour to be named as a child of the most high. Walk with dignity and honour God with your life. Your reasonable act of worship.

Worship is not something God lacks. Revelation tells us He is surrounded by Cherubs, Angels, and Elders bowing in worship and adoration, crying Holy, Holy, Holy. If you, despite your sinful nature, are called to worship, consider it a privilege.

Due to the privilege of being in covenant with God, you have received mercy. The mercy and grace to preach the gospel of our Lord Jesus Christ has been entrusted to you. Do not grow weary or lose heart in fulfilling the responsibilities entrusted to you by God. Do it with a good conscience. Selah

PRAYER

Thank you, Father, for entrusting me with your truth. Holy Spirit, thank you for leading me to those who I have to reach out to today. Amen.

JANUARY

Day 21

For it is not ourselves that we preach; we preach Jesus Christ as Lord, and ourselves as your servants for Jesus' sake. The God who said, "Out of darkness the light shall shine!" is the same God who made his light shine in our hearts, to bring us the knowledge of God's glory shining in the face of Christ. Yet we who have this spiritual treasure are like common clay pots, in order to show that the supreme power belongs to God, not to us.
2 Corinthians 4:5-7 GNT

The Gospel of our Lord Jesus Christ is a life-giving truth. The kind of knowledgeable truth that liberates you from bondage and curses and heals your soul and body.

Being called to proclaim the Gospel, you are in the service of our Lord Jesus. As the Word goes forth, light comes into the situation and dispels the darkness. The darkness has no option but to yield to the overpowering light. Hallelujah, praise God. Receive the light of God now in Jesus' name. Amen.

This supreme power belongs to God! But it is entrusted to you to represent God through His son Jesus. Be encouraged. God is with you. Amen. Selah.

PRAYER

Thank you, Lord, for entrusting me with the gospel. As I preach your truth and light, may every darkness disappear in Jesus' name. Amen.

JANUARY

Day 22

We are often troubled, but not crushed; sometimes in doubt, but never in despair; there are many enemies, but we are never without a friend; and though badly hurt at times, we are not destroyed. At all times we carry in our mortal bodies the death of Jesus, so that his life also may be seen in our bodies.
2 Corinthians 4:8-10 GNT

You are not alone! What a friend we have in Jesus—the very one who took your place, bore your pain, and sacrificed His perfect life for yours so you can have life more abundantly. He is Emmanuel, God with us. Amen.

It is because you are not of this world that the world does not know you. You may face troubles, but you won't be completely crushed. There might be doubts about God's presence, yet despair won't overcome you. Despite having enemies, you'll never be without a friend. Even if you experience pain, it won't lead to your destruction. Hallelujah, Amen.

Why do you go through these seasons of life challenges? 1 Peter 1:7 says this; "So that the proven character of your faith-more precious than gold, which perishes even though refined by fire-may result in praise, glory, and honour at the revelation of Jesus Christ. Selah.

PRAYER

As you are, I am. Abba, thank you for Jesus, Amen.

JANUARY

Day 23

For this reason, we never become discouraged. Even though our physical being is gradually decaying, yet our spiritual being is renewed day after day. And this small and temporary trouble we suffer will bring us tremendous and eternal glory, much greater than the trouble. For we fix our attention, not on things that are seen, but on things that are unseen. What can be seen lasts only for a time, but what cannot be seen lasts forever.
2 Corinthians 4:16-18 GNT

Challenges, troubles, storms, and pain are necessary in our lives. The wisdom of God is known and seen when we go through different situations. The whole earth is subjected to the rule of the enemy, but to the one who has accepted Jesus as your Savior, you have hope.

It is hope that you are not alone, hope that everything you suffer will bring you a tremendous and eternal glory far greater than your troubles. Fix your attention and faith on the one who called you out, justified you and purified you to be a son. What you see is temporal. God will reward you eternally. Selah.

PRAYER

Father, I keep my eyes on you. Help me to stay focused on you through Christ our Lord. Amen.

JANUARY

Day 24

For we know that when this tent we live in-our body here on earth-is torn down, God will have a house in heaven for us to live in, a home he himself has made, which will last forever. God is the one who has prepared us for this change, and he gave us his Spirit as the guarantee of all that he has in store for us.
2 Corinthians 5:1:5 GNT

"And if Christ has not been raised, then our preaching is vain [useless, amounting to nothing], and your faith is also vain [imaginary, unfounded, devoid of value and benefit-not based on truth]."
1 Corinthians 15:14 AMP

Our hope is founded on the resurrected Christ. He was raised on the third day from death, seen and dined with many, and taught them, too.

This is the same God we believe in, the same Spirit that raised Jesus from the dead. It is a guarantee that when you die, you will live again in a resurrected body like Christ. Death and grave have no power over a child of God.

God prepares this change. You are in Him. Hold on to your faith and rest in your Salvation. You have a heavenly inheritance. Selah.

PRAYER

Heavenly Father, my hope is in you. As Jesus was resurrected, I believe I will be when I die and live with you forever. Thank you.

JANUARY

Faith

JANUARY

Day 25

We live by what we believe, not by what we can see. Our only goal is to please God whether we live here or there, because we must all stand before Christ to be judged. Each of us will receive what we should get- good or bad-for the things we did in the earthly body.
2 Corinthians 5:7, 9-10 NCV

The Spirit life is a life of believing, walking by faith and not what you see. <u>Sight is a limitation to your spiritual walk</u>. Living a victorious life is achieved by seeing and believing in things that are not visible. In living by faith, you please God.

"The just shall live by faith," Hebrews 10:38. For without believing it is impossible to please God. Remember, we will all stand before God to be judged. You will receive the reward of your works whether good or bad. *"Be careful to walk circumspect, not as fools but wise."* Ephesians 5:5-20.

Galatians 3:11: *"Now it is clear that no one is justified before God by the law, because the righteous will live by faith."* Live to glorify God by believing He is God, good, kind and faithful to His Word. Shalom.

PRAYER

Father, I believe, help my unbelief. Amen.

JANUARY

Wisdom

JANUARY

Day 26

We know what it means to fear the Lord, and so we try to persuade others. God knows us completely, and I hope that in your hearts you know me as well. We are not trying again to recommend ourselves to you; rather, we are trying to give you a good reason to be proud of us, so that you will be able to answer those who boast about people's appearance and not about their character. Are we really insane? It is for God's sake. Or are we sane? Then it is for your sake.
2 Corinthians 5:11-13 GNT

Apostle Paul testifies that the fear of the Lord is the foundation of his wisdom. With this wisdom he convinces others about the importance of reverencing God. He further cautions us about the importance of boasting about the character of a person rather than appearance. The one who has the Spirit of God knows his nature is that of Christ. Through Jesus, you are glorified, Amen.

The content in a vessel is as important as the vessel itself. As a child of God, be careful not to be deceived by people's appearance, but examine their character. Amen.

PRAYER

Father may my life be a testament for the glory of your name. If there be anything in me that is not pleasing to you, take it away in Jesus' name Amen.

JANUARY
Day 27

I do not pray that You should take them out of the world, but that You should keep them from the evil one. They are not of the world, just as I am not of the world. Sanctify them by Your truth. Your word is truth.
John 17:15-17 NKJV

Jesus when He was on earth not only taught how we should pray, but also prayed for us. One of his earnest prayers was that the Father would keep His own from the evil one. This prayer is also my desire and prayer for you.

That as the storms in life blow so fiercely and aggressively to destroy you, because He knows His time is short, your faith will stand. Not only that, but you also allow the Word of Truth to sanctify and keep you.

My brethren, keep your eyes on Jesus and work what he has given unto you. The end of all things is nigh, and evil is so much alive.

PRAYER

Father, as I keep my eyes on you, I know you can keep me until the coming of our Lord Jesus, Amen.

JANUARY

Day 28

And, behold, there came a leper and worshipped him, saying, Lord, if thou wilt, thou canst make me clean. And Jesus put forth his hand, and touched him, saying, I will; be thou clean. And immediately his leprosy was cleansed.
Matthew 8:2-3 KJV

God is always willing to make you whole; the evidence is that He gave you Jesus (Isaiah 9:6) and His Holy Spirit without measure (John 3:34).

There is something divine when you worship (bow down) to God sincerely. Scriptures say it like this to worship the Father in spirit and in truth. For He searches the heart, mind, and intent of a person. When your heart is right before God answers your prayers, it happens quickly.

Today, believe God wants to make you whole.

Ask Him, believe, and if you have any sin or unforgiveness in your heart, let it go. And receive God's love, divine healing, and restoration.

PRAYER

Lord, as I worship today, I let go of anything that can hinder my prayers. I believe you have heard so I believe and receive my answers in Jesus' name Amen.

JANUARY

Day 29

I stand silently to listen for the one I love, waiting as long as it takes for the Lord to rescue me. For God alone has become my Savior. He alone is my safe place; his wraparound presence always protects me. For he is my champion defender; there's no risk of failure with God. So why would I let worry paralyze me, even when troubles multiply around me? But look at these who want me dead, shouting their vicious threats at me! The moment they discover my weakness, they all begin plotting to take me down. Liars, hypocrites, with nothing good to say— all their energies are spent on moving me from this exalted place. Pause in his presence.

I am standing in absolute stillness, silent before the one I love, waiting as long as it takes for him to rescue me. Only God is my Savior, and he will not fail me.
Psalms 62:1-5 TPT

God is your Champion defender, there is no failure in Him. Stand still and wait for the one you love. He is your Saviour, Amen.

PRAYER

Abba, I know you will save me. You have done it before, I believe you are doing it again Amen.

JANUARY

Day 30

I will bless the LORD at all times: His praise shall continually be in my mouth. My soul shall make her boast in the LORD: The humble shall hear thereof, and be glad. O magnify the LORD with me, And let us exalt his name together.
Psalm 34:1-3 KJV

King David behaved like a madman in Abimelech's presence, fearing for his life because his fame had gone before him. Just like Abraham feared for his life and said his wife Sarah was his sister when he came to Gerar in Genesis 20, interestingly, the king's name was also Abimelech.

Couldn't God have delivered these kings into the hands of Abraham or David? Yet they had to lie or behave otherwise to live. Selah.

After this, they bless God, for they believed He intervened and spared their lives; the humble will hear this and be glad. Tempt not your God but seek Him and His wisdom and strength. Amen.

PRAYER

Abba, I trust in your wisdom. Holy Spirit, I know you will guide me through. I believe and receive your grace, Amen.

JANUARY

Day 31

I sought the LORD, and he heard me, And delivered me from all my fears. They looked unto him, and were lightened: And their faces were not ashamed.
Psalm 34:4-5 KJV

The Lord is with you while you are in Him. If you seek him, you will find him, but if you forsake him, he will forsake you (2 Chronicles 15:2b).

There is something about knowing that you are wanted or needed, and so it is with God. If you need Him, you will seek Him, and He promises you will find Him. How desperate are you?

He continues to affirm His visibility. As you look, focus, and concentrate on Him, you will be enlightened. Hallelujah, amen.

Brethren, you are not without; you are not an orphan. Look to God, keep your gaze on Him, and you will not be disappointed. God wants to be known. Amen.

PRAYER

My Daddy, I look for as a deer pants for the brooks. My soul longs for her maker. As I seek you, may I find you in everything. Teach me your ways, that I may know you
Through Christ our Lord, Amen.

FEBRUARY

Free From Sin

FEBRUARY

Day 32

We are ruled by the love of Christ, now that we recognise that one man died for everyone, which means that they all share in his death. He died for all, so that those who live should no longer live for themselves, but only for him who died and was raised to life for their sake.

2 Corinthians 5:14-15 GNT

You are ruled by the love of God. Allow the love of God to be the drive, reason and foundation of your life and your decisions. Recognize that sin entered the world through one man, it was also through one man that we received redemption. This truth gives you a blessed assurance.

Romans 5:15 writes, "*But the gift is not like the trespass. For if the many died by the trespass of the one man, how much more did God's grace and the gift that came by the grace of the one man, Jesus Christ, abound to the many!*"

You are gifted with the life of God not to live for yourself. But through Jesus Christ, you are raised from death to life. Live this victorious life to glorify God. You are light called to shine. Shine brighter for God. Selah!

PRAYER

Father, thank you for your gift of life. I live to bring you glory; help me, Holy Spirit, to live a victorious life through Christ our Lord. Amen.

FEBRUARY

Day 33

Sin must no longer rule in your mortal bodies; so that you obey the desires of your natural self. Nor must you surrender any part of yourselves to sin to be used for wicked purposes. Instead, give yourselves to God, as those who have been brought from death to life; and surrender your whole to him to be used for righteous purposes.
Romans 6.12-13 GNT

"For sin will have no dominion over you; since you are not under law but under grace."
Romans 6.14 ESV

To sin is a choice! Your new nature in Christ is dead to sin. You are no longer ruled by the desires of your flesh but led by your spirit. Yours is to feed your spirit to dominate your flesh. Surrender the members of your body to be used by the Holy Spirit for righteous purposes.

Sin will not have dominion over you because you are not under the law but under grace. Live your best life now. You are under God's grace. Don't allow sin to rule over you! Ask the Holy Spirit to fill you daily and lead you in the path that pleases the Father. Shalom

PRAYER

Holy Spirit, lead me in my everyday choices so that I can please God in all my ways. Amen.

FEBRUARY

Christian Life

FEBRUARY

Day 34

No longer, then, do we judge anyone by human standards. Even if at one time we judged Christ according to human standards, we no longer do so. Anyone who is joined to Christ is a new being; the old is gone, the new has come. All this is done by God, who through Christ changed us from enemies into his friends and gave us the task of making others his friends also.
2 Corinthians 5:16-18 GNT

Judge no one by human standards. Anyone born of God overcomes the World through faith (1 John 5:4). The extent of someone's faith is usually unknown. Our duty is to love everyone, and by doing so, we attract God's blessing.

One who is joined with Christ is a new being, and you have a new nature where there is no seed of sin. (1 John 3:9.) 2 Corinthians 3:6 tells us *"And He has qualified us as ministers of a new covenant, not of the letter but of the Spirit; for the letter kills, but the Spirit gives life."*

This new standing makes you a friend and not an enemy. Your union with Christ is the best gift God gave to you. Allow the Spirit of God to lead you. Selah.

PRAYER

This life I have is God's life in me. I see no evil and do no evil. I love as Christ loved me, Amen.

FEBRUARY

Day 35

In our work together with God, then, we beg you who have received God's grace not to let it be wasted. Hear what God says: "When the time came for me to show you favor, I heard you; when the day arrived for me to save you, I helped you." Listen! This is the hour to receive God's favor; today is the day to be saved!
2 Corinthians 6:1-2 GNT

The price you are willing to pay for something determines the value you place on it. No one can buy the grace of God. It is priceless. The scriptures caution us not to waste God's grace on our lives. You have this grace because of your union with God. Acts 11:23: *"When he arrived and saw the grace of God, he rejoiced and encouraged them all to abide in the Lord with all their hearts."*

Remaining in the vine gives you rest. The Lord says, I have a set time to favour you, and I have heard you. Until you remain in God's grace, it might be difficult to determine the time acceptable and receiving from Him.

God works in seasons and times so don't waste God's grace. Remain in the vine. You are victorious. Amen.

PRAYER

Father God, thank you for hearing me and the plan you have for me. Help me Holy Spirit to wait on you and the knowledge of your visitation, Amen.

FEBRUARY

Day 36

We do not want anyone to find fault with our work, so we try not to put obstacles in anyone's way. Instead, in everything we do we show that we are God's servants by patiently enduring troubles, hardships, and difficulties.

We have been beaten, jailed, and mobbed; we have been overworked and have gone without sleep or food. By our purity, knowledge, patience, and kindness we have shown ourselves to be God's servants-by the Holy Spirit, by our true love, by our message of truth, and by the power of God. We have righteousness as our weapon, both to attack and to defend ourselves.
2 Corinthians 6:3-7 GNT

Who is a proven servant of God? One who patiently endures troubles, hardships, and difficulties. Through your purity, knowledge, patience, love and kindness, you will be known as God's servant. These attributes are done by the Holy Spirit. Through the power of the Holy Spirit, we can overcome the weakness of the flesh and obtain victory over the enemy. Through the blood of Jesus Christ, we live triumphantly.

Whatever you go through, have faith in God to make it work for your good and to establish you in every good work. Perfecting His good work, His wrought in Christ.

PRAYER

Holy Spirit, work in me till I am beholding Christ as in a mirror. Amen.

FEBRUARY

Day 37

Do not try to work together as equals with unbelievers, for it cannot be done. How can right and wrong be partners? How can light and darkness live together? How can Christ and the Devil agree? What does a believer have in common with an unbeliever?
2 Corinthians 6:14-15 GNT

Your worth is priceless. Your worth was the blood of Jesus Christ. No amount of money can buy the blood of Christ. He gave up His life to cleanse the church, His bride, for Himself. Let this be your truth and foundation, Apostle Paul gave us insight as to why you can't be equally yoked with an unbeliever.

Ephesians 5:11 says, *"Have no fellowship with the fruitless deeds of darkness, but rather expose them."* You have a duty also to expose them, therefore do not be partakers of them (Ephesians 5:7). You can't expose the darkness you enjoy and participate in. 1 John 1:6 says, *"If we say we have fellowship with Him yet walk in the darkness, we lie and do not practice the truth."*

God desires us to live in the light He provides. Be careful because if you associate with unlawful and ungodly men, you will forget what God requires of you.

PRAYER

Lord, I desire to do your will and stand for the truth of your Word. Help me to live rightly and expose the darkness around me for the glory of your name, Amen.

FEBRUARY

Day 38

All these promises are made to us, my dear friends. So then, let us purify ourselves from everything that makes body or soul unclean, and let us be completely holy by living in awe of God. But God, who encourages the downhearted, encouraged us with the coming of Titus. It was not only his coming that cheered us, but also his report of how you encouraged him. He told us how much you want to see me, how sorry you are, how ready you are to defend me; and so I am even happier now.
2 Corinthians 7:1, 6-7 GNT

The promises of God are for those who have accepted Jesus as their Lord and Saviour. We are called to be Holy as He is Holy, for without holiness, it is impossible to see God. We are to live in awe of God, revere His presence and live right to honour Him.

In our daily walk with the saints, Apostle Paul admonishes us to be encouraging and kind-hearted. Use the encouragement you received from the Lord to build others. *"He comforts us in all our troubles so that we can comfort others. When they are troubled, we will be able to give them the same comfort God has given us."* 2 Corinthians 1:4. Your experiences become your testimony. For we know God through the things we go through in and with Him.

PRAYER

Lord I will not despise the things you bring in my life, that through it I will be built and know your ways. Thank you.

FEBRUARY

Day 39

So I thought I should send these brothers ahead of me to make sure the gift you promised is ready. But I want it to be a willing gift, not one given grudgingly. Remember this -a farmer who plants only a few seeds will get a small crop. But the one who plants generously will get a generous crop. You must each decide in your heart how much to give. And don't give reluctantly or in response to pressure. "For God loves a person who gives cheerfully."

And God will generously provide all you need. Then you will always have everything you need and plenty left over to share with others.
2 Corinthians 9:5-8 NLT

Giving is a ministry and we are all encouraged to give willingly. Some people are anointed to give. May you receive that grace of giving in Jesus' name. Amen. Whatever you sow is what you reap. The measure you give, is the same measure you will receive. Do not limit your giving to only money.

Plan carefully what you want to give in the name of the Lord, God loves that you give cheerfully. Remember to give what you have bearing in mind that it's God who gives the seed to the sower. If you are willing and obedient, God is kind and faithful.

PRAYER

Lord, thank you for entrusting me with your seed. As I give, may it bring honour and glory to your name. May it multiply and further your Kingdom on earth.

FEBRUARY

Challenges

FEBRUARY

Day 40

Indeed, we live as human beings, but we don't wage war according to human standards; for the weapons of our warfare are not merely human, but they have divine power to destroy strongholds. We destroy arguments and every proud obstacle raised up against the knowledge of God, and we take every thought captive to obey Christ.
2 Corinthians 10:3-5 NRSV

It is true that we live in the world, but we do not fight from worldly motives nor fight as the world does. Knowing who you are, why you do something, for who you do it for and what motivates you steers your victory. You are a child of God; your living standards are not of this world. Likewise, your weapons of warfare are not carnal.

The weapons God gave you have divine power to destroy strongholds. Long outstanding issues, including anything that argues with you, or proud obstacles raised up against the "knowledge of God", can be destroyed with these weapons. Your duty is to bring these thoughts to the obedience of Christ. Anything that wants to destroy the intent of God for you is an enemy. You have power in Christ to disallow its operation. Use your weapons (Ephesians 6).

PRAYER

Lord, thank you for the weapons of warfare. Amen.

FEBRUARY

Day 41

Well, no wonder! Even Satan can disguise himself to look like an angel of light!
2 Corinthians 11:14 GNT

"Stay alert! Watch out for your great enemy, the devil. He prowls around like a roaring lion, looking for someone to devour."
1 Peter 5:8 NLT

The main purpose of the enemy is to devour man. Each moment is an opportunity for him to conquer someone else into his territory. Be wise!

With this aim, the scriptures have made us aware of his motives, to steal, kill and destroy. Anytime you see these activities surrounding you, be wise and discerning because the devil may be close by. You are equipped with the Holy scriptures and the Holy Spirit to conquer him. He has given you weapons.

With this truth, Apostle Paul also warns us. Apart from other devices that cause you to disobey God, he can also disguise himself as an angel of light to deceive you.

One of his strongest weapons is deception, making things look like the truth, but the real Spirit of truth lives inside of you. Allow that light to guide you. Selah.

PRAYER

With your help, Holy Spirit, I will defeat every darkness that comes my way through Christ our Lord. Amen.

FEBRUARY

Day 42

Three times I was whipped by the Romans; and once I was stoned. I have been in three shipwrecks, and once I spent twenty-four hours in the water. In my many travels I have been in danger from floods and from robbers, in danger from my own people and from Gentiles; there have been dangers in the cities, dangers in the wilds, dangers on the high seas, and dangers from false friends. There has been work and toil; often I have gone without sleep; I have been hungry and thirsty; I have often been without enough food, shelter, or clothing.
2 Corinthians 11:25-27 GNT

Our walk with the Lord is not devoid of adventure. It is a journey for the strong-willed. Be determined that you will hold on to the hand of Jesus and trust Him, whatever may come your way. The scriptures have made us aware that Jesus is the only way, the truth, and the life. John 14:6: *"He will not forsake you."*

Jesus told us, if they persecuted me, they will come after you too (John 15:20). No servant is greater than the master. Through the challenges and storms of life, we have hope that God is with us and will never leave us alone. He is Emmanuel. Selah.

PRAYER

Holy Spirit, I know you will not allow anything I cannot handle to come my way. I thank you that you are my helper in Christ, Amen.

FEBRUARY

Day 43

If I must boast, I will boast about things that show how weak I am. The God and Father of the Lord Jesus-blessed be his name forever!-knows that I am not lying. When I was in Damascus, the governor under King Aretas placed guards at the city gates to arrest me. But I was let down in a basket through an opening in the wall and escaped from him.
2 Corinthians 11:30-33 GNT

Any time I read about the escapades and exploits of the Apostles, I am marvelled at the acts of the Holy Spirit. It's amazing how boldly God will use our lives for His glory.

How is it possible for one to boast in his weakness? How likely are you to be confident in boasting about how weak you are in a particular area of your life? It is not natural for a human being to boast. Yet God says in 2 Corinthians 12:9, *"Each time he said, "My grace is all you need. My power works best in weakness." So now I am glad to boast about my weaknesses, so that the power of Christ can work through me."*

God's power works best in your weakness. His grace is all you need. If you have any challenge in any area of your life, God is waiting for you to ask for His strength. Selah.

PRAYER

Holy Spirit, thank you for making me your vessel. I know that when I am weak then I am strong because you are my helper, Amen.

FEBRUARY

Day 44

But to keep me from being puffed up with pride because of the many wonderful things I saw, I was given a painful physical ailment, which acts as Satan's messenger to beat me and keep me from being proud. Three times I prayed to the Lord about this and asked him to take it away. But his answer was: "My grace is all you need, for my power is greatest when you are weak." I am most happy, then, to be proud of my weaknesses, in order to feel the protection of Christ's power over me. I am content with weaknesses, insults, hardships, persecutions, and difficulties for Christ's sake. For when I am weak, then I am strong.
2 Corinthians 12:7-10 GNT

God is a gracious and good Father who knows what is best for His children. When you trust Him, you are not consumed by pride because your life holds a greater purpose.

God's grace is all you need. He has given His Word to help us know what He wants and what's possible if we believe and abide. You have the Holy Spirit, too. Be content with what you have. Believe God is with you. Be not afraid. Shalom.

PRAYER

Father, I trust with all of me. I know you will lead me beside still waters. Amen.

FEBRUARY

Commit to God

FEBRUARY

Day 45

I hope that you don't assume that all this time we have simply been justifying ourselves in your eyes? Beloved ones, we have been speaking to you in the sight of God as those joined to Christ, and everything we do is meant to build you up and make you stronger in your faith.
2 Corinthians 12:19 TPT

"All the ways of a man are pure in his own eyes, and Jehovah is pondering the spirits."
Proverbs 16:2 YLT

The other version says God weighs the motives of the heart. It is interesting that the Young Translation uses Spirit. Spirit is your real disposition, your intentions, and why you do what you do. God weighs these things because He can see and understand without you uttering a word.

As children of God, this verse reminds us that we are positioned in God's presence through Christ. You need to be careful in your daily interactions.

1 Samuel 2:3 says, *"Do not boast so proudly, or let arrogance come from your mouth, for the LORD is a God who knows, and by Him actions are weighed."* This is to build your faith, to cause you to walk in humility and consistently ask the Holy Spirit's guidance and direction. Selah.

PRAYER

Holy Spirit, if it is not pleasing to you, take it out from me. Amen.

FEBRUARY

Day 46

For we cannot do anything against the truth, but only for the truth. Finally, brothers and sisters, rejoice! Strive for full restoration, encourage one another, be of one mind, live in peace. And the God of love and peace will be with you.
2 Corinthians 13:8, 11 NIV

Truth is the person of the Holy Spirit, and He delights in manifesting this truth in your life. The Holy Spirit is the Spirit of truth. He is the power and mind of God. You can only stand for truth and not against truth. Truth is powerful. Truth always prevails.

No human wisdom, understanding or plan can stand against the LORD (Proverbs 21:30). No power in darkness can stand against our Lord. No human intelligence or intentions can thwart the counsel of the Almighty. Child of God, rest in Jesus.

Behold, rejoice in the God of your salvation, and strive for full restoration of anything the enemy stole from you. Jesus Christ has redeemed your life, take your restoration bountifully and glorify God. Encourage others and live in peace with others. When we strive to do these, God's love and peace will be with us. In Jesus' name, Amen.

PRAYER

Jesus, thank you for loving me. Thank you for saving me. Thank you for keeping me. Amen.

Day 47

FEBRUARY

From Paul, whose call to be an apostle did not come from human beings or by human means, but from Jesus Christ and God the Father, who raised him from death.
Galatians 1:1 GNT

The knowledge and acceptance of who you are, who you belong to and who made you is an essential part of your success on this earth. I believe the productive life and journey of Apostle Paul sprang from this truth of who he is and who sent him. He was confident in the God he served. No trial or persecution that came his way deterred his focus and purpose.

It is my prayer that you become confident in your position as a child of the Most High. Blood washed, sanctified, and seated with Christ in heavenly places Ephesians 2:6. You are loved.

PRAYER

Heavenly Father, thank you for making me your own. I thank you for the blood of Jesus that gives me access to you and raised me from death to life with everything that concerns me. Amen.

FEBRUARY

Day 48

For I would have you know, brothers, that the gospel that was preached by me is not man's gospel. For I did not receive it from any man, nor was I taught it, but I received it through a revelation of Jesus Christ.
Galatians 1:11-12 ESV

God wants to reveal Himself to you. The purpose of Jesus on earth was to reconcile you back to God, your Father, whom you did not know. Jesus revealed the Father to us (Luke 11:2, John 20:17). When Jesus took His last breath on the cross, the veil in the temple was torn. This signified a doorway had been created to the holy of holies, where the priest was the only one who could enter into the presence of God. Now you and I can enter boldly to obtain mercy in times of need (Mathew 27:5 1). This is a privilege, Amen.

Jesus reveals God's intent through the scriptures to you. He says search for me with all your heart, and you will find me (Jeremiah 29:13). God wants you to pursue him. He pursued you through Christ, how much would you seek Him to know?

PRAYER

Father God, I bless your name for the sacrifice of Calvary. As I seek you with all my heart, reveal yourself to me in Jesus' name. Amen.

FEBRUARY

Day 49

We know full well that we don't receive God's perfect righteousness as a reward for keeping the law, but by the faith of Jesus, the Messiah! His faithfulness, not ours, has saved us, and we have received God's perfect righteousness. Now we know that God accepts no one by the keeping of religious laws!
Galatians 2:16 TPT

The law has no power to save a soul. Romans 3:20 says, "*Therefore no one will be justified in His sight by works of the law. For the law merely brings awareness of sin.*" God's perfect righteousness by faith is in Jesus Christ. Through Him, you have redemption and the forgiveness of sins. Through Him, you can obtain mercy. It is His faithfulness that has saved you, not what you achieved through keeping some laws. It is a gift of God.

Remember God accepts no one by keeping the law. It is only by faith in Jesus Christ, the Son of God, that saves. *"The just shall live by faith,"* Galatians 3:11. Accept what Jesus did for you to be saved. Believe, and you will be justified. Amen.

PRAYER

Father God, thank you for Jesus; through His faithfulness, I stand justified and redeemed. Amen.

Daily Hope | 63

FEBRUARY

Day 50

Christ died on the cross on my behalf. It is like I died there with him. So I do not live my own life any more. Instead, Christ lives in me. The life that I live now in my body, I live because I trust what he has done for me. He has loved me so much that he died on my behalf.
Galatians 2:20 ESV

One of the most powerful scriptures that vividly depicts your new nature is this verse in Galatians. This verse explains the change from your old life to your life now, which is the nature of your life after the cross. You are a unique individual, specially designed to manifest the phases of God. You are blessed, favoured, and envied by Satan. Hallelujah Amen.

Christ lives in you richly. You do not live your own life, act the way you used to before you received Christ, and are born again. You live to glorify Him alone, living by His Word in faith.

What is living by faith? Adhering to, relying upon, total and complete obedience to God's word, direction, and counsel. When you do that, your life is assured of constant victory. Walk in love as He has loved you. Selah.

PRAYER

Heavenly Father, thank you for Jesus. I am who l am because of His sacrifice. Grant me the grace to live for you every day. Amen.

FEBRUARY

Day 51

I wish you would tolerate me, even when I am a bit foolish. Please do! I am jealous for you, just as God is; you are like a pure virgin whom I have promised in marriage to one man only, Christ himself. I am afraid that your minds will be corrupted and that you will abandon your full and pure devotion to Christ-in the same way that Eve was deceived by the snake's clever lies. For you gladly tolerate anyone who comes to you and preaches a different Jesus, not the one we preached; and you accept a spirit and a gospel completely different from the Spirit and the gospel you received from us!
2 Corinthians 11:1-4 GNT

You are betrothed to one man, our Lord and Saviour Jesus. You are His bride, the Church. He refers to you as His temple, His dwelling. He is jealous of your affection. I beseech you, please don't be deceived by any other gospel other than the one you received when you accepted Jesus. *"The Word of the Lord is Spirit and life,"* John 6:63.

When you accept the Word, you accept His Spirit. When you accept another gospel, you accept another spirit to rule over you. Selah.

PRAYER

Father God, you have the Words of life. I have your Spirit; I will serve you alone and live by your Word in Jesus' name. Amen.

FEBRUARY

Day 52

Dear friends, let us love one another, because love comes from God. Whoever loves is a child of God and knows God. Whoever does not love does not know God, for God is love. And God showed his love for us by sending his only Son into the world, so that we might have life through him. There is no fear in love; perfect love drives out all fear. So then, love has not been made perfect in anyone who is afraid, because fear has to do with punishment. We love because God first loved us. If we say we love God, but hate others, we are liars. For we cannot love God, whom we have not seen, if we do not love others, whom we have seen. The command that Christ has given us is this: whoever loves God must love others also.
1 John 4:7-9, 18-21 GNT

God is love. You are a product of love. Love lives inside of you. As you abide in Him, only love can flow through you. You are love!

Love is not made perfect in anyone who is afraid, for perfect love casts out fear. Do not fear. Loving people is your new nature. God expresses His love through you to others. You are loved.

PRAYER

My Father in heaven, as you are so I am here on this earth, a child of love. Help me, Holy Spirit, to live by this truth through Christ our Lord. Amen.

FEBRUARY

Day 53

The angel of the LORD encampeth round about them that fear him, And delivereth them. O taste and see that the LORD is good: Blessed is the man that trusteth in him. O fear the LORD, ye his saints: For there is no want to them that fear him.
Psalm 34:7-9 KJV

One of the tremendous benefits of being born into the Kingdom of Light is walking in the fear of the LORD. The Psalmist says the fear of the Lord is the beginning of Wisdom, but fools despise discipline. The fear of the Lord will teach, protect, and lead you. You will also benefit from the Lord's correction.

Angels harken to the voice of God. They thrive in obedience; they grow in loyalty. You can host their presence when you fear God. They will encamp around you and show you wondrous things. Amen.

Brethren I encourage you to grow in the word of God, meditate on it, by it you mature your spirit and the angels of God can encamp around you feeding on His word - command.

PRAYER

Father, thank you for your goodness over me and mine in Jesus' name, Amen.

FEBRUARY

Day 54

How excellent is thy loving-kindness, O God!

Therefore the children of men put their trust under the shadow of thy wings. For with thee is the fountain of life: in thy light shall we see light.
Psalm 36:7, 9 KJVAAE

I believe God is kind to all his creation. He is the Father of goodness. In Mark 10:18, Jesus answered, "Why do you call me good?" No one is good except God alone.

The enemy cannot do good, there is no kindness in him. Anything that looks good from him is a bait to trap you so he can steal, kill and destroy you.

Be wise. Trust only in God's kindness and acknowledge Him when you are the recipient of his kindness.

Jesus is the fountain of life. In Him is the light, and He is also the light of the world. Live in Him. Learn from Him and trust Him to light your path. Shalom.

PRAYER

I will say of my God, you are a good God. Your name is excellent that is why I trust in you, The fountain of life.
Amen.

FEBRUARY

Day 55

Deliver me from all my transgressions: make me not the reproach of the foolish.
Psalm 39:8 KJV

Have you ever felt so helpless that you need a delivery or a defender, so bad you can cry out in anguish?

This was a psalm in which King David asked for forgiveness and presented his complaints and requests to the Lord, who was able to deliver.

What is disturbing you? What is making you feel so guilty that you can't even pray? What do you need deliverance from?

This is the good news. Jesus, our Messiah, can be all that for you now if you will believe him, accept, ask for forgiveness, and present your case. He is able to help save you from foolish men. Those who are saying there is no help for him in God. That is a good place to be. Call on Jesus now!
Ezekiel 18:30-32

PRAYER

My God and Saviour, my help from ancient past. I know you are in charge, thank you for victory on every side, Amen.

FEBRUARY

Day 56

And Hezekiah received the letter of the hand of the messengers, and read it: and Hezekiah went up into the house of the Lord, and spread it before the Lord. And Hezekiah prayed before the Lord, and said, O Lord God of Israel, which dwellest between the cherubims, thou art the God, even thou alone, of all the kingdoms of the earth; thou hast made heaven and earth.
2 Kings 19:14-15 KJV

I do not know what kind of report you have received, or what makes you so fearful. But King Hezekiah showed us what to do when you are under attack, receive a threat from the devil, and are overwhelmed. You go to the Lord in prayer and supplication. You talk to God!

God has commanded victory concerning you in Christ. If you will only believe and trust the Judge of all creation to defend you. Amen. Shalom.

Peace has a name, and that name is Jesus. He is the Prince of Peace and He promises to be with you always. When your heart is overwhelmed, may you be led to the rock that is higher than you.

PRAYER

Daddy, your hand is not short to save. I believe you are my fortress and protection, my healer and comfort. I know you will save me in Jesus' name. Amen.

Day 57

But I say unto you which hear, Love your enemies, do good to them which hate you, Bless them that curse you, and pray for them which despitefully use you. But love ye your enemies, and do good, and lend, hoping for nothing again; and your reward shall be great, and ye shall be the children of the Highest: for he is kind unto the unthankful and to the evil.
Luke 6:27-28, 35 KJV

The first line of what Jesus said makes you want to sit down and pay real attention to what He is saying. It's amazing that you might think you hear what is being said, but you don't. I pray that today you will hear what the Lord is saying. Amen.

Loving your enemy and those who hate you is not a joke, but to be called a child of God, these are what your Father expects. The Kingdom life is different. Be the burning light in the darkness.

Matthew 5:45-48 tells us we are only our Father's children when we love our enemies; in this love we are perfected. May the Lord grant us the grace to love all.

PRAYER

Lord, teach my heart to love my enemies. Help me to bless those that curses me and do good to those who despitefully use me, Amen.

FEBRUARY

Day 58

Make the weak arms strong again. Strengthen the weak knees. People are afraid and confused.

Say to them, "Be strong! Don't be afraid!" Look, your God will come and punish your enemies. He will come and give you your reward. He will save you.
Isaiah 35:3-4 ERV

May the Lord strengthen your weak arms. You shall be strong again, Amen. Every weak knee is being strengthened to overtake, in Jesus' mighty name. Amen.

Remember, let the weak say, 'I am strong'. You need to believe and declare it with your mouth. For we believe with our heart ans with our mouth confession is made unto salvation. Romans 10:40.

For God did not give us the spirit of fear, but of power and of a sound mind. I say to your soul, do not be afraid. Confusion is not your portion; you have wisdom in you, for Jesus is your wisdom.

Be strong and be of good courage. God is coming! He is coming in power and might to save you and punish your enemies. Not forgetting your reward is with Him. Rejoice. Shalom.

PRAYER

I will not be afraid, for God is as my right hand. He encamps around me and all that belongs to me, Amen.

FEBRUARY

Day 59

In the fourteenth year of King Hezeki'ah, Sennach'erib king of Assyria came up against all the fortified cities of Judah and took them. Do not let Hezeki'ah make you rely on the LORD by saying, "The LORD will surely deliver us; this city will not be given into the hand of the king of Assyria." But they were silent and answered him not a word, for the king's command was, "Do not answer him."
Isaiah 36:1,15,21 RSV

There are times when the enemy comes to you to attack your mind and life with words. He brags about his achievements, and these often sap your courage.

This was what the king of Assyria was doing to King Hezekiah: taunting him with words and daring him to see if what he believed would save him. Brethren, sometimes hold your piece and trust in God. Although in this case, God had already spoken, God speaks on your behalf. Be still.

PRAYER

God, I know you have my best interest at heart. As the enemy wages war against me, I will trust in you. Amen.

Any time the enemy begins to wage war of doubt both in God and in yourself, remember who you are; a child of the lion of Judah. You will always prevail. You are more than a conqueror. Amen.

MARCH

God's Promise to Abraham

Day 60

For as many as are the promises of God, in Christ they are [all answered] "yes." so through him we say our "amen" to the glory of God.
2 Corinthians 1:20 AMP

Happy New Month. This month, our focus will be on reminding ourselves of God's promises. He Himself said to put Him to remembrance (Isaiah 43:26). But how can you remember God if you don't know what He has promised you?

God gave our father Abraham several promises (Genesis 12:2-3). They are ours as well because we are the seed of Abraham through Jesus Christ. We have become heirs with Christ. God, through His Word, has also given us different kinds of blessings, it is yours to partake.

The above scripture informs us that God has already answered all His promises through Christ. All you need to do is say Amen (so be it or it is so). Align your will with His so He can work on your behalf.

PRAYER

Heavenly Father, thank you for qualifying me to receive your promises. Amen.

MARCH

Day 61

Now the lord had said unto Abram, get thee out of thy country, and from thy kindred, and from thy father's house, unto a land that I will shew thee:
Genesis 12:1 KJV

We are redeemed by the blood of the Lamb and by the word of our testimony (Revelation 12:11). We are also in a covenant, grafted into the blessings of God by the faith of our father, Abraham. His obedience to God. When God called him out, He gave him and to us spiritual blessings.

God called him out of the country he knew, from his father's house, unto a place he did not know. Yet he believed in God. What is God calling you out from, but you find it challenging to part with? What has he called you to do that appears unreasonable to obey?

There is always a blessing attached to separation. Dare to believe in God. By Abram's obedience, we are now children of God through Christ Jesus. His obedience made it possible for the purpose of God for mankind to be fulfilled. Your obedience can usher your generation to permanent blessings from God. Be obedient and sensitive to His leadings.

PRAYER

Heavenly Father, I bless your name for your promises. Help me to obey you at all times and in all I do in Jesus' name. Amen.

MARCH

Day 62

And I will make of thee a great nation, and I will bless thee, and make thy name great; and thou shalt be a blessing.
Genesis 12:2 KJV

God had asked Abram to leave his home and family to a place He will show him. The only thing God gave Abram was His Word. He dared to believe, which was credited to him as faith (Genesis 15:6). What impossible situation have you believed God for? It is to your credit.

God gave these seven promises to him. First, I will make you a great nation. You can learn from our father Abraham. He decided to trust God and left what was familiar and dear to him, because of this, God blessed him and gave him more than what he gave up. As you have believed in the message of salvation by accepting Jesus as your Lord, He will make you a great nation. Amen.

If you have given anything up for the love of God, He will repay you. He said anyone who has left family or houses for my sake, will receive a hundred times much more in this life and eternally – Matthew 19:29. Receive the abundance of God in Jesus name. Amen.

PRAYER

Father God, thank you for making me a great nation. Help me to stay in obedience to you in Jesus' name. Amen.

MARCH

Day 63

And I will make of thee a great nation, and I will bless thee, and make thy name great; and thou shalt be a blessing:
Genesis 12:2 KJV

The second promise God gave Abraham was, 'I will bless you.' This blessing entails consecration to God, setting him apart for His use. Through this covenant with Abraham, all the nations of the earth will be blessed. Abraham needed to possess this kind of blessing for it to be transferred to his generation to come.

The other side of this kind of blessing is divine favour. When we obey God, we attract divine favour. Luke 11:28 AMP: *"But He said, "On the contrary, blessed (happy, favored by God) are those who hear the word of God and continually observe it."* If you want to enjoy divine favour from God, keep, meditate, and do what the Word of God says.

Now if you will obey me and keep my covenant, you will be my own special treasure from among all the peoples on earth; for all the earth belongs to me. Exodus 19:5 NLT. That is His promise to obedience to His word.

PRAYER

Heavenly Father, thank you for making me a special treasure. Help me, Holy Spirit, to be obedient to His every Word. Amen.

MARCH

Day 64

And I will make of thee a great nation, and I will bless thee, and make thy name great; and thou shalt be a blessing:
Genesis 12:2 KJV

'I will make your name great' was the third promise. A name is what identifies you from another of your kind. It defines who you are, your lineage, your family, your habits and many more. God gave this promise to Abram informing him that His plan was to make Him a new lineage with God Himself as His source. This is likened to becoming a new creation when you accept Christ, all things have passed away behold He makes things new (2 Corinthians 5:17).

The Hebrew word for the name shêm implies position, honour, authority. This promise means, although you have left everything for my name's sake, I, the Lord, will honour you. I will cause your name to be great and give you authority even over your enemies.

God will make your name great, even in a foreign land (this earth is not your home), because He holds everything by the power of His Word. He will nourish you in a foreign land, giving you lands and blessed nations (people) through your obedience. 1 Samuel 2:9.

PRAYER

Father God, I bless your name for making my name great and establishing me even in a foreign land. In Jesus' name, Amen.

MARCH

Day 65

AND THOU SHALT BE A BLESSING:
Genesis 12:2 KJV

God says you shall be a blessing. Amen. *"Everyone agrees a person who gives a blessing is greater than the one who receives the blessing,"* Hebrews 7:7.

To be a blessing is to be a source of happiness to everyone around you, to enrich the lives of those who come around you with blessedness. You cannot hide a blessed person. They transmit the glory of God. It is not only about money or what it can buy, but your life is a gift to those who are connected to you. You are a blessing!

Hebrews 7:6: *"But Melchizedek, who did not trace his descent from Levi, collected a tenth from Abraham and blessed him who had the promises."* This fourth promise is your presence being a blessing to others and prosperity. It is important for me to add that giving is a blessing. In giving to the things of God and others, you arouse God to bless you. Your obedience to God allows Him to be gracious and merciful to you, according to the promise. Don't be afraid to be the light. God bless you to become the blessing. Do not let your blessing control you; use the blessing, give to others, and give for a good cause. In doing so, people will give glory to God for meeting their needs.

PRAYER

Father God, I bless your name for making me a blessing to my generation in Jesus' name. Amen.

MARCH

Day 66

And I will bless them that bless thee, and curse him that curseth thee: and in thee shall all families of the earth be blessed.
Genesis 12:3 KJV

God provides a blessed assurance in His promises to you if you will believe and obey Him. He is in control over the affairs of men and is capable of keeping His word.

The fifth promise says, 'I will bless those who bless you and curse those who curse you.' It tells you that the Lord is your covering. He will determine what comes your way because you obey Him.

Exodus 23:22: *"But if thou shalt indeed obey his voice, and do all that I speak; then I will be an enemy unto thine enemies, and an adversary unto thine adversaries."* You are the object of God's affection. He made you like Himself, and through His word (Jesus Christ), He will bless those who bless you and likewise curse those who curse you.

He is the one who will fight your battles and bless even the water you drink. Trust and have faith in His Word.

PRAYER

Heavenly Father, thank you for being my shield and protector. I trust in your unfailing love. Amen.

MARCH

Day 67

Blessed be the lord, who bears our burden day by day, the God who is our salvation! Selah.
Psalms 68:19 AMP

The burdens we carry are not always loads that are physical. They come in different shapes, shades, and forms. It could be a load of debt, sickness, finance, employment, children, marriage, etc. Every person has a load they bear. But praise be to our Lord who bears our burdens day by day.

His divine power has given us everything we need for life and godliness, through the knowledge of Him who called us by His own glory and excellence. Through these He has given us His precious and magnificent promises, so that through them you may become partakers of the divine nature, now that you have escaped the corruption in the world caused by evil desires (2 Peter 1:3-4).

The Lord is a good Shepherd, and you are the sheep of His pastures. He has made provisions for your burdens, but his provision is through the knowledge of Him by faith that you know. Through knowledge, you become a partaker of His divine nature; he carries your burden and gives you His perfect peace. But do you know? Are you aware of the promise of God that addresses the circumstance you are in now? It's up to you to seek the provision in His word. Amen.

PRAYER

Heavenly Father, thank you for being my burden bearer. I bless you for the gift of salvation and knowledge of you in Jesus' name. Amen.

MARCH

His Promise

MARCH

Day 68

So don't be impatient for the lord to act; keep moving forward steadily in his ways, and he will exalt you at the right time. And when he does, you will possess every promise, including your full inheritance. You'll watch with your own eyes and see the wicked lose everything.
Psalms 37:34 TPT

Patience is a virtue. It is an essential part of our walk with the Lord. Pace your life according to the Word and counsel of God. Move steadily in His ways not wavering on what you see. For faith does not walk by sight.

<u>The word of God can be trusted. His faithfulness gives you a reason to be patient</u>. That is trusting God, knowing that the testing of your faith produces patience. *"But let patience have its perfect work, that you may be perfect and complete, lacking nothing."* James 1:3-4 NKJV.

Patience tests our faith. When this testing is complete, it brings us to the promise of our full inheritance. Not only will you receive your inheritance from the Lord, but you will also see the wicked lose everything. Keep trusting God and taking Him by His word.

PRAYER

Father God, thank you for the gift of patience. I trust you to bring me to the place where my life is for your glory in Jesus' name, Amen.

MARCH

Day 69

The Lord knows the days of the upright, and their inheritance shall be forever. They shall not be ashamed in the evil time, and in the days of famine they shall be satisfied.
Psalms 37:18-19 NKJV

The Lord knows the way of the righteous, but the wicked will perish (Psalm 1:6). The Lord is a good Shepherd, He knows His sheep and His sheep knows His voice (John 10:14). 2 Timothy 2:19 says, *"Nevertheless, God's firm foundation stands, bearing this seal: "The Lord knows those who are His,"* and *"Everyone who calls on the name of the Lord must turn away from iniquity."*

Because you are His, your inheritance is eternal. You shall not be ashamed of evil times. Turn away from iniquity, the plans of the enemy can never succeed over you and yours.

God promises to sustain you in the time of famine. He will redeem you from death, and in battle from the stroke of the sword (Job 5:20). The salvation of the righteous is from the LORD; He is their stronghold in times of trouble (Psalm 37:39).

Take the word of the Lord as it says. Believe it and see it work for you.

PRAYER

Thank you, Father God, that you know the way that I take. Thank you for your provision on the day of famine in Jesus' name. Amen.

MARCH

Day 70

The Lord will fight for you; you need only to be still.
Exodus 14:14 NIV

The LORD is a warrior, the LORD is His name.
Exodus 15:3 NIV

The Lord is a man of war. He holds the strategies of spiritual battles because victory belongs to Jesus and they bring God glory. You need to learn to depend on Him and trust His ways.

A warrior is skilful and fierce on the battlefield. Remember the nature of God as you walk through life. The enemy is cunning and manipulative, but God is all wise and you are God's warrior.

In His Word, He has promised never to leave nor forsake you (Deuteronomy 31:6). Don't doubt what God has said or promised you. Today, if you will only believe His word, stand on it and refuse to back down no matter what comes your way, you will see the faithfulness of God.

Jesus has paid the price. You need to only follow His stead and obey. Your battle is the Lord's. Pay attention and obey Him in every situation. You will see the salvation of the Lord (2 Corinthians 10:6), when your obedience is complete every evil will be punished. Your obedience plays a role. Amen.

PRAYER

Heavenly Father, thank you for fighting my battles for me. I will trust and obey even when I don't understand; in Jesus' name I pray, Amen.

MARCH

Day 71

Do not be deceived, my beloved brethren. Every good gift and every perfect gift is from above, and comes down from the father of lights, with whom there is no variation or shadow of turning.
James 1:16-17 NKJV

The Lord is a just God, yet He is merciful. The Bible says, *"He has not dealt with us as our sins require"* (Psalm 103:10). He loves us and His love suffers long, but do not be deceived, God is not mocked. He is the source of everything!

Every good and perfect gift is from God. He is the Father of light which implies He is dependable and can be trusted. His ways are flawless. Make a choice to hold on to God's word because His promises are sure.

Everything you need that pertains to life and godliness is found in Him and His word. The Holy Spirit is your guide, trust His leading. He desires to supply your needs, prosper you and glorify Himself in you.

PRAYER

Heavenly Father, thank you for your promises. Thank you for every good and perfect gift you have given me in Jesus' name, Amen.

MARCH

Day 72

He gives power to the weak, and to those who have no might he increases strength.
Isaiah 40:29 NKJV

God is a good Father. His wisdom is fathomless and mysterious. His mercy echoes His sovereignty. He is all powerful yet generous and kind.

He holds all power in His hands. He is the God who judges, exalting one and bringing another down (Psalm 75:7). It is He that weighs the motives of men, giving power and strength when needed.

He gives you power and endurance for that which you need to go through. 2 Corinthians 4:16: *"Therefore we do not lose heart. Though our outer self is wasting away, yet our inner self is being renewed day by day."*

He makes the weak stronger. His strength is made perfect in our weakness (2 Corinthians 12:7). Ask for His strength when you need it. The strength He provides might come in different ways, so be sensitive to His leading. He is your ever-present help.

PRAYER

Heavenly Father, thank you for your power and strength. May your will be done in my life as it is in heaven in Jesus' name Amen.

MARCH

Day 73

But those who wait for the lord [who expect, look for, and hope in him] will gain new strength and renew their power; they will lift up their wings [and rise up close to God] like eagles [rising toward the sun]; they will run and not become weary, they will walk and not grow tired.
Isaiah 40:31 AMP

The act of waiting is a posture that does not come to our human nature easily, especially when one is helpless in a situation. You would rather do something whilst waiting on God to come to your aid. This verse is emphatically letting us know the importance of waiting on God.

To wait is the action of staying where one is or delaying action until a particular time or event. Are you willing and obedient to stay in a place until God tells you to move? If you are, then He promises to give you new strength and renew your power.

You will mount up with wings like the eagles, soaring above your enemies. You will run and not be weary for He will be your strength. You will walk and not grow weary for He will be with you, guiding and carrying you in His arms. He will be your burden bearer. Trust in God for He cares for you.

PRAYER

Heavenly Father, thank you for being my Lord. Thank you for strength and might. I will trust and obey you in Jesus' name Amen.

MARCH

Day 74

For I, the lord your God, will hold your right hand, saying to you, 'fear not, I will help you.'
Isaiah 41:13 NKJV

The Bible teaches that it is important to be honest and reliable, even when it is difficult or painful (Psalm 15:4). Similarly, God is always faithful to His promises and will keep His every Word to you. He is a covenant-keeping God.

He is the great I AM. He reigns in the affairs of men, and He has said I will hold your right hand. If you have accepted Jesus as your Lord, then be rest assured He will hold your hand when you need Him. Holding the hand can imply guiding, leading, and being beside you to accompany you always.

What is in the right hand of God? Jesus is seated at the right hand of God. You are in Him as God holds your right hand. He is making known to you the path of life and pleasures (Psalm 16:11). Let the Word dwell in you richly, it is the word in you that will light your path in His promises. And you will never be afraid. His presence with you cast all fears away.

PRAYER

Heavenly Father, thank you for holding me by the right hand. I decree and declare I am in Christ, seated far above principalities and powers in heavenly places. Amen.

MARCH

Day 75

But now, o Jacob, listen to the Lord who created you. O Israel, the one who formed you says, "Do not be afraid, for I have ransomed you. I have called you by name; you are mine.

When you go through deep waters, I will be with you. When you go through rivers of difficulty, you will not drown. When you walk through the fire of oppression, you will not be burned up; the flames will not consume you.

For I am the Lord, your God, the Holy one of Israel, your Savior. I gave Egypt as a ransom for your freedom; I gave Ethiopia and Seba in your place.

Others were given in exchange for you. I traded their lives for yours because you are precious to me. You are honored, and I love you.
Isaiah 43:1-4 NLT

This is what God declares over you as His child. Agree with the Lord and speak these blessings over your life, until you see yourself just as God sees you. You are precious. You are His, He paid a price for your redemption. He will not withhold any good thing from you.

PRAYER

Heavenly Father, thank you for ransoming my life and giving me your name. Amen.

MARCH

Day 76

"Just as I swore in the time of Noah that I would never again let a flood cover the earth, so now I swear that I will never again be angry and punish you.

For the mountains may move and the hills disappear, but even then my faithful love for you will remain. My covenant of blessing will never be broken," says the Lord, who has mercy on you.
Isaiah 54:9-10 NLT

The Words of the promises of God are God Himself. Whenever you take any promise of God you are eating His bread of life. Eat it with faith, you will definitely see results.

The Lord has sworn not to punish you in anger like in the days of Noah. Furthermore, because of the sacrifice of Jesus, the wrath of God was satisfied His covenant of blessings is sure. It will never be broken. Your father is merciful. He looks at you with grace, desiring that even when you do something wrong, you boldly come to Him and repent. He will forgive and clean you up. Fear not, you are loved just like the prodigal son. Come home. Amen.

PRAYER

Heavenly Father, thank you for your promises. Thank you for keeping your promises to me. Amen.

Day 77

See how very much our Father loves us, for He calls us His children, and that is what we are! But the people who belong to this world don't recognize that we are God's children because they don't know Him. Dear friends, we are already God's children, but he has not yet shown us what we will be like when Christ appears. But we do know that we will be like Him, for we will see Him as He really is. And all who have this eager expectation will keep themselves pure, just as he is pure.
1 John 3:1-3 NLT

You are a child of God and God loves you so much. Just imagine being adopted by the President of the United States of America. Now wherever you go, you are recognized and given special treatment. That is exactly how it is with the kingdom of God. You are a royal priesthood, a holy nation (1 Peter 2:9).

The world cannot recognize us because they don't know our Father. Your home is not in this world. Nevertheless, hold your head high and know you are a child of the King of kings and Lord of lords. You are loved.

You are a holy nation; a peculiar people made for wonders (1 Peter 2:9). Believe what your Father says you are.

PRAYER

ABBA Father, thank you for making me your child. I celebrate you as my father today and always. Happy Father's Day Lord.

MARCH

Day 78

"Sing, o barren, you who have not borne! Break forth into singing, and cry aloud, you who have not laboured with child! For more are the children of the desolate than the children of the married woman," says the lord. "enlarge the place of your tent, and let them stretch out the curtains of your dwellings; do not spare; lengthen your cords, and strengthen your stakes. For you shall expand to the right and to the left, and your descendants will inherit the nations, and make the desolate cities inhabited. "Do not fear, for you will not be ashamed; neither be disgraced, for you will not be put to shame; for you will forget the shame of your youth, and will not remember the reproach of your widowhood anymore. "for a mere moment I have forsaken you, but with great mercies I will gather you.
Isaiah 54:1-4, 7 NKJV

Faith without works is dead. Show me your faith by how you live and by your actions. When the word of the Lord comes to you, act in faith. Standing firm in the word causes the Spirit of God to work on your behalf. Alignment with God's promises reduces friction.

Faiith works when you have an object of focus. What are you focusing on? Jesus, who is the word of God, should be your focus. Through Him all things were made (Colossians 1:16). With Him all things are possible (Matthew 19:26).

PRAYER

Father, thank you for the capacity to enlarge to receive and keep what you give me in Jesus' name, Amen.

MARCH

Day 79

If any of you lacks wisdom [to guide him through a decision or circumstance], he is to ask of [our benevolent] God, who gives to everyone generously and without rebuke or blame, and it will be given to him.
James 1:5 AMP

Wisdom is the principal thing; therefore, get wisdom: and with all thy getting, get understanding (Proverbs 4:7). And He said to man, *"Behold, the fear of the Lord, that is wisdom, and to turn away from evil is understanding"* Job 28:28. To have this principal thing called wisdom begins with having a reverential fear of God.

Wisdom is what guides your decisions. The Bible says, at any point in your life when you lack this ability, ask God, because He gives freely without rebuke. Don't be afraid to ask. Don't doubt whether He will answer your prayer.

Ecclesiastes 7:12: *"For wisdom is a defence, and money is a defence: but the excellency of knowledge is, that wisdom giveth life to them that have it."*

Wisdom gives life to knowledge and even money. For through wisdom your days will be multiplied, and years will be added to your life. If there is anything you need in these times, ask for wisdom. Godly wisdom. Selah.

PRAYER

Father, thank you for the Spirit of wisdom in Jesus' name, Amen.

MARCH

Day 80

If my people, which are called by my name, shall humble themselves, and pray, and seek my face, and turn from their wicked ways; then will I hear from heaven, and will forgive their sin, and will heal their land. Now mine eyes shall be open, and mine ears attend unto the prayer that is made in this place.
2 Chronicles 7:14-15 KJV

God is a just God. He created the universe and all that is in it. He takes care of His creation, raining and shinning both on the righteous and unrighteous. He feeds even the birds of the air, implying He provides for all.

This promise is for those who are called by His name, His children. If only you will call on His name in humility and pray. Seek His face, be willing to obey Him, and turn from your wicked ways. God promises to hear your prayers from heaven and forgive your sins and also heal your land. Hallelujah.

This is good news. Would you call His name today? Are you willing to forsake your own ways and follow Him? He is waiting.

PRAYER

Father God, thank you for the privilege to be called by your name, knowing that you will answer. I am calling on you Father, hear me now in Jesus' name. Amen.

Day 81

For God so loved the world that He gave His only begotten Son, that whoever believes in Him should not perish but have everlasting life. He who believes in the Son has everlasting life; and he who does not believe the Son shall not see life, but the wrath of God abides on him.
John 3:16, 36 NKJV

God is love. He loves what He made. He looked at His creation and said it was good. He so loved the world that He was willing to sacrifice Himself to redeem us back to Himself. Only the perfect sacrifice of Jesus was sufficient to redeem mankind from sin and pay the price of redemption.

You are valuable. The Son of God was the one who gave His life so you can have eternal life. When you believe in His sacrifice and accept His Lordship, you will not perish. Death is already defeated. It will be a blissful transition to be with the Lord eternally.

It is important to know that if you choose not to believe in Jesus Christ, God's son, you cannot have everlasting life. The wrath of God rests with you. His peace is not your portion, and you are cut off from His grace and mercies.

PRAYER

Heavenly Father, thank you for your Son Jesus. Thank you for redeeming me and giving me everlasting life. Amen.

MARCH

Day 82

Jesus replied, you are slaves of sin, every one of you. And slaves don't have rights, but the Son has every right there is! So if the Son sets you free, you will indeed be free.
John 8:34-36 TLB

Anyone who has not accepted Jesus as his Lord is living in sin (Acts 4:12). Anyone who lives in disobedience to God's Word is a sinner (John 5:24). You become a slave to the one you obey. Sin is a slave in itself. It only oppresses, kills, steals, and destroys. Slaves begot slaves. Slaves have no rights. Come to Jesus and have life. Your slavery will only be to righteousness.

The Son, who is Jesus, has every right. In fact, it pleased the Father that all the fullness of the God in bodily form be entrusted in Him (Colossians 2:9). He is the way, the truth, and the life, He is the only one that can set you free indeed.

He says, today when you hear my voice do not harden your heart, repent and come to your Father. His arms are open wide, He loves and wants to restore back everything that sin took from you. God is merciful and kind-hearted, slow to anger. Confess and accept Him He will set you free.

PRAYER

I accept Jesus as my Lord and Saviour. Forgive my sins. Come live in my heart and take absolute control. Set me free from everything that does not please you. Thank you for loving me. Amen.

MARCH

Day 83

I am the Lord All-Powerful, and I challenge you to put me to the test. Bring the entire ten percent into the storehouse, so there will be food in my house. Then I will open the windows of heaven and flood you with blessing after blessing.
Malachi 3:10 CEV

Our walk on this earth is a walk of trust and obedience to the Word of God. His Word is Jesus made flesh, making His dwelling among and in us (John 1:14).

The Lord commands us to follow Him, He gave His Son so we could have life and have it more abundantly. He encourages us to dedicate a part of what we earn to Him. This can be interpreted as literally putting physical food in His house. He promises to reward our trust.

Tithe is not given because a man of God asked you to, nor is it given by force. You give from the place of honour, faith, understanding, and trust in God. You give because God commands us to give.

Today, as you prepare to give your tithe and offering, remember who you are giving to. Give in faith and He will give it back to you in good measure, pressed down, shaken together, and running (Luke 6:38). Do not forget He gave it to you first.

PRAYER

Heavenly Father, thank you for blessing me so I can give. I honour you with my substance in Jesus' name, Amen.

MARCH

Day 84

I've commanded you to be strong and brave. Don't ever be afraid or discouraged! I am the Lord your God, and I will be there to help you wherever you go.
Joshua 1:9 CEV

When you are an emissary on a journey for the Kingdom of God, He sends you with the backing of heaven, the authority, and anointing to fulfil His purpose for His glory. He is with you and in you. He leads you on the path that will glorify Him.

He commands you to be strong in your election and brave in your purpose. Refuse to be afraid of anything or anyone. For God did not give you the spirit of fear, but love, power and a sound mind -2 Timothy 1:7.

He affirms His presence with you. You are surrounded by a great cloud of witnesses (Hebrews 12:1), cheering you to completion. Keep your eyes on the prize. Focus on Jesus, who for the joy set before Him, endured the cross despising the shame (Hebrews 12:2). Your faith in God will be rewarded. Be strong and courageous.

PRAYER

Heavenly Father, thank you for your presence. I decree and declare I am strong and brave. I can do all things through Christ who gives me strength in Jesus' name, Amen.

MARCH

Day 85

And the angel of the LORD appeared to the woman and said to her, "Behold, you are barren and have no children; but you shall conceive and bear a son. Therefore beware, and drink no wine or strong drink, and eat nothing unclean."
Judges 13:3-4 RSV

There is no other teacher I know who is so willing to teach than the Holy Spirit. If you are ready to be taught, he will teach, guide, correct, and instruct you for the glory of God. Amen.

Manoah and his wife had a barren situation, and when she least expected it, an Angel showed up with great tidings. You shall bear a son. May this news be your testimony, too, Amen. Not only a child but a deliverer. May your blessings bring you many deliverances in Jesus' name. Our blessings come with instructions. Beware, as you keep them, you maintain your blessings. Shalom (peace).

Sometimes these blessings come in a seed form. As you nurture it with the Word of God, prayer, fasting and spiritual exercises, it grows beautifully into the glory of God.

PRAYER

Lord, as I receive your promise, help me to know your instructions and obey them, Amen.

MARCH

Day 86

In the beginning was the Word, and the Word was with God, and the Word was God. The same was in the beginning with God. All things were made by him; and without him was not anything made that was made. In him was life; and the life was the light of men.
John 1:1-4 KJV

If Elon Musk, the richest man on earth as of 27/12/2022, came to show you his way of making money, I bet you would be thrilled, take notes, listen over and over again, and then do exactly what he said.

Well before the beginning, God was. His Word was and did make everything and everyone, including the world's richest people you admire. If this God is showing you how He made the world, why don't you pay attention, listen, watch, practice, and learn what He is showing you? Selah.

Today, ask prayerfully, 'Lord, show me the things that make it difficult for me to obey you. Reveal my weakness and strength to me. I receive your grace for knowledge and the spirit of correction and truth.' Through Jesus Christ Our Lord, Amen.

PRAYER

Thank you, Spirit of truth. I open myself to receive from all wisdom, Amen.

MARCH

Day 87

All things were made by him; and without him was not any thing made that was made. In him was life; and the life was the light of men. And the light shineth in darkness; and the darkness comprehended it not.
John 1:3-5 KJV

All things were made by the Word, and nothing was made without the Word. Simply, if you do not say the Word nothing will be made or change. God's Word is the maker of the world and everything in it. Without the Word, there would be no creation. Learn to speak the Word of God!

The Scriptures show us that in this Word is Life, and in this life is the light of men. You desire to have this light, the Word of God in you. This light purifies your soul and regenerates your heart and mind. It dispenses all darkness to bring clarity and direction to the glory of God. Amen.

Believe this light lives in you; it works through you. When you acknowledge the deeds of this light, you will notice you are no ordinary person, but the light of the world. Amen.

PRAYER

Father, thank you for giving me power through your Word, Amen.

MARCH

Day 88

John came to declare the truth about the light so that everyone would become believers through his message. [8] John was not the light, but he came to declare the truth about the light. [9] The real light, which shines on everyone, was coming into the world.
John 1:7-9 GW

Anytime you declare something, I believe you desire to see the result of your declaration. Whether your declaration means an announcement or acknowledging possession of something, it has to be heard by another.

This is the truth about the Word which is both truth and light. The truth about who you truly are is that you have a light to illuminate your path and oil your lamp (as His glory is in you). You, like John, should declare the truth of about the light of God. Be the light as He lives in you. You are light! Hallelujah, Amen.

Now that you know you are light, speak as the light; live like light and exemplify the life of light. Child of God, you cannot be hidden. Light up your world. Amen.

PRAYER
I am the light of the world. Thank you, Father, for making me just like you. Amen.

MARCH

Day 89

He was in the world, and the world was made by him, and the world knew him not. He came unto his own, and his own received him not. But as many as received him, to them gave he power to become the sons of God, even to them that believe on his name:
John 1:10-12 KJV

I cannot get my head around the idea of my children being unable to recognise me under whatever circumstances. Even babies can detect their mothers with their senses and smell.

How come the world could not recognise its maker and His own rejected Him? That is how powerful sin is. The Prince of this world has blinded them and they also love darkness to light because it will expose their deeds.

Good news to those who believe they have been given the invitation to become a son. A son of truth and light. What a privilege.

PRAYER

Lord, thank you for finding me worthy to become your own, Amen.

MARCH

Day 90

But as many as received him, to them gave he power to become the sons of God, even to them that believe on his name: Which were born, not of blood, nor of the will of the flesh, nor of the will of man, but of God. And the Word was made flesh, and dwelt among us, (and we beheld his glory, the glory as of the only begotten of the Father,) full of grace and truth.
John 1:12-14 KJV

Anyone who has accepted Jesus as their Saviour has a new birth. The Scriptures above show us the kind of Birth you have—one not determined by flesh, blood, or the will of man. You are God's choice.

You carry His seed; He calls you His offspring. Hallelujah, praise God. He lives in you, He dwells among your family, and you can behold his glory every day as you become conscious of him. He is full of grace and truth. Selah (pause and meditate).

Power lives in the inside of you. It is the knowledge of this power in you that can make it effective. Believe you are powerful – power full. Amen.

PRAYER
Abba (father), thank you for giving me your name. A child of God, heir with Christ, Amen.

APRIL

Christ Our Example

APRIL

Day 91

But he gave up his place with God and made himself nothing. He was born as a man and became like a servant. And when he was living as a man, he humbled himself and was fully obedient to God, even when that caused his death- death on a cross.
Philippians 2:7-8 NCV

Letting go of your identity, especially when it's a fundamental part of who you are, can be extremely painful. It is tough to give up something substantial and integral to who you are. But Jesus did it. He gave up Himself so we could be reconciled back to God.

He humbled Himself not having His own way but surrendered to the will of the Father. He submitted Himself to God's sovereignty on earth. He became obedient even to death on the cross. As we celebrate His choice, humility, obedience, and suffering, what are you willing to give up for Christ?

Meditate on these and let the Holy Spirit help you make the necessary changes. Change begins with you. Shalom.

PRAYER

Holy Spirit, help me identify the things I need to give up, and teach me to humble myself. Grant me the grace to be obedient. Amen.

Day 92

APRIL

If you've gotten anything at all out of following Christ, if his love has made any difference in your life, if being in a community of the Spirit means anything to you, if you have a heart, if you care –then do me a favor: Agree with each other, love each other, be deep- spirited friends. Don't push your way to the front; don't sweet-talk your way to the top. Put yourself aside, and help others get ahead. Don't be obsessed with getting your own advantage. Forget yourselves long enough to lend a helping hand.
Philippians 2:1-4 MSG

Living the life Christ paved for us is not for the faint-hearted, but He promised never to leave us nor forsake us. It is the working of the Holy Spirit in you that quickens your mortal body to align with, and equip you for everything. Your part is to trust and obey.

"Christ is the anointing that equips". As we celebrate this Easter, how has Christ influenced your life? Does His Spirit mean anything to you, apart from speaking in tongues? Do you agree with and honour the brethren?

Jesus brought the Kingdom of God to us. It is in you (Luke 17:21). It is not outside of you. Let us reflect and meditate on the reason God gave Jesus as a ransom. Your worth is in the cross. Selah.

PRAYER

Father, open the eyes of my heart to know the mystery of the cross that will usher me to the grace of redemption. Amen.

APRIL

Day 93

So God raised him to the highest place. God made his name greater than every other name so that every knee will bow to the name of Jesus- everyone in heaven, on earth, and under the earth. And everyone will confess that Jesus Christ is Lord and bring glory to God the Father.
Philippians 2:9-11 NCV

Today marks one of the most profound celebrations for those who believe in and follow our Lord Jesus Christ — Resurrection Day. We remember when Christ came back to life and left the tomb. He was a prophet and knew God had promised him that he would make a descendant from David's family a king, just as he was.

David had talked about Christ rising from the dead. He said: 'He was not left in the grave. His body did not rot.' Jesus is the One whom God raised from the dead, and we are all witnesses to this (Acts 2:30-32 NCV).

Jesus is the only name that saves! He has risen from the dead! In Him is redemption, the forgiveness of sin. You are forgiven and loved, hallelujah, Amen. Romans 8:11 says, *"Yet God raised Jesus to life! God's Spirit now lives in you, and he will raise you to life by his Spirit. You are risen to life!"*

PRAYER

Heavenly Father, thank you for your Son Jesus who is my life now. Thank you for the Holy Spirit who helps me lead my new life. Amen.

Day 94

APRIL

For we have already experienced "heart-circumcision," and we worship God in the power and freedom of the Holy Spirit, not in laws and religious duties. We are those who boast in what Jesus Christ has done, and not in what we can accomplish in our own strength. It's true that I once relied on all that I had become. I had a reason to boast and impress people with my accomplishments—more than others- for my pedigree was impeccable.
Philippians 3:3-4 TPT

Circumcision of the heart is the work of the Holy Spirit. Be holy as He is holy (1 Peter 1:16). Our call to holiness is not achieved by works or any external factors. It is the Spirit of God who will sanctify your heart by washing you with the Word.

Our worship of God is of the power and freedom of the Holy Spirit. As you allow Him to work on you, then He can trust you with His power. Power doesn't come before circumcision, it comes after. When you have learned to humble and submit under the authority of the Spirit of God. The work of the Spirit is not only to speak in tongues but to present you pleasing just like Christ to the Father.

The work of Christ, which is the Anointing, is the working of the Spirit. Believe and rely on Him totally.

PRAYER

Holy Spirit, circumcise my heart. Cause me to walk in your precepts, line upon line. Amen.

APRIL

Day 95

I don't mean to say that I have already achieved these things or that have already reached perfection. But I press on to possess that perfection for which Christ Jesus first possessed me. No, dear brothers and sisters, I have not achieved it, but I focus on this one thing: Forgetting the past and looking forward to what lies ahead, I press on to reach the end of the race and receive the heavenly prize for which God, through Christ Jesus, is calling us.
Philippians 3:12-14 NLT

We are called to become like Jesus. He is the model we pattern our life after. The scriptures in 2 Corinthians 3:18 says, *"But we all, with open face beholding as in a glass the glory of the Lord, are changed into the same image from glory to glory, even as by the Spirit of the Lord."*

As we behold Him through His Word and spend time in the secret place, we become like Him by the work of the Holy Spirit. *You believe to become.* As you trust the Holy Spirit to lead you, He will guide and strengthen you to fulfil the Father's purpose for you. Press on to that perfection.

As we walk with the Lord, focus on what is ahead. Hebrews 12:2 says, *"Looking unto Jesus the author and finisher of our faith; who for the joy that was set before him endured the cross […] Whatever you are enduring for Christ sake will earn you a reward."*

PRAYER

Father, help me to focus on you. Victory is on the horizon.
Amen.

APRIL

Paul Exhorts

APRIL

Day 96

Don't be pulled in different directions or worried about a thing. Be saturated in prayer throughout each day, offering your faith-filled requests before God with overflowing gratitude. Tell him every detail of your life, then God's wonderful peace that transcends human understanding, will make the answers known to you through Jesus Christ.
Philippians 4:6-7 TPT

God is interested in the details of your life. From your choice of clothes to the course you want to study, from who you like to date to choosing a spouse, from what makes you happy to what makes you sad. He knows when you are weak and angry, and when you are at peace and happy. He is aware of all your worries.

That is intimacy. It is sharing every part of your life with the one who cares for you. You are called to a kingdom lifestyle and cannot afford to be pulled in different directions. Your focus is on God and the leading of His Spirit.

The scripture is encouraging you today to ask God for everything in faith, with gratitude. And His wonderful peace that surpasses human understanding will guard your heart. Selah.

PRAYER

Heavenly Father, thank you for being interested in my everyday life. I thank you for providing my every need, according to your riches in Christ, and guiding me to glory.
Amen.

APRIL

Day 97

I know what it is to be in need and what it is to have more than enough. I have learned this secret, so that anywhere, at any time, I am content, whether I am full or hungry, whether I have too much or too little. I have the strength to face all conditions by the power that Christ gives me.
Philippians 4:12-13 GNT

Wealth and poverty have the ability to bring out your nature that you would not have otherwise known existed. The wisdom of God teaches us to live to bring him glory. Baptism into the suffering of Christ is part of sharing in his glory. There is a kind of glory that can only be experienced in being a *partaker of the sufferings of Christ*. 2 Corinthians 4:17 says, *"For our light and momentary troubles are achieving for us an eternal glory that far outweighs them all."* Amen.

As a child of a King, all the heavenly resources are available to you. God may choose to train your hands for battle through having nothing, little or more (Psalm 144:1). But you need to believe you are complete in him. You are the blessed of the Lord. The anointing that is in you gives you the power to live in all conditions. Hallelujah, praise God. Selah. Bearing in mind He will never send anything your way that is meant to destroy you, or you cannot bear. HE IS A GOOD FATHER. The Abba you can trust.

PRAYER

Heavenly Father, thank you for the anointing to thrive in all situations. I know I can do all things through Christ who strengthens me. Amen.

APRIL

Day 98

Now ye Philippians know also, that in the beginning of the gospel, when I departed from Macedonia, no church communicated with me as concerning giving and receiving, but ye only. Not because l desire a gift: but I desire fruit that may abound to your account. But I have all, and abound: I am full, having received of Epaphroditus the things which were sent from you, an odour of a sweet smell, a sacrifice acceptable, well pleasing to God. But my God shall supply all your need according to his riches in glory by Christ Jesus.
Philippians 4:15, 17-19 KJV

You cannot expect to receive without giving (Luke 6:38). Your giving is a measure, and your motives are the weights by which God gives back to you. Whether it will be pressed down, shaken together, and running over depends on what, how, who you give to. Your giving is a fruit that goes to your heavenly account. *You can always trade your giving with the other things you lack or need.* Acts 9:36-34 tells us of Dorcas. Her generosity brought her back from the dead because her generosity interceded for her.

Your giving can be a sacrifice acceptable and well pleasing to God. Give from a generous heart. When you have done that, God in turn supplies all your needs according to His riches in glory by Christ Jesus. Your giving gives you access to abundance.

PRAYER

Father, thank you for a heart of generosity in Jesus' name, Amen.

APRIL

Day 99

I am convinced and confident of this very thing, that He who has begun a good work in you will [continue to] perfect and complete it until the day of Christ Jesus [the time of His return].
Philippians 1:6 AMP

The life of the kingdom involves growth. We are commanded to mature into the full stature of Christ. Ephesians 4:13 says it like this *"This will continue until we all come to such unity in our faith and knowledge of God's Son that we will be mature in the Lord, measuring up to the full and complete standard of Christ."*

Be confident that you don't disappoint God in any way. Not in your shortcomings, failures, transgressions, or anything. He made provision for that in Jesus Christ. This is part of the mystery of Christ. Confess your sins to Him, repent, turn away from that sin, and continue your journey.

God uses all these things to mature and perfect you. The enemy is only mad because he knows there is therefore no condemnation for those in Christ. You are justified. You are free. Praise God. Rejoice and live. Our God reigns.

PRAYER

Thank you, Holy Father, for justifying me as your child. You have made me a new birth by your Spirit. I live a glorified life now through Christ our Lord Amen.

APRIL

Day 100

I pray that your love will overflow more and more, and that you will keep on growing in knowledge and understanding. For I want you to understand what really matters, so that you may live pure and blameless lives until the day of Christ's return. May you always be filled with the fruit of your salvation-the righteous character produced in your life by Jesus Christ –for this will bring much glory and praise to God.
Philippians 1:9-11 NLT

Love is the single most powerful force on earth. The whole law of God is summed up in this one word: love. You can love truly when you have God in you, He is love.

It is good to have knowledge of the Word of God, but how would that profit you if you lack understanding? A man of understanding is a stable man. So, in all your getting, understanding (Proverbs 4:7). Understanding will show you what really matters in life. It will guide you to live a pure and blameless life until Christ returns.

The salvation you have also believed has to produce fruits. This fruit of righteousness is by Jesus Christ. As you daily plunge into Him, he prunes you, building in you a righteous character. This is to the glory of the Father through his Son Jesus. Selah.

PRAYER

Heavenly Father, thank you because Jesus is revealed in me, and I am bearing the fruit of righteousness to the glory of your name. Amen.

APRIL
Day 101

For now the elite Roman guards and government officials overseeing my imprisonment have plainly recognized that I am here because of my love for the Anointed One. And what I'm going through has actually caused many believers to become even more courageous in the Lord and to be bold and passionate to preach the Word of God, all because of my chains.
Philippians 1:13-14 TPT

The Christ-like journey we are called to, is not an uninteresting one. It is full of adrenaline. The ups and downs, the happy and sad times, the deaths and healing, the miracles and everything in between makes it more meaningful than anything on this earth.

How can someone's imprisonment lead many hearts to turn to the Lord? And others bold enough to preach the gospel? Today, can you see your challenges as something that can glorify God? Do you believe He can use it for your good and transform other lives too? Is it possible that your trial is going to encourage somebody else into this kingdom? Selah.

In these times of self-love, it is difficult for us to see God amidst the chaos. But today, be encouraged. God is for you. Even in your chains, something wonderful can happen. Shalom.

PRAYER

Abba, this truth is wonderful to me, I believe you are working everything for your glory. I trust you. Amen.

APRIL

Day 102

Meanwhile, live in such a way that you are a credit to the Message of Christ. Let nothing in your conduct hang on whether l come or not. Your conduct must be the same whether I show up to see things for myself or hear of it from a distance. Stand united, singular in vision, contending for people's trust in the Message, the good news, not flinching or dodging in the slightest before the opposition. Your courage and unity will show them what they're up against: defeat for them, victory for you-and both because of God. There's far more to this life than trusting in Christ. There's also suffering for him. And the suffering is as much a gift as the trusting. You're involved in the same kind of struggle you saw me go through, on which you are now getting an updated report in this letter.
Philippians 1:27-30 MSG

The suffering of this present age cannot be compared to the glory that awaits you (Romans 8:18). Live in a way that your life is a credit to Christ. There is more to this Christian walk than trusting God, there is also suffering. *"For unto you it is given in the behalf of Christ, not only to believe on him, but also to suffer for his sake;"* Philippians 1:29. Selah. You are equipped to endure. As you endure, know that no situation is permanent. This one too will pass.

PRAYER

Father, may my every suffering be a sacrifice acceptable and pleasing to you. I love you, Lord. Amen.

APRIL

Day 103

Paul, a prisoner of Jesus Christ, and Timothy our brother, Unto Philemon our dearly beloved, and fellow-labourer, and to our beloved Apphi-a, and Archippus, our fellow soldier, and to the church in thy house: Grace to you, and peace, from God our Father and the Lord Jesus Christ.
Philemon 1:1-3 KJV

May the grace and peace of our Lord Jesus be multiplied to you. Apostle Paul, in his letter, identified himself by the call of God in his life. He had accepted the truth that he had been chosen to send the mystery of the gospel to the Gentiles. That acceptance placed him in a position where he was totally sold out to the purpose of the Lord. His identity was a prisoner of Jesus Christ.

Whose prisoner are you? Your flesh or Jesus Christ? Or is it Satan the Prince of this world, and all its earthly gains? Selah.

In Paul's letter to Philemon, he acknowledged some people in the body. He identified some as dearly beloved, fellow labourers, fellow soldiers, and the Church. This tells us we aren't identified the same. The next time you get offended by what you are called, remember even God weighs your labour and calls you by what you do in and for His body. Focus on your purpose. Shalom.

PRAYER

Father, thank you for the grace and peace to do your will. Amen.

APRIL

Claim the Word

Day 104

APRIL

Happy are those who do not follow the advice of the wicked, or take the path that sinners tread, or sit in the seat of scoffers; but their delight is in the law of the Lord, and on his law they meditate day and night. They are like trees planted by streams of water, which yield their fruit in its season, and their leaves do not wither. In all that they do, they prosper.
Psalms 1:1-3 NRSV

There is a better way to live a happy fulfilled life that glorifies God. God's desire is for you to prosper and be in good health. He instructs us to not follow the counsel of the ungodly, or tread in the seat of the sinner. You can't tread the same path with ungodly people if you want to be happy.

You are called to delight (that is enjoy, be happy) in the laws of the Lord. Meditate on it day and night, and you shall be like a tree, yielding fruit in season. You will not be outdated meaning throughout the seasons of life you will know what to do at the right time. You will be effective and productive because the Word is your foundation.

Not only that, but He assures that you will also prosper in all areas of life. As we honour God's Word, He will remain faithful and committed to keeping you in perfect peace. Selah.

PRAYER

Father, thank you for the comfort of your Word. Amen.

APRIL

Day 105

I will declare the decree: the Lord hath said unto me, Thou art my Son; this day have I begotten thee. Ask of me, and I shall give thee the heathen for thine inheritance, and the uttermost parts of the earth for thy possession. Thou shalt break them with a rod of iron; thou shalt dash them in pieces like a potter's vessel.
Psalm 2:7-9 KJV

The only thing you need to hear and say is what God is saying about you, so you can align your faith to reality. Your real life is hidden in Christ since you resurrected with Him (Colossians 3:3).

The scriptures guide us in establishing God's will over our lives on this earth through decreeing and declaring what God is saying. James 1:25 MSG tells us, *"God's revealed counsel gives the life that is free."* Therefore, it is essential for you to listen correctly in order to declare accurately. What has God revealed to you? What has He said that scares you? What are you believing him to do for you and others? Open your mouth, decree, and declare and He that watches over His Word will make it happen. Do what you have to do, and in obedience, He will always honour His Word.

PRAYER

Father, thank you for the revealed word. I decree and declare it over me and mine in Jesus' name Amen. Shalom.

Day 106

Lord, how they have increased who trouble me! Many are they who rise up against me. Many are they who say of me, "There is no help for him in God." Selah But You, O Lord, are a shield for me, My glory and the One who lifts up my head. I cried to the Lord with my voice, And He heard me from His holy hill. Selah.
Psalms 3:1-4 NKJV

I think there is a moment in life when it feels like everything is going wrong, and you perceive enemies all around you. Enemies are the necessary evil of life, and it is sometimes good to have them. Your enemies serve as a measure of God's protection over your life. Whenever you begin to experience such interference in your life, know God has also increased his angelic protection over you. I don't know if the enemy has been whispering that God will not come to your aid. Believe it when I say God knows, and he has already taken charge, hallelujah, Amen.

Believe that God is for you, a Shield in times of trouble. Cry to the Lord, call on His name, tell him your need and believe he has heard and answered you. He is your shield and will deliver you. Until trouble blows, you will never know how protected you are. Selah.

PRAYER

Thou, oh Lord, are a shield for me, my glory, and the lifter up of my head. Amen.

APRIL

Day 107

May we never forget that the Lord works wonders for every one of his devoted lovers. And this is how I know that he will answer my every prayer. Lord, prove them wrong when they say, "God can't help you!" Let the light of your radiant face break through and shine upon us! The intense pleasure you give me surpasses the gladness of harvest time, even more than when the harvesters gaze upon their ripened grain and when their new wine overflows. Now, because of you, Lord, I will lie down in peace and sleep comes at once, for no matter what happens, I will live unafraid!
Psalms 4:3, 6-8 TPT

God is with those who believe. He works wonders with your faith in him. Let this blessed assurance give you rest. Do not keep iniquity in your heart and he will hear your prayers. Psalm 66:18. Harbouring sin hinders your prayers. May the Lord lift up the light of his countenance upon you as you stay in obedience to his word and let go of every sin.

There is a kind of pleasure that comes from being in unity with the Lord, and dwelling in his secret place, where he shepherds you. He will keep you in perfect peace no matter what comes your way. God delights in you. He is your shepherd. Shalom.

PRAYER

Thank you for the light of your radiant face breaking me through and shining on me. Amen.

APRIL

Repent

APRIL

Day 108

For thou art not a God that hath pleasure in wickedness: neither shall evil dwell with thee. The foolish shall not stand in thy sight: thou hatest all workers of iniquity. But as for me, I will come into thy house in the multitude of thy mercy: and in thy fear will I worship toward thy holy temple. Lead me, O Lord, in thy righteousness because of mine enemies; make thy way straight before my face.
Psalm 5:4-5, 7-8 KJVAAE

The righteousness and holiness of God is such that it cannot behold sin! Habakkuk 1:13 says *"Your eyes are too pure to look on evil; you cannot tolerate wrongdoing..."* He takes no pleasure in wickedness or those who do them. In fact, Psalm 34:16 says it like this: *"But the face of the LORD is against those who do evil, to wipe out all memory of them from the earth."*

He will wipe out those who do evil if they don't repent and accept his gift of salvation. What strikes me in the scriptures above is verse 5. It says the foolish shall not stand in thy sight! Selah

The foolish, boastful, proud and arrogant cannot dwell with God. Repent and change your ways, because it hinders your prayers, because God does not see you, and if He cannot see you neither does He hear your prayer. Selah.

PRAYER

Forgive me, Abba for my foolishness. I come to you in the multitude of your mercy. May my prayers not be hindered.
Amen.

APRIL

Day 109

For thou hast maintained my right and my cause; thou satest in the throne judging right. But the Lord shall endure for ever: he hath prepared his throne for judgment. And he shall judge the world in righteousness, he shall minister judgment to the people in uprightness. The Lord also will be a refuge for the oppressed, a refuge in times of trouble. And they that know thy name will put their trust in thee: for thou, Lord, hast not forsaken them that seek thee.
Psalm 9:4, 7-10 KJVAAE

The Lord is compassionate and merciful, but judges in righteousness. He supports what is right and advocates for the upright. He cautions us to walk in obedience and he will bless and protect us. The wicked, he tells us, will come to ruin.

Psalm 9 puts a lot of emphasis on the judgement of God. Verse 7 says the throne of God is prepared for judgement. Verse 20 establishes that when God judges, men will know they are but just mere men. God is in absolute control, fear not mere men but fear God.

The Lord is a refuge for the oppressed, a refuge in times of trouble. Do not feel alone. Those that are on your side are more than the opponents you see. God is your Father, the judge of all, your shepherd and salvation. Be confident in this hope and trust him always. Selah.

PRAYER

Abba, maintain my right and my cause for the glory of your name. Defend and protect me from danger. Amen.

APRIL
Day 110

Vindicate me, O God, and defend my cause against an ungodly people; from those who are deceitful and unjust deliver me! O send out your light and your truth; let them lead me; let them bring me to your holy hill and to your dwelling. Then I will go to the altar of God, to God my exceeding joy; and I will praise you with the harp, O God, my God. Why are you cast down, O my soul, and why are you disquieted within me? Hope in God; for I shall again praise him, my help and my God.
Psalms 43:1, 3-5 NRSV

John 8:15 tells us, *"God's judgments are different from our way of judgement." "His throne is established for judgement,"* Psalms 9:7. *"Righteousness and justice are the foundation of his throne,"* Psalms 89:14. l urge you to go to God with your challenges. He will hear your supplication. Make known to him your case, He is an honest judge and will vindicate you.

Make use of your Advocate the Holy Spirit. Jesus is also known as the Word of God. In any situation ask the Lord to send and grant you his light and truth. Light for illumination and truth for assurance and stability. These will be a guide and foundation you can stand on in any circumstance, as you wait on the Lord.

Then you can say to your soul, why are you cast down? Hope in the Lord, my help and my salvation. Selah.

PRAYER

You oh Lord, are my shield and my glory, the lifter of my head. Amen.

APRIL

Our Strength

APRIL

Day 111

I thirst for God, the living God. When can I go and stand before him? My heart is breaking as I remember how it used to be: I walked among the crowds of worshipers, leading a great procession to the house of God, singing for joy and giving thanks amid the sound of a great celebration! But each day the Lord pours his unfailing love upon me, and through each night I sing his songs, praying to God who gives me life.
Psalms 42:1-2, 4, 8 NLT

Discouragement is a massive tool of the enemy to discontinue doing whatever God has led you to do. It makes you pessimistic, where you only see the worst in everything. But God told us in John 16:33 that in him we will have peace. Joshua 1:9 commands us to be strong and be of good courage.

Your soul is the seat of your emotions, the coordinator of your senses. Its influence over your life is very powerful. The scriptures admonish us not to live by sight but by the spirit, because the spirit searches all things, even the deep things of God (1 Corinthians 2:10).

Your soul is a valuable asset. You can channel your emotions into the hands of your spirit to be led to please God. He says I pray that your soul prospers. The Holy one can lead you to still waters.

PRAYER

My soul thirsts for you oh Lord my King. Fill me till I overflow. Amen.

APRIL

Day 112

O clap your hands, all ye people; shout unto God with the voice of triumph. For the Lord most high is terrible; he is a great King over all the earth. He shall subdue the people under us, and the nations under our feet. He shall choose our inheritance for us, the excellency of Jacob whom he loved. Selah. For God is the King of all the earth: sing ye praises with understanding.
Psalm 47:1-4, 7 KJV

God did not reveal himself to us as Lord alone, as he did in the past. Not only is He the Lord over all, but he is the creator of all things. He also showed us he is a King, he rules even in the affairs of men. But above all, He is your Father, which has always been a mystery to some. The mighty, ever glorious Lord calls us his children.

It is therefore important to know who He is, why he called you, and made these promises to you. Shout his praise and worship him in triumph. Because He has already won the victory for you. Only believe to receive. The Lord most high is terrible to your enemies, a great king overall the earth. He will subdue for your peace. But most importantly, he has chosen your inheritance for you. Rejoice in the Lord of your salvation. Hallelujah. Selah.

PRAYER

Abba, thank you for being my Lord, my King and my Father. Amen.

APRIL

Day 113

God is our refuge and strength, a very present help in trouble. Therefore will not we fear, though the earth be removed, and though the mountains be carried into the midst of the sea; though the waters thereof roar and be troubled, though the mountains shake with the swelling thereof. Selah. The Lord of hosts is with us; the God of Jacob is our refuge. Selah.
Psalm 46:1-3, 7 KJVAAE

Through your knowledge of God, you have been taught that you are the temple of God and He dwells in you (1 Corinthians 3:16). You grow up believing that God lives in you. But have you paused to think that God is also your dwelling?

All over the scriptures, God makes us aware that we are in Him! You were in him before he brought you forth, and you will remain in him on this earth. Selah. He says, abide in me and I in you, for without me you can do nothing (John 15:4).

Psalm 90 tells us God has been our dwelling place from generation to generation. He is God from everlasting to everlasting. Take your place in God. Be seated in Christ and rest in his finished work. Selah.

PRAYER

Abba, thank you for being my home, my refuge and strength. Amen.

APRIL

Day 114

We have heard with our ears, O God, Our fathers have told us, The deeds You did in their days, In days of old: You drove out the nations with Your hand, But them You planted; You afflicted the peoples, and cast them out. For they did not gain possession of the land by their own sword, Nor did their own arm save them; But it was Your right hand, Your arm, and the light of Your countenance, Because You favored them. You are my King, O God; Command victories for Jacob. Through You we will push down our enemies; Through Your name we will trample those who rise up against us. For I will not trust in my bow, Nor shall my sword save me. In God we boast all day long, And praise Your name forever. Selah.
Psalms 44:1-6, 8 NKJV

Your Father will do anything for your peace. He said, *"I will give men in exchange for your life"* (Isaiah 43:4). He drove others out of places to give it to you. You didn't have to do anything because of his mighty arm and his favour over you. He granted you an advantage over your enemies.

Through God, you have overcome your enemies and trampled over those who rise against you. As you keep dwelling in His presence and trusting in Him, He will shepherd you through life. Make your boast in Him, for He is a good Father. Selah.

PRAYER

Father, thank you for giving me the best in this life. Amen.

APRIL

Day 115

This beginning of miracles did Jesus in Cana of Galilee, and manifested forth his glory; and his disciples believed on him. Now when he was in Jerusalem at the passover, in the feast day, many believed in his name, when they saw the miracles which he did.
John 2:11, 23 KJV

God delights in working miracles. He wants to give you good gifts (Matthew 7:11). Miracles manifest God's glory because no one can claim ownership of an act of a miracle. Miracles also increase people's faith and trust in God.

Why then would God not delight himself by giving you miracles? James 4:3: *"And even when you ask, you don't get it because your motives are all wrong—you want only what will give you pleasure."* The next time you pray about anything, you align your motives to His and make sure your miracle will bring the glory to Him alone amen.

PRAYER

God of miracles, as I go in your name, may miracles, signs and wonders follow me in Jesus' name, Amen.

APRIL

Day 116

The impotent man answered him, Sir, I have no man, when the water is troubled, to put me into the pool: but while I am coming, another steppeth down before me. Jesus saith unto him, Rise, take up thy bed, and walk.
John 5:7-8 KJV

To be in the same place with a want of strength, without help from another person, you cannot do anything; that is what infirmity does to a man. This is not God's will for anyone. The Scriptures described this man as impotent. May this never be your story. Amen.

Thirty-eight years is a long time to be impotent. No wonder he attracted Jesus's attention. The compassion of Christ for his creation always moves him to heal and restore. That is why if you desire any spiritual gifts, you need to love people. Selah.

Today, may Adonai see your affliction and cause you to rise again in Jesus' name, Amen.

PRAYER

Adonai, my Lord, I thank you that right now every arear in my life that is impotent receive strength right now in Jesus' name. Amen.

APRIL
Day 117

And Jesus took the loaves; and when he had given thanks, he distributed to the disciples, and the disciples to them that were set down; and likewise of the fishes as much as they would. When they were filled, he said unto his disciples, Gather up the fragments that remain, that nothing be lost.
John 6:11-12 KJV

God is the God of excellence and order.

Everything he made was done beautifully with precision. The season and times are in their cause, they do not elapse. So is the miracles and healing of God. Every one of the miracles in Scriptures were carefully done either by God or through others were done by instruction with compelling obedience.

If you seek to receive any form of miracles, signs, wonders, or healing, then be ready to follow God's instructions. In your obedience is your testimony, Amen. Shalom.

PRAYER

Thank you God for your Spirit of truth. Leading and showing me what to always do in Jesus' name, Amen.

Day 118

APRIL

When they kept on questioning him, he straightened up and said to them, "Let any one of you who is without sin be the first to throw a stone at her." Jesus straightened up and asked her, "Woman, where are they? Has no one condemned you?" "No one, sir," she said. "Then neither do I condemn you," Jesus declared. "Go now and leave your life of sin."
John 8:7, 10-11 NIV

The generosity of God transcends His provision for the living, but His mercies and grace are what keep you alive. But for grace, hallelujah, Amen.

I believe one of the most powerful demonstrations of God's love and grace towards a sinner is the story of the woman caught in adultery (John 8:1-11). Don't be quick to condemn or judge. His kindness leads us to repentance (Romans 2:4). Show someone kindness, mercy, forgiveness, and patience today. In so doing we demonstrate the love of God to his creation.

You are the salt and light of this world. You are meant to build up and demonstrate the love and kindness of God to all men.

PRAYER

Lord, make me merciful in all my ways, Amen.

APRIL

Day 119

For they loved human praise more than praise from God. "If anyone hears my words but does not keep them, I do not judge that person.

For I did not come to judge the world, but to save the world. There is a judge for the one who rejects me and does not accept my words; the very words I have spoken will condemn them at the last day.
John 12:43, 47-48 NIV

The work of Christ on earth and after is that of salvation. He has commissioned his disciples, you and I to go to the ends of the earth with the gospel, the good news that God (Jesus) became flesh, died and took our sins so that we will be made right with God.

After this, when the end of all things shall come then judgement. Jesus reminded us that what will judge us is His Word, which we did not pay heed to. If you hear his voice, harden not your heart.

PRAYER

Holy spirit, help me to always give heed to the Word of God, Amen.

Day 120

APRIL

Then Jesus said, "I am the true vine, and my Father takes care of the vineyard. He removes every one of my branches that doesn't produce fruit. He also prunes every branch that does produce fruit to make it produce more fruit. "You are already clean because of what I have told you. Live in me, and I will live in you. A branch cannot produce any fruit by itself. It has to stay attached to the vine. In the same way, you cannot produce fruit unless you live in me.
John 15:1-4 GW

Every child of God has two phases to the activities of their lives. The cut-off and pruning stage. The seriousness of the cut-off is like King Saul; although rejected by God, he was still a king.

Be wise and serve the Lord in reverence. The second one is pruning. Sometimes when we face tough times, we don't see it like the love and chastening of God. Not all difficulties/challenges are from the enemy.

You cannot live outside of Christ. Stay glued. Even in adversity you are being nurtured to His image.

PRAYER

Father, I trust your wisdom. I trust you with my life and I know as I stay in the vine I will bear much fruit. Amen.

MAY

Rejoice

Day 121

Great is the Lord, and greatly to be praised in the city of our God, in the mountain of his holiness. Beautiful for situation, the joy of the whole earth, is Mount Zion, on the sides of the north, the city of the great King. As we have heard, so have we seen in the city of the Lord of hosts, in the city of our God: God will establish it forever. Selah. For this God is our God forever and ever: he will be our guide even unto death.
Psalm 48:1-2, 8, 14 KJV

Praising the most high God is a good thing, to exalt his name above all things. Praise him in the beauty of holiness. "*The sceptre of his kingdom is righteousness and justice,*" Hebrews 1:8.

God is beautiful for every situation. He can manifest his power and act as he wills and desires. His judgments are true and pure. He is the king! Selah. If you can see him as the joy of the whole earth, then you can see his mighty arm working in everything. Do you trust he can turn it around for you? As you have heard now do you believe?

Salvation comes by hearing and hearing the word of the Lord. What are you hearing? Don't accept it if it is not in line with God's promises to you. God is your God forever. He is faithful, trustworthy and a good Father. He loves you, now and forever.

PRAYER

This God is my God forever. He will be my guide even to death. You are the joy for my situation, Amen.

Day 122

A happy heart is good medicine and a joyful mind causes healing, But a broken spirit dries up the bones.
Proverbs 17:22 AMP

To be cheerful is to be happy. The Bible says that it is good medicine. Peace begins with a smile, but I also know some smiles can be mischievous. But I hope yours is the former. Keep smiling. Choose to be cheerful in every situation. The joy of the Lord is your strength.

Strength appears when you make up your mind to remain happy despite challenges. If there are a million reasons to be unhappy, find one reason to be happy. And that is the breath of life. Don't allow brokenness, pain, and unforgiveness to suck the strength out of your life. You oversee your joy. Chad Sugg says it like this; *"If you're reading this... Congratulations, you're alive. If that's not something to smile about, then I don't know what is."*

Smile at the face of adversity; it confuses your enemies. A merry heart is a good medicine (Proverbs 17:22).

PRAYER

Heavenly Father, thank you for the gift of life. Thank you for the grace of remaining cheerful in spite of anything life may bring my way. Thank you for another month. Amen.

Day 123

Behold, I was brought forth in iniquity, and in sin did my mother conceive me. Behold, you delight in truth in the inward being, and you teach me wisdom in the secret heart. Create in me a clean heart, O God, and renew a right spirit within me. The sacrifices of God are a broken spirit; a broken and contrite heart, O God, you will not despise.
Psalm 51:5-6, 10, 17 ESV

I believe a lot of us Christians do not understand the new covenant we have with God. He has made Jesus who knew no sin to be sin for us. He says you are born again, your sins are forgiven and forgotten. You are the redeemed of the Lord, rejoice in your salvation and believe it. Hallelujah!

We usually quote these verses as a pacifier, to justify the wrongs we do instead of standing in the truth of what Jesus has done. We need to walk in the new nature that has no sin in it. Romans 6:14 says 'For sin will no longer be your master.' You are under the grace of God! Your sins now have been forgiven by the blood. Selah. The next time you read the scriptures recognize when it was written and who you are now. Remember what Jesus did and the Holy Spirit in you. You are bought with a price. Rejoice!

PRAYER

Heavenly Father, thank you for the benefits of my salvation. I rejoice in you, Amen.

MAY

Day 124

But I am like a green olive tree in the house of God. I trust in the steadfast love of God forever and ever. I will thank you forever, because you have done it. I will wait for your name, for it is good, in the presence of the godly.
Psalm 52:8-9 ESV

God really does delight in the prosperity of his people. (Psalms 35:27). Genesis 1 shows us how He made sure everything needed was available before He made Adam. So, it is with you, if you can believe and trust Him for your everyday need, He will lead you and bring you along the still waters.

The Psalmist declared he is a green olive. Who are you? What are you saying about yourself and your situation? Are you agreeing with what God is saying?

An olive tree is an emblem of prosperity. You are like a green olive-tree in the house of God. You are safe and happy. No effort made by your enemies to secure your destruction can prosper. You will be kept unharmed, like a green and flourishing tree, a tree protected in the very courts of the sanctuary. You are safe under the caring eyes of God.

Be thankful because God has done this for you and your household Amen. Selah.

PRAYER

Father, thank you for making me like a green olive tree. Amen.

Day 125

O God, save me by your name, and vindicate me by your might. Behold, God is my helper; the Lord is the upholder of my life. He will return the evil to my enemies; in your faithfulness put an end to them. With a freewill offering I will sacrifice to you; I will give thanks to your name, O Lord , for it is good. For he has delivered me from every trouble, and my eye has looked in triumph on my enemies.
Psalm 54:1, 4-7 ESV

Human beings have the inclination of being needed. Just like His nature, He desires us to need him in all aspects of our lives. The one who bears the name of the Lord should know that the Lord is his refuge, shield and a strong tower. He has given you His name by which you shall be saved. You need to identify which name of God you need, then call on him for manifestation.

He will answer and vindicate you by his might. He is delighted to help you. When evil men plan evil, he laughs and sends it back to them, they fall in their own pit (Proverbs 26:27).

Do not forget to praise and give thanks to him when he delivers you and gives you another testimony. Testify of his goodness to you. The Lord is kind. Give thanks.

PRAYER

Thank you for upholding my life in all the seasons of life Amen.

Day 126

It is good to give thanks to the Lord, to sing praises to the Most High. It is good to proclaim your unfailing love in the morning, your faithfulness in the evening, You thrill me, Lord, with all you have done for me! I sing for joy because of what you have done. O Lord, what great works you do! And how deep are your thoughts. Only a simpleton would not know, and only a fool would not understand this: But you have made me as strong as a wild ox. You have anointed me with the finest oil. But the godly will flourish like palm trees and grow strong like the cedars of Lebanon.
Psalms 92:1-2, 4-6, 10, 12 NLT

Thankfulness is an attitude stemming from contentment. When a person comes to the place of being content in the grace God has given him, thankfulness flows unequivocally. Your desire to worship and commune with the Lord becomes strong. You proclaim and declare that His love kept you through the dangers of the night. In the evening, you thank Him for His faithfulness.

The Lord does a lot of things to keep the upright joyful all the time. Like a man courting his bride, He beckons you to his chamber/presence and showers you with His love. He anoints you and strengthens you for what may come your way. He makes you strong like the wild ox. You are the child of God. Rejoice in your identity. Selah.

PRAYER

Father, your love is so wonderful to me, thank you. Amen.

MAY

His Mercies

MAY

Day 127

Have mercy on me, O God, have mercy! I look to you for protection. I will hide beneath the shadow of your wings until the danger passes by. I cry out to God Most High, to God who will fulfill his purpose for me. He will send help from heaven to rescue me, disgracing those who hound me. My God will send forth his unfailing love and faithfulness. My heart is confident in you, O God; my heart is confident. No wonder I can sing your praises!
Psalms 57:1-3, 7 NLT

The best place to be in time of trouble is to fall on the mercies of God. The mercy of God is his kindness. He bends or stoops in kindness to favour you. What an awesome father we have. Look to him for protection, our Jehovah Nissi.

The Lord can be your hiding place if you trust in Him and His word to hide and protect you from harm. He will shield you from evil. Why would he do that? So that he can fulfil his purpose for you. He will send help from heaven to rescue you and disgrace those who want to trample on you.

Make up your mind, be confident with all of your heart that God is faithful to His word. Psalm 53:2 echoes *"when I am afraid I will trust in you."* Whenever fear knocks at your door, send the Word to answer. Jesus is Lord. Selah.

PRAYER

Thank you, Lord, for your mercies. It is by your mercies I am not Consumed. Amen.

Day 128

My soul, wait thou only upon God; for my expectation is from him. He only is my rock and my salvation: he is my defence; I shall not be moved. In God is my salvation and my glory: the rock of my strength, and my refuge, is in God. Trust in him at all times; ye people, pour out your heart before him: God is a refuge for us. Selah.
Psalm 62:5-8 KJV

Training your soul to act and be steadfast in the Lord is a discipline. Sometimes the Holy Spirit enables one the grace, and by His mercies, manoeuvres one through situations to keep your hope alive.

When you decide that you have made the Lord your salvation, defence, strength, and refuge, you will always have situations that would challenge your beliefs. But you are encouraged to trust God at all times and pour your heart to him. When it becomes difficult to find hope, ask Him to be hope for you. He becomes your expectation. Hope is an expected end, when God becomes that expected end, he becomes your all in all. You shall not be in want. Selah!

Hebrews 6:19: *"We have this hope as an anchor for the soul, firm and secure. It enters the inner sanctuary behind the curtain."*

PRAYER

Father, thank you for being my hope, my expectation. When I cannot, I know you can. Amen.

MAY

Day 129

God presides in the heavenly council; in the assembly of the gods he gives his decision: "You must stop judging unjustly; you must no longer be partial to the wicked! Defend the rights of the poor and the orphans; be fair to the needy and the helpless. Rescue them from the power of evil people. You are gods,' I said; 'all of you are children of the Most High.
Psalm 82:1-4, 6 GNT

One of the attributes of God is that He is just. Whether you believe it or not the foundation of God's throne is justice and righteousness. He is the just judge! (Psalm 89:14).

In righteousness has He called you to be like him, ruling on earth with dominion and power.

God presides in the Heavenly Council, judging the wicked and protecting the poor. He commands you, who represents Him on this earth to do likewise.

He gave us His word to give us knowledge, His Spirit, to lead and guide us. He wants us to defend the rights of the oppressed in society, protect the widows and the orphans, and be fair to the needy and helpless. This is the heart of God. Proverbs 19:17 BSB says this: *"Kindness to the poor is a loan to the LORD, and He will repay the lender".* Selah.

PRAYER

Father, thank you for the grace to be kind-hearted and merciful. Amen.

MAY

Prayer and Praise

MAY

Day 130

O you who hear prayer, to you shall all flesh come. When iniquities prevail against me, you atone for our transgressions. Blessed is the one you choose and bring near, to dwell in your courts! We shall be satisfied with the goodness of your house, the holiness of your temple! By awesome deeds you answer us with righteousness, O God of our salvation, the hope of all the ends of the earth and of the farthest seas; You crown the year with your bounty; your wagon tracks overflow with abundance.
Psalm 65:2-5, 11 ESV

I do not know what would have happened to humanity if there was no prayer, where there was no channel in which one could speak to his maker.

"But thanks be to God, who calls us to himself and has given us this same ministry to reconcile others." 2 Corinthians 5:18.

Not only did God make a way for all flesh to come to him but also clean us up of every wrong. Those who choose to come near to God are blessed. Dwelling in his court, you will find rest and help in the day of adversity. You shall be filled with the goodness of His house. Selah.

Because God is awesome, He will always answer you in his righteousness. He will send forth his salvation as Jesus is the hope for the earth. He will crown you with a bounty and you will overflow with abundance. Amen.

PRAYER

Father, thank you for salvation, answers, and abundance
Amen.

MAY

Day 131

Sing the glory of his name; give to him glorious praise! Say to God, "How awesome are your deeds! So great is your power that your enemies come cringing to you. Come and see what God has done: he is awesome in his deeds toward the children of man. He turned the sea into dry land; they passed through the river on foot. There did we rejoice in him, who rules by his might forever, whose eyes keep watch on the nations- let not the rebellious exalt themselves. Selah.
Psalm 66:2-3, 5-7 ESV

God lives or occupies the place where His praise is. No wonder David had the Lord's heart. Even in absurd situations he will choose to praise God. May God grant you the heart of a worshipper at all times in every situation. Tell him how awesome His deeds are and testify to others how God has been good.

When you praise him, you take your eyes off yourself and circumstances into possibilities. The glory of God is beautiful, and as you gaze upon this beauty, you are changed, renewed, refined, and regenerated from glory to glory.

Remember the presence of God is His goodness. As you behold Him, you will experience all His goodness. You will pass through the river on foot without drowning. Selah.

PRAYER

Heavenly Father, thank you for your goodness, I wear your glory like a garment. Amen.

MAY
Day 132

How lovely is your dwelling place, Lord Almighty! My soul yearns, even faints, for the courts of the Lord; my heart and my flesh cry out for the living God. Even the sparrow has found a home, and the swallow a nest for herself, where she may have her young- a place near your altar, Lord Almighty, my King and my God. Blessed are those who dwell in your house; they are ever praising you. Blessed are those whose strength is in you, whose hearts are set on pilgrimage. As they pass through the Valley of Baka, they make it a place of springs; the autumn rains also cover it with pools. They go from strength to strength, till each appears before God in Zion.
Psalms 84:1-7 NIV

Anyone who has tasted the presence of Yahweh knows it is like nothing ever experienced on earth. Words cannot describe it. The Psalmist tells us even the swallow has made its nest in thy dwelling. Blessed and happy are those that dwell in your house, whose strength is in you.

As you pass through the valley of challenging and unprecedented times, it shall be as a spring because you know you are on a pilgrimage. God is your home. He is your dwelling place, and He will make your way prosperous. Selah.

PRAYER

Abba, all the days of my life I will dwell in your house beholding your beauty and worshipping you. Amen.

Day 133

O Lord God of hosts, hear my prayer: give ear, O God of Jacob. Selah. Behold, O God our shield, and look upon the face of thine anointed. For a day in thy courts is better than a thousand. I had rather be a doorkeeper in the house of my God, than to dwell in the tents of wickedness. For the Lord God is a sun and shield: the Lord will give grace and glory: no good thing will he withhold from them that walk uprightly. O Lord of hosts, blessed is the man that trusteth in thee.
Psalm 84:8-12 KJV

It is not the desire of the Lord to withhold anything good from you. But the scriptures emphatically tell us that an heir, as long as he remains a child, is no different from a slave Galatians 4:1. If you want to see your inheritance in Jesus, grow up in the kingdom of God. Selah.

God hears our prayers, if he doesn't, he wouldn't have said call on me and I will answer and show you great and mighty things (Jeremiah 33:3).

Any time spent in the presence of God is better than anything else you can do. He is the giver of undeserved favours and glory. He will never withhold any good thing from the one who walks upright. Trust in God. Selah.

PRAYER

Abba, you are my dwelling, my grace, and my glory. Amen.

MAY

God of Justice

MAY

Day 134

How long, O Lord? How long will the wicked be allowed to gloat?

They kill widows and foreigners and murder orphans. Is he deaf-the one who made your ears? Is he blind-the one who formed your eyes? He punishes the nations-won't he also punish you? He knows everything-doesn't he also know what you are doing? The Lord knows people's thoughts; he knows they are worthless! Joyful are those you discipline, Lord, those you teach with your instructions.

You give them relief from troubled times until a pit is dug to capture the wicked. The Lord will not reject his people; he will not abandon his special possession.
Psalms 94:3, 6, 9-14 NLT

God knows everything; doesn't he know what you do? Is he deaf he who made the ear? Is he blind, he who made the eye? He punishes the nations; won't he punish you? Don't be ignorant. God is not mocked; whatever you sow is what you will reap.

The Lord knows people's thoughts. He knows how worthless they are. The Lord's discipline brings joy, he teaches his instructions. He will give you relief from trouble. The Lord will not abandon his possession. You are his child, be confident in this truth. Selah.

PRAYER

Father, thank you for your discipline and your instructions.

Day 135

Mighty King, lover of justice, you have established fairness. You have acted with justice and righteousness throughout Israel. Exalt the Lord our God! Bow low before his feet, for he is holy! Moses and Aaron were among his priests; Samuel also called on his name. They cried to the Lord for help, and he answered them. He spoke to Israel from the pillar of cloud, and they followed the laws and decrees he gave them. O Lord our God, you answered them. You were a forgiving God to them, but you punished them when they went wrong.
Psalms 99:4-8 NLT

God is a lover of justice. He has established fairness throughout the earth. The Lord is holy! There is no shadow of falsehood in him that is why you can trust him. He is faithful and true.

The scriptures show us here that Moses and Aaron were priests, God spoke to Moses face to face. He answered their prayers. Moses was an intercessor for Israel, yet they did not escape God's punishment although God is forgiving.

Samuel was a priest and called on God's name. No words of his fell to the ground unhindered, God still punished his wrong. Be careful, lest you feel the Lord does not see your unrepentant wrongdoing. He is a righteous judge. Selah.

PRAYER

Abba, forgive me of all my wrongs in Jesus' name. I repent of my sins. Amen.

MAY

Hurt

MAY

Day 136

For it is not an enemy who taunts me then I could bear it; it is not an adversary who deals insolently with me- then I could hide from him. But it is you, a man, my equal, my companion, my familiar friend. We used to take sweet counsel together; within God's house we walked in the throng. Cast your burden on the Lord, and he will sustain you; he will never permit the righteous to be moved.
Psalm 55:12-14, 22 ESV

Our most painful experiences and hurts are wounds from loved ones. These are people we trusted, people we expected to love and protect us and people we have learnt to be vulnerable with. The betrayal and wrong from these kinds of people cut really deep. But for the mercies and love of God, you can trust and love again.

It is therefore necessary to be informed it is a part of our life's journey. Jesus himself experienced this in John 13:18: *"I speak not of you all: I know whom I have chosen: but that the scripture may be fulfilled, He that eateth bread with me hath lifted up his heel against me."*

This referred to His experience with Judas, which eventually led to our salvation. The Lord is asking you to give him that burden today and he will sustain you through the pain, loss, grief, and betrayal. Will you allow him? Selah.

PRAYER

Abba, I give to you all my burden, sustain my life in Jesus' name.

Day 137

They don't belong to the world any more than I belong to the world. "Use the truth to make them holy. Your words are truth. I'm dedicating myself to this holy work I'm doing for them so that they, too, will use the truth to be holy.
John 17:16-17, 19 GW

Being in a place with the knowledge that you don't belong can be unsettling. Jesus consistently informed us he did not belong to this world. He also told us that this world is not our home; we are foreigners. You know why you are unsettled?

Because if God allows you to be so comfortable, you might forget you are passing through. Don't mistake peace for comfort. He allows things in our journey on this earth to remind us we are passing through. His truth, which you know and accept, makes you holy, sanctified for his presence to be in you. The truth sets you apart for his glory. Amen.

PRAYER

Lord, I thank you for your truth abides in me always, guiding me to do right till I come home. Amen.

MAY

Day 138

And Simon Peter followed Jesus, and so did another disciple: that disciple was known unto the high priest, and went in with Jesus into the palace of the high priest. But Peter stood at the door without. Then went out that other disciple, which was known unto the high priest, and spake unto her that kept the door, and brought in Peter.
John 18:15-16 KJV

I believe in the daily bread of God, and I also know men do not live on bread alone but by every word of God. This means that the bread you need to Nourish both your spirit and soul is more spiritual than physical.

Jesus knew his time had come to die. But on his journey to the cross, he was not alone. His Father was with him, and Angels ministered to him until he carried our sins. But you see when the soldiers arrested him, another disciple went with him and made way for Peter to come into the courtyard. You are never alone.

You have God, Angels, and men to minister to you. There are times you have experienced these miracles but because God manifested through a human form you could not discern. You have numerous helpers on every side. Amen.

PRAYER

Lord, I thank you for men that you have sent to help me.
Amen.

MAY

Day 139

And after this Joseph of Arimathaea, being a disciple of Jesus, but secretly for fear of the Jews, besought Pilate that he might take away the body of Jesus: and Pilate gave him leave. He came therefore, and took the body of Jesus. And there came also Nicodemus, which at the first came to Jesus by night, and brought a mixture of myrrh and aloes, about an hundred pound weight.
John 19:38-39, KJV

Jesus's humility is evident not only because he was God but also because he took on the nature of flesh to die in our stead. His humility is also evident in how he treated people and how welcoming he was to all.

He could relate to everyone, rich or poor, sick or healed, children or adults, young or old. That was true humility.

Because of his nature, he secured for himself a burial place. People like Joseph, who secretly believed in him, bold enough to ask for his body and Nicodemus, who would give without thinking of the cost. May God grant you men like these. Amen.

PRAYER

Lord, thank you for making me bold like Joseph and also to stand up for truth for others, Amen.

MAY

Listening to God

Day 140

MAY

"Love your enemies! Do good to them. Lend to them without expecting to be repaid. Then your reward from heaven will be very great, and you will truly be acting as children of the Most High, for he is kind to those who are unthankful and wicked. You must be compassionate, just as your Father is compassionate.
Luke 6:35-36 NLT

The Kingdom of God has principles and a way of life that identifies and differentiates you from the rest. One of those principles is to love people (1 John 3:14) and the world because God made them.

We can live like Jesus when we first acknowledge that we are like him on this earth. As he is, so are we (1 John 4:16-17). He dwells in you because you are compatible with him. You are amazing.

Love others as Jesus did and lend without expecting anything from others. Your great reward is in giving. Don't forget to be merciful. Like Dorcas, her gift spoke for her when she couldn't (Acts 9:38). She was described as merciful and of good works. How would people describe you? Pause and meditate on this. Selah.

PRAYER

Holy Spirit, teach me how to love others more and more. Amen.

Day 141

But wisdom is justified of all her children.
Luke 7:35 KJV

Wisdom is the use of knowledge—the ability to use what you know, how, and when. Wisdom is personified in Scripture, mostly in the book of Proverbs, as a woman who calls on her children to seek her like treasure hidden (Proverbs 1:20-33).

In 1 Corinthians 1:30-31, it says: *"Instead, credit God with your new situation: you are united with Jesus the Anointed. He is God's wisdom for us and more. He is our righteousness and holiness and redemption."*

As the Scripture says: "If someone wants to boast, he should boast in the Lord."

Jesus is your wisdom. If you follow his leadership, you will be vindicated. He will lead you in truth for the glory of His name. Wisdom is the right application of knowledge. He will lead you in the path you should take, and the good thing about Jesus is that He stays with you through it all. He is the friend that stays closer than a brother (Proverbs 18:24).

PRAYER

Abba, thank you for giving me Jesus who is my wisdom. I declare wisdom has His home in my heart, Amen.

Day 142

Pay attention, therefore, to how you listen. Whoever has will be given more, but whoever does not have, even what he thinks he has will be taken away from him.
Luke 8:18 BSB

Take heed of how you hear Jesus warning us. You might think you heard something, but how did you hear it? Did you hear with understanding, or did you perceive that is what was said? This Scripture creates the importance of hearing right. Having the spirit of understanding and being careful of the source of what you hear.

He also added to be careful to use what has been given to you freely. For if you do not use that which is given to you for others, by telling them about the truth of the gospel, even what you think you have will be taken away from you. Selah.

You have the power and grace to tell others about Jesus. This lamp of yours cannot be hidden, You cannot put your lamp under a bushel (Matthew 5:15).

When God lights up your lamp, share your radiance; through it others can also shine and give glory to God. Amen.

PRAYER

Lord, help me to be a witness to others Teach me Holy Spirit to hear right, Amen.

Day 143

And he answered and said unto them, My mother and my brethren are these which hear the word of God, and do it.
Luke 8:21 KJV

Jesus taught us the importance of heeding to how you hear. It is equally necessary to your growth as a child of God to be doers of the Word heard. In that, you will be natured, and the Spirit of God can use you in different aspects regarding the issues of life.

Jesus, in the above verse, shows us that those he calls relations are those who listen and act on the Word. He himself does what he sees the Father do in John 5:17-30. So, it relates to you, you are his brethren if you do what he commands you to do. In your obedience, you inherit the blessings and are found in him. Also, in his righteousness, hallelujah, Amen. Shalom.

PRAYER

Father God, teach my heart to wait on because I know you heard my prayer, Amen.

MAY

Day 144

O love the LORD, all ye his saints: for the LORD preserveth the faithful. Be of good courage, and he shall strengthen your heart, all ye that hope in the Lord. Amen.
Psalm 31:23-25 KJV

O you saints, love the Lord, love him faithfully because he is worthy to be loved, honour and adored. The Lord preserves the one who is faithful.

He gives strength to guard you from the evil one, for his name's sake. Halleluiah amen.

Be of good courage, and he will do this; *"But look, God will not reject a person of integrity, nor will he lend a hand to the wicked. He will once again fill your mouth with laughter and your lips with shouts of joy. Those who hate you will be clothed with shame, and the home of the wicked will be destroyed."* Job 8:20-22 NLT. Amen.

Never be afraid to tell and show you love the Lord. He said, *"Whoever denies me before men, I also will deny before my Father."* Matthew 10:33 ESV.

Be courageous for the one who died for you.

PRAYER

Father, you are good and kind. Thank you for taking care of me and my family.
Amen.

MAY

Day 145

For I considered all this in my heart, so that I could declare it all: that the righteous and the wise and their works are in the hand of God. People know neither love nor hatred by anything they see before them. [2] All things come alike to all: One event happens to the righteous and the wicked; To the good, the clean, and the unclean; To him who sacrifices and him who does not sacrifice. As is the good, so is the sinner; He who takes an oath as he who fears an oath.
Ecclesiastes 9:1-2 NKJV

It is an error to think that opportunities do not happen to all. Verse two tells us all things come alike to all. One event happened to the righteous and the wicked alike. This makes me fear God, he is not unjust. His judgment is. true.

Your advantage as a believer after Salvation is the indwelling Holy Spirit that can teach you all things that pertain to life and godliness and also be your wisdom. Make use of this truth.

Making use of the Holy Spirit who is already in you is by feeding on the word of God and having a clear conscience. Know the truth, as He is the Spirit of truth. He will lead you by His truth through your spirit and your conscience.

PRAYER

Thank you Daddy for Giving me all I need. Because Jesus lives in me, I will not be afraid of workers of iniquity, Amen.

Day 146

The LORD is my shepherd. I will always have everything I need.
Psalm 23:1 ERV

Shepherds are accountable; they protect, direct, and lead. When you have a Shepherd,, you learn to follow. You need a submissive heart and an obedient, childlike trust. Our human nature finds it difficult to obey without knowing, but that is what faith is about—trusting that the one who has called and led you is truth-worthy.

When you have grasped the truth about the nature and character of God, you don't just say He is your Shepherd, but you declare to the hearing of every living creature The LORD is my Shepherd. Hallelujah, Amen.

Shepherd watches during the night; while you sleep, He watches over you. He neither sleeps nor slumbers. Trust your Shepherd. Amen.

PRAYER

I declare I have good shepherd leading me, Amen.

Day 147

Yea, though I walk through the valley of the shadow of death, I will fear no evil; For You are with me; Your rod and Your staff, they comfort me. [5] You prepare a table before me in the presence of my enemies; You anoint my head with oil; My cup runs over.
Psalm 23:4-5 NKJV

I have a Shepherd! Although I will walk through the valley of what looks like it is going to kill me, I will not be afraid, for my Shepherd is with me.

Your love and mercy comfort me always. You have prepared victory for me in the presence of my enemies. You have anointed my head with fresh oil.

As you hold me together, I will live in abundance. Amen.

Sometimes you have to read His words to your soul, body and mind; even your environment. Declare what He has said over you. He overcame by the word of our testimonies (Revelations 12:11-12). Testify that the valley is a walk-through. Hallelujah, praise God. Amen.

PRAYER

Lord, I am so grateful for you being my shepherd. I am loved and comforted in Jesus' name, Amen.

Day 148

Surely your goodness and unfailing love will pursue me all the days of my life, and I will live in the house of the LORD forever.
Psalm 23:6 NLT

Because I have a Shepherd, only goodness and mercy will follow me. His unfailing love pursues me all day long. I am blessed all the days of my life, when I sleep and when I awake.

I declare I live in the house of my Shepherd all the days of my life. I am blessed. I am highly favoured. Because I have a good Shepherd.

PRAYER

Lord, thank you for your goodness and mercy that follows me everywhere I go, Amen.

I have a good shepherd,
His banner over me is love;
God pursues me in everything I do.
His love wakes me up and
Guides me through and through.
I live in my Father's house.
I have a good shepherd.

Amen.

MAY

Day 149

Hear my cry, O God; attend unto my prayer. From the end of the earth will I cry unto thee, when my heart is overwhelmed: lead me to the rock that is higher than I.

For thou hast been a shelter for me, and a strong tower from the enemy.
Psalm 61:1-2 KJV

My God and Father hear my cry. He attends to my prayers. Amen.

From the ends of the earth, I cry to you regardless of where I am. My heart is overwhelmed; lead me to the rock that is higher than I.

For you, oh God, are my shelter. My strong tower from the enemy. Lead me to the rock that is higher than I. Amen.

PRAYER

Lead me, Lord. Amen.

Day 150

I have set watchmen on your walls, O Jerusalem; They shall never hold their peace day or night. You who make mention of the LORD, do not keep silent, And give Him no rest till He establishes And till He makes Jerusalem a praise in the earth.
Isaiah 62:6-7 NKJV

I declare God has set watchmen on my walls. They will never hold their peace day and night until what He has said about you comes to pass, Amen.

I declare Jerusalem's walls are protected. Their watchmen will not hold their peace day and night. Amen.

You who mention the name of the Lord, do not keep silent. Do not give Him rest until He establishes and make Jerusalem a praise on earth, Amen.

PRAYER

Father, I thank you for watchmen. I thank you also for making me a watchman in Jesus' name Amen.

MAY

Day 151

Be humble under God's powerful hand so he will lift you up when the right time comes. Give all your worries to him, because he cares about you. Control yourselves and be careful! The devil, your enemy, goes around like a roaring lion looking for someone to eat.
1 Peter 5:6-8 NCV

There is a way to live in God's kingdom to experience the things He has promised.

For you to enjoy His powerful hands you need to humble yourself under Him. Trusting in His time. God is not bound and limited by human timing. He is divine, when He promise He keeps it.You should learn to trust Him with your worries and be assured He cares for you.

Be self control knowing that the enemy will come after you but be steadfast. Amen.

PRAYER

Father God, thank you for the Spirit of humility. I trust you with my life and all the things that belongs to me, As it is in heaven let it be unto me amen.

JUNE

Praise God

JUNE

Day 152

Let all that I am praise the Lord; with my whole heart, I will praise his holy name. Let all that I am praise the Lord; may l never forget the good things he does for me. He forgives all my sins and heals all my diseases. He redeems me from death and crowns me with love and tender mercies. He fills my life with good things. My youth is renewed like the eagles. I the Lord gives righteousness and justice to all who are treated unfairly.
Psalms 103:1-6 NLT

Praise flows freely from a grateful heart. Sometimes when it becomes difficult to praise God, remember what he did for you. That you have breath. And that also is free. Hallelujah! God be praised Amen.

Don't forget and lose sight of all that God does for you. Let me remind you of how He forgave all your sins and healed all your diseases. How that sickness should have killed you, but God stepped in and snatched you from the clutches of death and said not this one! Praise him!

He redeemed you from death and after he crowned you with his love and tender mercies. He made sure he filled your life with good things so that you are renewed like the eagles. Because he is righteous, he treated you fairly in spite of your unfaithfulness. Pause and meditate. Give thanks with a grateful heart.

PRAYER

Father, may I never lose the wonder of your mercies to me. Amen.

JUNE

God's Love

JUNE

Day 153

He revealed his character to Moses and his deeds to the people of Israel. The Lord is compassionate and merciful, slow to get angry and filled with unfailing love. He will not constantly accuse us, nor remain angry forever. He does not punish us for all our sins; he does not deal harshly with us, as we deserve. For his unfailing love toward those who fear him is as great as the height of the heavens above the earth. He has removed our sins as far from us as the east is from the west.
Psalms 103:7-12 NLT

When you were a child, you thought like a child but as you grew you put aside childish ways (1 Corinthians 13:11). The Lord will deal and reveal things to you according to the power at work in you (Ephesians 3:20). God revealed his ways, his plans of redemption to Moses but to Israel he revealed his acts, what he could do. The Lord is slow in getting angry and filled with unfailing love. It is not in his nature to constantly accuse you although he will convict you of sin and lead you to repentance. He does not deal harshly with you as your sins deserve.

The love God has towards those who fear him is great as the heights of heaven. He has removed your sins and the love of it from you, as far as the East is to the West. Rejoice. Selah.

PRAYER

Abba, thank you for loving me this much. Amen.

Day 154

JUNE

And the Lord multiplied the people of Israel until they became too mighty for their enemies. The Lord blanketed Egypt in darkness, for they had defied his commands to let his people go. The Lord brought his people out of Egypt, loaded with silver and gold; and not one among the tribes of Israel even stumbled.

The Lord spread a cloud above them as a covering and gave them a great fire to light the darkness. They asked for meat, and he sent them quail; he satisfied their hunger with manna-bread from heaven. [...] Praise the Lord!
Psalms 105:24, 28, 37, 39-40, 44-45 NLT

God is love. It is love that causes him to go to the extreme to protect his beloved. God's dealing with the Egyptians concerning Israel shows us the extent he will go to protect His people, purpose and will. You are in good hands Amen.

He did not leave them empty-handed when they left Egypt. God made sure he restored all the years they spent working as slaves, unpaid and unappreciated. He gave them more than enough to sacrifice to him.

Whatever you need, God is able to provide it. He has done it before and will do it again. If He did it for the children of Israel, He will do it for you. Believe to receive in Jesus' name. Amen.

PRAYER

Father, I believe you are for me. I will not fear. With you I have all I need. Amen.

JUNE
Day 155

Let everyone everywhere shine with praise to Yahweh! Let it all out! Go ahead and praise him! For he has conquered us with his great love and his kindness has melted our hearts. His faithfulness lasts forever and he will never fail you. So go ahead, let it all out! Praise Yah! O Yah!
Psalms 117:1-2 TPT

When you have the knowledge that you are truly loved, it changes your life. Love makes the difference. You can love and be loved but you must love God first, then love man. We love because God first loved us. He demonstrated this love by sending Jesus to die for you whilst you were a sinner.

The truth is that Jesus, who knew no sin became sin for you, took your penalty of death and trespasses to give you eternal life. This is life-changing! When you believe this message, God gives you the right to become his child, born of him into his kingdom. Hallelujah, what a love.

This should melt your heart. God is faithfully committed to you growing to become like Christ. Put your praise on this truth and rejoice. You are loved. Amen. Selah.

PRAYER

Abba, thank you for loving me and giving me your life.

JUNE

Give Thanks

JUNE
Day 156

Give thanks to the Lord, for he is good! His faithful love endures forever. Has the Lord redeemed you? Then speak out! Tell others he has redeemed you from your enemies. For he has gathered the exiles from many lands, from east and west, from north and south. Some wandered in the wilderness, lost and homeless. Hungry and thirsty, they nearly died. " Lord, help!" they cried in their trouble, and he rescued them from their distress. He led them straight to safety, to a city where they could live. Let them praise the Lord for his great love and for the wonderful things he has done for them. For he satisfies the thirsty and fills the hungry with good things.
Psalms 107:1-9 NLT

Has the Lord been good to you? Have you thanked Him today for his goodness? For his faithfulness and love towards you? Has the Lord redeemed you? Then speak out. Tell others of his loving kindness. God is good all the time.

You were far away, in exile by sin and transgressions, but he redeemed your life. Give thanks. He fed you when you were hungry and thirsty, give thanks. You were homeless and lost your way, he shepherded you, give thanks. The Lord is good. You cried for help, and he rescued you from anything that distressed you, and gave you His peace, His shalom. Nothing broken, nothing missing, give thanks. Selah.

PRAYER

Thank you, Lord, for your kindness unto me. I am grateful.
Amen.

JUNE

Day 157

Give thanks to the Lord, for he is good! His faithful love endures forever. Let all who fear the Lord repeat: "His faithful love endures forever." In my distress I prayed to the Lord, and the Lord answered me and set me free. The Lord is for me, so I will have no fear. What can mere people do to me? Yes, the Lord is for me; he will help me. I will look in triumph at those who hate me. It is better to take refuge in the Lord than to trust in people. It is better to take refuge in the Lord than to trust in princes.
Psalms 118:1, 4-9 NLT

The dead cannot praise God, so we must acknowledge that being alive is a gift from God. He is delighted by your praise. Are you living in gratitude? Do you have a thankful heart?

Give the Lord thanks for his faithful love which has endured throughout your years. When you live in gratitude, the Lord will be your helper and deliverer in the time of distress. He will set you free.

You will not be afraid because of sudden terror because God is with you. What can mere men do to you? God who created all things is your salvation. You are secured and covered in Christ, Hallelujah, Amen. It is better to take refuge in God than any other name.

PRAYER

Heavenly Father, thank you for keeping charge over me and granting me your salvation. I am blessed in Christ. Amen.

JUNE

Our Help and Confidence

Day 158

JUNE

My heart is confident in you, O God; no wonder I can sing your praises with all my heart! For your unfailing love is higher than the heavens. Your faithfulness reaches to the clouds. Oh, please help us against our enemies, for all human help is useless. With God's help we will do mighty things, for he will trample down our foes.
Psalms 108:1, 4, 12-13 NLT

Where do you place your confidence? In whom does your heart's confidence rest? How do you place your confidence?

When God is your confidence, you can not be or stay in fear. "*There is no fear in love but perfect love casts away every fear*," 1 John 4:18. God is love, as you make him your confidence, His love encamps around you and works in you to bring him glory. His love is unfailing. You can trust him with your life. His love for you is as high as the heavens, deep like the ocean's depth. His love always seeks to do good to you, give you the best and make you the best. Taking his word, believing, and acting on it makes your life beautiful, and you, in turn, reflect his glory.

God is faithful. He will help you against your enemies. The flesh cannot help you but with God's help you can do great exploits and trample down on your foes. Amen.

PRAYER

Father, thank you for your love and help, now and forever, Amen.

JUNE
Day 159

O God, whom I praise, don't stand silent and aloof.
Psalms 109:1 NLT

O God, do not keep silent; do not hold Your peace; do not be still, O God.
Psalm 83:1 ESV

The pain you feel is the determinant of how you will ask for help from the Lord. When you know your help is from the Lord, then today he says do not keep silent. Call on me. Selah.

Isaiah 42:14 says, *"I have kept silent from ages past; I have kept quiet and restrained. But now I will groan like a woman in labor; I will at once gasp and pant."*

Is the Lord your salvation? Is he your strength? Then sing his praise, magnify his name, tell of his faithfulness to you. As you bless Him and are grateful for what He has done, miracles will never cease from you.

Exodus 15:2: *"The LORD is my strength and my song, and He has become my salvation. He is my God, and I will praise Him, my father's God, and I will exalt Him."*

PRAYER

Heavenly Father, I thank you for thinking about me. Thank you for sending me help and helpers. Thank you for being a good father to me in Jesus' name. Amen.

JUNE

Day 160

The Lord will extend your powerful kingdom from Jerusalem; you will rule over your enemies. When you go to war, your people will serve you willingly. You are arrayed in holy garments, and your strength will be renewed each day like the morning dew. The Lord stands at your right hand to protect you. He will strike down many kings when his anger erupts. But he himself will be refreshed from brooks along the way. He will be victorious.
Psalms 110:2-3, 5, 7 NLT

To God belongs all power. He is all powerful. "God has spoken plainly, and I have heard it many times: Power, O God, belongs to you:" Psalms 62:11. He is the one who can cause you to rule over your enemies. He is in charge. When you go to war, it is God who will let people and even your enemies serve you willingly.

He promises to array you in holy garment, renewing your strength each day like a morning dew. He will stand at your right hand to protect you. Amen.

He will strike down Kings and change systems for your sake. You will be refreshed from unusual sources, causing you to be victorious all the way. God be praised Amen.

PRAYER

Thank you, Father, for being my good shepherd. Amen.

JUNE

Speak the Word

Day 161

JUNE

I believed, therefore I spoke, "I am greatly afflicted." Psalms 116:10 NKJV

We are made as speaking beings. To create our world through thoughts and words. What do you believe? Have you imagined it? Have you spoken it yet? *"Now to him who is able to do immeasurably more than all we ask or imagine, according to his power that is at work within us,"* Ephesians 3:20. The process of speaking your desires is God's way of creating. He created from Himself, agreeing with Himself, and speaking it forth. So are you. Agree, believe, and declare (Genesis 11:6).

What you are seeing is a result of your thoughts. Whether you are speaking according to God's will for you or not, change the course of your life with your words and imagination, according to his power at work in you. Selah.

PRAYER

Father, thank you for making me like you to create my world and live like heaven. Amen.

JUNE

Day 162

Though hostile nations surrounded me, I destroyed them all with the authority of the Lord. Yes, they surrounded and attacked me, but I destroyed them all with the authority of the Lord. They swarmed around me like bees; they blazed against me like a crackling fire. But I destroyed them all with the authority of the Lord. My enemies did their best to kill me, but the Lord rescued me. The Lord is my strength and my song; he has given me victory.
Psalms 118:10-14 NLT

The authority of the Lord has been given to the child of God to enforce the will of God in everything. This authority both in heaven and on earth has been invested in the name Jesus who is also the Word of God. Philippians 2:9-11 and John 1 tells us that.

The enemy will wage war against you but know and believe your victory is in the name of our Lord Jesus. They will surround you to destroy you, but you will overcome through the authority of Jesus.

Is Jesus your strength and salvation? Then know you are more than a conqueror. If he is not, then this is the day to invite him into your life.

PRAYER

Jesus, I am yours both now and forever Amen. I believe in Jesus the saviour of the world. Thank you, Jesus, for redeeming my life Amen.

JUNE

Faithfulness

JUNE

Day 163

I will sing of your love and justice, Lord. I will praise you with songs. I will be careful to live a blameless life- when will you come to help me? I will lead a life of integrity in my own home. I will refuse to look at anything vile and vulgar. [...] I will search for faithful people to be my companions.

Only those who are above reproach will be allowed to serve me. I will not allow deceivers to serve in my house, and liars will not stay in my presence.
Psalms 101:1-7 NLT

You cannot love the Lord and not hate injustice. Every lover of God should be a just person, standing for the truth and defending the helpless in society.

The Lord expects us to live a life of integrity even in our own homes where no other eyes may be watching and judging. You should strive to live a blameless life. Hating what is vile and vulgar. Let us not tolerate people who slander their neighbours.

The king showed us in the above scriptures, he will search for faithful people as companions. Those that will serve him are above reproach. If even an earthly king has these qualities to look out for, how much more our father in heaven? Who are your companions? Pause and think about it.

PRAYER

Father, thank you for reminding me how peculiar I am and what you expect from me; lead me, Holy Spirit, to live like Christ. Amen.

JUNE

Names of God

JUNE

Day 164

Have you not known? Have you not heard? The everlasting God, the Lord, The Creator of the ends of the earth, neither faints nor is weary. His understanding is unsearchable.
Isaiah 40:28 NKJV

We begin our new phase of our devotion with the study of the names of God. The knowledge of the character of God helps you to identify yourself and situations with Him.

Elohim known in the bible as the LORD God or God means the Living God, Supreme and Mighty One. It emphasises God's power and mighty acts. He is the creator of the heavens and the earth and all that is in it (Genesis 1:1).

Do you thus deal with the Lord, O foolish and unwise people? Is He not your Father, who bought you? Has He not made you and established you? (Deuteronomy 32:6 NKJV). It shows that God made you and has established you. He made you in His likeliness to rule and have dominion. He promises never to let anything harm you or hurt you. Believe He is for you. You are for God's pleasure. He loves you. Cast all your cares on Him for He cares for you (1 Peter 5:7). He will not allow any harm to befall you.

PRAYER

"Now therefore, Arise, O Lord God, to Your resting place, You and the ark of Your strength. Let Your priests, O Lord God, be clothed with salvation, And let Your saints rejoice in goodness." (II Chronicles 6:41 NKJV)

Amen.

Day 165

Then Moses said to God, "Indeed, when I come to the children of Israel and say to them, 'The God of your fathers has sent me to you,' and they say to me, 'What is His name?' what shall I say to them?" Moreover God said to Moses, "Thus you shall say to the children of Israel: 'The Lord God of your fathers, the God of Abraham, the God of Isaac, and the God of Jacob, has sent me to you. This is my name forever, and this is My memorial to all generations.'
Exodus 3:13-15 NKJV

Yahweh, I AM THAT I AM. The all sufficient one. He is all in all. In Him comprises everything. You cannot explain Him but can trust Him. You cannot understand Him, but you can believe His Word, for He is faithful to His promises.

He keeps His covenant even to the fourth generation that is why He can't swear by any other than Himself. There is none close to His equal. No rival. He is God by Himself.

"And Asa cried unto the LORD his God, and said, LORD, it is nothing with you to help, whether with many, or with them that have no power: help us, O LORD our God; for we rest on you, and in your name we go against this multitude. O LORD, you are our God; let not man prevail against you." 2 Chronicles 14:11 KJV.

PRAYER

Yahweh is a jealous God and avenges. Yahweh avenges and is full of wrath. Yahweh takes vengeance on his adversaries, and he maintains wrath against his enemies. Amen.

Nahum 1:2 WEB

JUNE

Day 166

And because you are sons, God has sent forth the Spirit of His Son into your hearts, crying out, "Abba, Father!"
Galatians 4:6 NKJV

ABBA means Daddy, Father, and is the favourite name of God. Abba is the most intimate form of God's name, showing us His character as our loving daddy. He is the One who can be fully trusted, the One we can lean on, the One who cares about all that concerns us. Just as a godly father's presence in our daily lives is one of protection, security, and unconditional love, the constant presence of our heavenly Father is what gives us the strength and covering we need for this life's journey.

Luke 11:2: *"So He said to them, "When you pray, say: Our Father in heaven, Hallowed be Your name. Your kingdom come. Your will be done on earth as it is in heaven.""*

This is the privilege we have to call the maker of the heavens and the earth as our Father.

"I myself said, "I want very much to make you my sons. I want to give a good country to you. It is more beautiful than the country that any other people enjoy." And I said, "You will call me 'Father', and you will not stop obeying me."" Jeremiah 3:19. He only desires your obedience to His Word and honouring Him.

PRAYER

Abba Father, thank you for making me your child. I will honour you with my life in Jesus' name, Amen.

JUNE

Day 167

I will praise the Lord according to his righteousness: and will sing praise to the name of the Lord most high.
Psalms 7:17 KJV

And blessed be the most high God, which hath delivered thine enemies into thy hand. And he gave him tithes of all.
Genesis 14:20 KJV

El Elyon means God Most High. Nothing is more sacred on the earth than Him. His name is above all gods. He is indeed the Lord Most High, the One who reigns supreme. He is greater than any force of darkness in this world, He is bigger than any problem we might come up against in this life. In life's struggles and battles, we sometimes need to be reminded that God is still in control.

He is the one that is blessed to give blessings. He is the gift to give gifts. He is merciful to give mercy. He is love to express love. He is all things so He will be all things to you. He is the Lord Most High, the ever faithful God, the unchanging. He is able to keep you from falling and uphold you and to deliver you from your enemies. Trust His faithfulness.

PRAYER

El Elyon, my God Most High. My Father and God, thank you for being my source. Because you own everything, I lack nothing. In Jesus' name, Amen.

JUNE

Day 168

And she called the name of the Lord that spake unto her, Thou God seest me: for she said, Have I also here looked after him that seeth me?
Genesis 16:13 KJV

El Roi, the one who sees me. This was the name Hagar, Sarah's servant called the Lord when the angel of the Lord came to her in the wilderness after she fled from her mistress. Hagar is Ishmael's mother, the son of Abraham. She was scorned by Sarah and mistreated. As she fled her home, she found herself in a desert, alone, sacred to the point of death. It was at this point of desperation the angel appeared to her.

She didn't expect to see an angel come to her aid. But the Lord who is a covenant keeping God had His eyes on the seed of Abraham. So He sent forth His Word to instruct and comfort her.

It is never too dark for you to see. For you, the night has as much light as the day. Darkness and light are the same to you! Psalms 139:12 EASY.

So it is with you. No situation, no challenge, no storm can take you from the watchful eye of El Roi. He is watching over your going in and coming out. You are covered by the blood of Jesus. His sovereign hand is your guide.

PRAYER

El Roi, the one who sees me. Thank you for your covering over me and mine. I bless you for being a good Shepherd. I love you.

Day 169

JUNE

And when Abram was ninety years old and nine, the Lord appeared to Abram, and said unto him, I am the Almighty God; walk before me, and be thou perfect.
Genesis 17:1 KJV

El Shaddai, means God Almighty. He is the God who sees all, knows all, and has the power to go before you, walk with you daily, and cover you from behind. Dwelling in God's presence gives you shelter and rest. That is why He urges you to walk blameless before Him because He cannot behold sin.

For a day in thy courts is better than a thousand. I had rather be a doorkeeper in the house of my God, than to dwell in the tents of wickedness. For the Lord God is a sun and shield: the Lord will give grace and glory: no good thing will he withhold from them that walk uprightly. Psalms 84:10-11 KJV

When you choose to walk blameless, El Shaddai becomes your secret place. Within the Rock. "Shaddai" is to be traced, not to the Hebrew, but to an Accadian word that means "mountain".

Psalm 91:1 says;

"He who dwells in the secret place of the Most High Shall abide under the shadow of the Almighty. When you dwell in Him He becomes your refuge, shield and refuge, a safety you can trust."

PRAYER

El Shaddai, I thank you for being safe for me. My secret place, my hiding place against the storms of life, until all my enemies are defeated in Jesus' name Amen.

JUNE

Day 170

And said, If thou wilt diligently hearken to the voice of the Lord thy God, and wilt do that which is right in his sight, and wilt give ear to his commandments, and keep all his statutes, I will put none of these diseases upon thee, which I have brought upon the Egyptians: for I am the Lord that healeth thee.
Exodus 15:26 KJV

Jehovah Rapha or Rophe means the Lord who heals. We are reminded that God Himself is the great physician who has the power to heal our physical, emotional and spiritual needs. He is our mighty healer. Rophe in Hebrew means cure, heal, and make whole or to restore.

This name brings comfort and hope to many of us who have prayed for healing and deliverance from disease, illness, brokenness, or painful circumstances. It reminds us that God knows we need help and healing, and He promises to redeem and restore every broken place in our lives. He never leaves us to fend for ourselves.

Today, as He has reminded us of this promise, why don't you take His word and remind Him? Thank Him for being your healer in every aspect, physically, emotionally, mentally, and spiritually.

PRAYER

Jehovah Rapha, thank you for healing all my diseases. May your name be praised Through Christ our Lord, Amen.

JUNE

Day 171

And the Lord said unto him, Peace be unto thee; fear not: thou shalt not die. Then Gideon built an altar there unto the Lord, and called it Jehovah-shalom: unto this day it is yet in Ophrah of the Abi-ezrites.
Judges 6:23-24 KJV

Jehovah Shalom meaning the Lord is Peace. The word for peace, shalom, goes deeper than the lack of conflict or being calm. It means wholeness in all of life or completeness, safety and welfare. God is the source of these blessings.

As a result of Israel's disobedience, God delivered them to the Midianites and they prevailed against the Israelites. They were so greatly impoverished that they dwelt in caves for the fear of the Midianites. But as they cried to the Lord He sent an Angel who found Gideon and commissioned him a deliverer.

God is a God of peace. His ways are peaceful to those who know Him. He is the Peace giver. He calms the ocean waves with a word. He calms our hearts with a whisper. Jesus said in Luke 14:27 "Peace I leave with you, my peace I give to you; not as the world gives do I give to you. Let not your heart be troubled, neither let it be afraid". Abba is your peace. Amen.

PRAYER

Jehovah Shalom, you are my peace. I decree and declare your peace in me, over me and around me in Jesus' name Amen. Read Judges 6. Don't be afraid.

JUNE

Day 172

It was round about eighteen thousand measures: and the name of the city from that day shall be, The Lord is there.
Ezekiel 48:35 KJV

Jehovah Shammah means the Lord is there. Is the name to be given to the new Jerusalem, restored and glorified, as seen in the vision of Ezekiel. The name indicates that God has not abandoned Jerusalem, leaving it in ruins, but that there will be a restoration.

When Jesus died and redeemed our lives, He conquered sin and death, and gave us a new nature of Himself, where His spirit in us relates to the Father. We call Him Abba. Gal 4:6. Like the new Jerusalem, we are resurrected with Jesus if we died with Him. We are therefore admonished to live a life worthy of our calling. Philippians 1:27.

Jehovah Shamma holds significance for Christ followers because it reminds us that God has not abandoned Jerusalem. It's a reminder to us also that he has not abandoned us in our darkest hour either. Again that God reveals himself to us incessantly. He is always there. Ever present, unchanging, and trustworthy.

PRAYER

Jehovah Shammah, I believe you are there for me, you are in me, and you are with me. Thank you for never leaving me in Jesus' name Amen.

JUNE

Day 173

The Lord is my shepherd; I have all that I need.
Psalms 23:1 NLT

Jehovah Raah, the Lord my Shepherd. In Hebrew, Raah means friend or companion. It can be translated as "The Lord my friend." In this passage we are reminded of just how much God cares for us. He is our friend, our confidant, our leader, provider and Shepherd.

As your Shepherd, the first thing the Lord addresses is lack or want. He says because I AM your companion you will not lack. Hallelujah Amen. He owns the World and all that is in it. How can you walk with Him, and be deprived of what you want? He is the good shepherd. (Micah 5:4).

This is what the Lord says: *"A shepherd who tries to rescue a sheep from a lion's mouth will recover only two legs or a piece of an ear..."* Amos 3:12. So it will be for God to rescue His children from the traps of the enemy. He will rescue you from every snare of the fowler (Psalm 91:3).

On that day the Lord their God will rescue his people, just as a shepherd rescues his sheep. They will sparkle in his land like jewels in a crown. How wonderful and beautiful they will be! The young men will thrive on abundant grain, and the young women will flourish on new wine.

(Zechariah 9:16-17 NLT)

PRAYER

This is your portion; in Jesus' name, Amen.

JUNE

Day 174

And this will be his name: 'The Lord Is Our Righteousness.'
In that day Judah will be saved, and Israel will live in safety.
Jeremiah 23:6 NLT

"O Israel, keep hoping, keep trusting, and keep waiting on the Lord, for he is tenderhearted, kind, and forgiving. He has a thousand ways to set you free! He himself will redeem you; he will ransom you from the cruel slavery of your sins!"
Psalms 130:7-8 TPT

It is in God's nature to be just and deal righteously with His creation. The verse above encourages you to keep hoping and trusting in God's kind-heartedness to save you from sin and any cruelty of slavery.

Even the righteousness of God which is by faith of Jesus Christ unto all and upon all them that believe: for there is no difference between Jews and Gentiles. (Romans 3:22). He does not discriminate and withhold justice. He is our righteousness, through Christ HE has imputed this nature into you. He calls you righteous.

We believe God is righteous, through Jesus Christ. whatever you believe the Justice of God for, approach the throne room of grace through the blood and make your request known in the court of heaven. Let us believe the one who did not spare His son but gave Him as a sin offering and ask for help and mercy. I know He will answer in Jesus' name Amen.

PRAYER

Jehovah Tsidkenu, my righteous judge. Arise and defend my case in your righteousness and mercy, in Jesus' name, Amen.

Day 175

And this man went up out of his city yearly to worship and to sacrifice unto the Lord of hosts in Shiloh. And the two sons of Eli, Hophni and Phinehas, the priests of the Lord, were there.
1 Samuel 1:3 KJV

Jehovah Sabaoth, which can also mean the LORD of heaven's armies. He is in charge! Both in heaven and on earth. He rules in the affairs of men. He directs the stars, planets, and the armies of heaven according to His pleasure. That is the LORD we serve.

Lift up your heads, O ye gates; even lift them up, ye everlasting doors; and the King of glory shall come in. Who is this King of glory? The Lord of hosts, he is the King of glory.
Psalms 24:9-10

He is the King of glory yet He desires to have His dwelling in you. Selah.

No wonder Psalm 91 says, when you dwell in the secret place of God, He will be your refuge and you will abide under His shadow, which is an awesome privilege.

PRAYER

Jehovah Sabaoth, my LORD of heaven's armies. Thank you for choosing to dwell in me and being my refuge; in Jesus' name, Amen.

JUNE
Day 176

And Abraham planted a grove in Beer-sheba, and called there on the name of the Lord, the everlasting God.
Genesis 21:33 KJV

El Olam, the Everlasting God. Although translated as God of ages and generations. El Olam shows us that God is the God of all ages; everything that happens is under His control. His revelation and manifestations are shown through His Son Jesus Christ. (Hebrews 1:1-2).

Jesus has eternal attributes. *"He is the same yesterday, today, and forever."* Hebrews 13:8. *"He obtained eternal redemption for us."* Hebrews 9:12. This name teaches us that God created time yet exists outside of and beyond it. Before the creation of the universe, there was God with no beginning and no end.

All things we know of change through time, yet our Father never does. This means the character of God, His Word, His Kingdom, and all He stands for never change and never end. That means we have a dependable, trustworthy, and consistent God! God has eternity in view for you. (Psalm 90:1-2). You have a Father and a God who is proven to be dependable.

PRAYER

El Olam, my Everlasting Father. Thank you for your eternal purpose for my life. I consecrate my life to you. May my life be a living sacrifice, holy, acceptable, and pleasing to you. Amen.

Day 177

JUNE

Speak thou also unto the children of Israel, saying, verily my Sabbaths ye shall keep: for it is a sign between me and you throughout your generations; that ye may know that I am the Lord that doth sanctify you.
Exodus 31:13 KJV

Jehovah Mekoddishkem, The Lord Who Sanctifies you. God instituted the Sabbath to show His favour to His people and as a sign that He had distinguished them from all other people. Their observance of the Sabbath was a duty and obedience to Him. God rested on the seventh day and also sanctified the Sabbath as a day of rest, which set His people apart for Himself and His service.

Blessed is the man who does this, and the son of man who holds it fast, who keeps the Sabbath without profaning it, and keeps his hand from doing any evil.
Isaiah 56:2 ESV

Keep God's Sabbath, and He will bless you, bringing you to the place of rest. Amen.

When you rest, God works. He gave you rest, to trust Him for increase. Meditate on a seed in the soil on the ground. In the dark is where maturity and growth occur. He is the Lord of the Sabbath.

PRAYER

Jehovah Mekoddishkem, the Lord who sanctifies me.
Thank you for making me your treasured possession,
sanctified, refreshed, and blessed in Jesus' name, Amen.

JUNE

Day 178

Thou shalt not bow down thyself to them, nor serve them: for I the Lord thy God am a jealous God, visiting the iniquity of the fathers upon the children unto the third and fourth generation of them that hate me;
Exodus 20:5 KJV

Qanna means jealous. It can be translated as 'jealous', 'zealous', or 'envy'. The fundamental meaning is of a marriage relationship. God is depicted as Israel's husband; He is a jealous God, wanting all our praise for Himself and no one else.

"For thou shalt worship no other god: for the Lord, whose name is Jealous, is a jealous God" Exodus 34:14. You are designed for intimacy with God, your maker. There is a part of you only He can satisfy. When you try to replace Him, He is jealous of your affection. What a loving Father and Lord we have.

You adulterers! Don't you realise that friendship with the world makes you an enemy of God? I say it again: If you want to be a friend of the world, you make yourself an enemy of God. Do you think the Scriptures have no meaning? They say that God is passionate and that the spirit he has placed within us should be faithful to him. (James 4:4-5 NLT). You are called into God Himself, worship Him alone with your life as a living sacrifice.

PRAYER

Qanna, The One who is jealous about the object of my affection and zealous for my attention, thank you for loving me too much. May my worship rise to you. Amen.

Day 179

JUNE

Abram said, "Lord God, what reward will You give me, since I am [leaving this world] childless, and he who will be the owner and heir of my house is this [servant] Eliezer from Damascus?"
Genesis 15:2 AMP

Adonai means LORD, from the derivation of the word 'Sovereignty'. May they know that you alone, whose name is the LORD, are Most High over all the earth. Psalm 83:18. He is the LORD of Lords, so He calls us to walk before Him and be blameless.

"Thus says the LORD who made the earth, the LORD who formed it and established it, the LORD is His name." Jeremiah 33:2. *"The LORD is a warrior, the LORD is His name."* Exodus 15:3. Reverence the Lord and He shall show Himself strong.

"Then you, my people, will know that I am the LORD, when I open your graves and bring you up from them." Ezekiel 37:13. When you know who you belong to and whom you have trusted, He will make impossible situations possible. He promises to open graves and bring you out, implying every dead thing will come back to life in Jesus' name. Amen.

PRAYER

Adonai, LORD of Lords. The Sovereign Lord, open thou every grave in my life. With you nothing is impossible. Thank you for my miracle sign and wonders, in Jesus' name, Amen.

JUNE

Day 180

God is full of grace. From him we have all received grace in place of the grace already given. [17] In the past, God gave us grace through the law of Moses. Now, grace and truth come to us through Jesus Christ.
John 1:16-17 NIRV

Grace is divine influence or the influence of the spirit that renews the heart and restrains sin. It is the favourable influence of God. What amazing grace. Thank God for Jesus.

You are not meant to live in this world by yourself. A world where Satan is the Prince, where darkness is increasing, wrong is right, and sin is a lifestyle. You need grace and truth and that is what God has given you. Favouring you among others when you need it, whilst influencing you to live and do right.

You are not without; you are Holy Spirit fed and divinely protected. A Prince of God, Amen.

PRAYER

Abba, thank you for giving me all I need in your son Jesus to be victorious. I receive grace to live this life, Amen.

JUNE

Day 181

f2Keep on loving each other as brothers and sisters. Remember to welcome strangers, because some who have done this have welcomed angels without knowing it. Remember those who are in prison as if you were in prison with them.
Hebrews 13:1-3 NCV

Remember those who are suffering as if you were suffering with them. It is not hard to be polite and nice to each other. Human beings' need for love is essentially important for thriving. Loving comes in different forms, sometimes it might be needed through forgiveness, patience, tolerance, kindness to name but few.

We are all called to love others because we might be the only image of God they might know. God is in you. You have love to give.

Remember to do good to strangers. Most Angels sent on assignment on Earth appear as strangers.

PRAYER

The world needs more people to love than to hate. Lord, help me to be the instrument of love everywhere I go.
Amen.

JULY

Victory

JULY

Day 182

My enemies did their best to kill me, but the Lord rescued me. The Lord is my strength and my song; he has given me victory. Songs of joy and victory are sung in the camp of the godly. The strong right arm of the Lord has done glorious things! The strong right arm of the Lord is raised in triumph. The strong right arm of the Lord has done glorious things! I will not die; instead, I will live to tell what the Lord has done.
Psalms 118:13-17 NLT

The fear of death has crippled a lot of people so much so that they cannot live the abundant life Jesus has redeemed them for. You will not die! The strong right arm of the Lord is raised in triumph. Amen.

When the Lord sets a table before you, you will need your enemies to see and be present. But don't fret yourself over them. They are defeated, and you have the victory. Rejoice in the God of your salvation. You are seated in heavenly places in Christ, far above rulers and authorities, principalities and powers, and every name in this world and the one to come. Hallelujah. (Ephesians 1:21).

PRAYER

Thank you, Father, for granting me life and access. Amen.

JULY

Day 183

Before I was afflicted I went astray, but now I keep your word. It is good for me that I was afflicted, that I might learn your statutes. The law of your mouth is better to me than thousands of gold and silver pieces. Your hands have made and fashioned me; give me understanding that I may learn your commandments. Forever, O Lord, your word is firmly fixed in the heavens.
Psalm 119:67, 71-73, 89 ESV

Christ's love controls us. Since we believe that Christ died for all, we also believe that we have all died to our old life. (2 Corinthians 5:14).

It is because we love him as he first loved us that helps us to live right and do right for His name's sake. One of the ways the enemy can have his way into your life to afflict you is when you go astray from the precepts of God when you decide to live your own way and not obey his voice. The devil will get hold of you.

But sometimes, it is good to go through these afflictions to learn the benefits of staying and abiding under the shadow of the Almighty. You are protected in Christ in God. Abide!

PRAYER

Father, help me keep your laws. They are settled in heaven. Amen.

JULY

Peace and Blessing

JULY

Day 184

Too long have I had my dwelling among those who hate peace. I am for peace, but when I speak, they are for war!
Psalm 120:6-7 ESV

The Peace of God is priceless. Jesus gave us his peace which the world doesn't have. This is an advantage for the child of God. Don't let anyone or anything take your peace. Jesus paid a price for your peace. He is our Prince of peace.

Psalm 34:14 admonishes us to depart from evil, and do good; seek peace, and pursue it. It is our duty to maintain the peace of God everywhere. But it's not so with evil doers.

Psalm 35:20 says they speak not peace: but they devise deceitful matters against them that are quiet in the land. Although you seek peace, anytime you speak of the peace which is Jesus, they are against it. Don't worry. It is not you they are rejecting, It is the light of Christ in you.

"Blessed are the peacemakers for they shall be called the children of God." Matthew 5:9.

PRAYER

Abba, thank you for giving me your peace. Nothing broken, nothing missing. I am blessed. Amen.

JULY

Day 185

Blessed is everyone who fears the Lord, who walks in his ways! You shall eat the fruit of the labor of your hands; you shall be blessed, and it shall be well with you. Your wife will be like a fruitful vine within your house; your children will be like olive shoots around your table.

Behold, thus shall the man be blessed who fears the Lord. The Lord bless you from Zion! May you see the prosperity of Jerusalem all the days of your life! May you see your children's children! Peace be upon Israel!
Psalm 128:1-6 ESV

The faculty to enjoy the fruit of your labour is a gift from God. You are happy and blessed when you revere the Lord and delight in His ways. You become like Mount Zion, which can never be moved.

The Lord does not only bless the one who fears him, He extends it to your spouse. He promises the wife will be like a fruitful vine in your household. Hallelujah, Amen! Your children will be like olive shoots around you. You will be a partaker of them that inherit the prosperity of Jerusalem.

Oh, how blessed you are, you who fear the Lord. Rejoice.

PRAYER

My soul magnifies the Lord, who delights in my well-being.
Amen.

JULY

God's Work

JULY

Day 186

The very stone the masons rejected as flawed have turned out to be the most important capstone of the arch, holding up the very house of God. The Lord himself is the one who has done this, and it's so amazing, so marvellous to see! This is the very day of the Lord that brings gladness and joy, filling our hearts with glee.
Psalms 118:22-24 TPT

You are not a mistake! You are God's special creature. God made you with purpose in mind. He designed you to be whole, unique, fearful, and wonderful. You are exceptional!

When you face any form of rejection, it is not the end of your life but a beginning, full of possibilities. The scriptures are saying to you where they thought you were flawed, defective, wrong, erroneous, God has made you a cornerstone. This is marvellous in His eyes, hallelujah.

This is good news. The Lord did it. He completed it in Christ. Do you believe it? This is the day the Lord has made, get up, rejoice and be glad in it. He made it for you and calls you his own. YOU ARE A CHILD OF GOD!

PRAYER

Abba, thank you for making me your own. Amen.

JULY

Day 187

Unless the Lord builds the house, the builders labor in vain. Unless the Lord watches over the city, the guards stand watch in vain. In vain you rise early and stay up late, toiling for food to eat- for he grants sleep to those he loves.
Psalms 127:1-2 NIV

Unless the Kingdom of God is the reason for whatever you do, it will not last forever!

God has placed eternity in the hearts of men (Ecclesiastes 3:11) and made everything beautiful in its time. You carry an incorruptible seed (1 Peter 1:23), meaning you have eternal life as a born-again child. You cannot live with an earthly mindset. You cannot do anything with a myopic mentality.

You are called to have a Kingdom perspective, where God is the master builder. Let Christ build you a house. Let him be your foundation and builder that will stand through eternity. This attitude gives you rest. He gives sleep to his beloved. You won't strive as the world does. He provides for His vision according to his riches in glory through Christ Jesus. Amen.

PRAYER

Father God, take the wheels of my life and let your will be done in me through Christ Jesus our Lord Amen.

JULY

Great God

JULY

Day 188

If you, O Lord, should mark iniquities, O Lord, who could stand? But with you there is forgiveness, that you may be feared. My soul waits for the Lord more than watchmen for the morning, more than watchmen for the morning.

O Israel, hope in the Lord! For with the Lord there is steadfast love, and with him is plentiful redemption. And he will redeem Israel from all his iniquities.
Psalm 130:3-4, 6-8 ESV

I am glad God's mercies are new every day. Iniquity means being wicked or immoral in nature or character, not conformed to the nature of Christ. We all fall short of God's glory and fall into Iniquity. But for His mercies, we are not consumed.

With the Lord, there is forgiveness so that we may fear and love him. Psalm 130:4 NLT writes, *"But you offer forgiveness, that we might learn to fear you."* He teaches you, when you forgive others, they learn to fear you. Selah.

No matter what kind of sin or wrongdoing you have committed, come to God and ask for His forgiveness. He is waiting; His love is open to all.

Wait on the Lord. Keep your eyes steadfast on his truth. His truth is his word, and His word is His bond. Hold on; change is coming. God bless you for trusting in Him. Shalom.

PRAYER

Heavenly Father, thank you for forgiving me and teaching me to forgive others. Amen.

JULY
Day 189

Lord, remember David and all his self-denial.
Psalms 132:1 NIV

Lord, please don't forget all the hardships David had to pass through.
Psalms 132:1 TPT

Remember, O Lord, in David's favor, all the hardships he endured,
Psalm 132:1 ESV

Lord, remember David, and all his afflictions:
Psalm 132:1 KJV

Today, if the Lord was to remember you for anything, what would that be? If the Lord was to show you favour for one thing, will he find anything to remember you for? What have you endured for his name's sake? What have you not compromised on? What is it in the spirit that has your name on as an altar?

Sometimes we go through life thinking that God is responsible for everything that happens to us. Well l am sorry to inform you, he gave you dominion and rulership, but with his guidance if you so choose. How have you used it? Selah.

PRAYER

Oh Abba, make me willing and obedient to your will Amen.

JULY

Day 190

I know the greatness of the Lord- that our Lord is greater than any other god. The Lord does whatever pleases him throughout all heaven and earth, and on the seas and in their depths.
Psalms 135:5-6 NLT

Do you know the Lord our God is greater than any other God? Not that there is any other close to him. He is the all-wise God, immortal, invincible, the I Am, the creator of the universe. He is our God and Lord overall. Hallelujah, Amen.

Psalm 95:3: *"For the LORD is a great God, a great King above all gods."* Psalm 97:9: *"For You, O LORD, are Most High over all the earth; You are exalted far above all gods."* Psalm 115:3: *"The Lord does whatever it pleases him.* Selah.

Isaiah 46:10: *"I distinguish the end from the beginning, and ancient times from what is still to come, saying: My purpose will be established, and I will accomplish all My good pleasure."*

Fear the Lord and shun evil, his ways are not your ways. Seek him in all you do, and you will prosper.

PRAYER

Psalm 33:9, 11: For He spoke, and it came to be; He commanded, and it stood fast... Amen.

JULY

Day 191

God remembered us when we were down, His love never quits. Rescued us from the trampling boot, His love never quits. Takes care of everyone in time of need. His love never quits. Thank God, who did it all! His love never quits!
Psalm 136:23-26 MSG

The thought that God's love never quits is life changing. God's mercy endures throughout your life and in eternity, rejoice in the Lord your God again I say rejoice. Amen.

Still, when God saw the trouble they were in and heard their cries for help, He remembered his Covenant with them, and, immense with love, took them by the hand. He poured out his mercy on them while their captors looked on, amazed.
Psalm 106:44-46 MSG

His Covenant love will do everything for your safety. Trust Him!

Psalm 103:14 says, *"For He knows our frame; He is mindful that we are dust."* He made you; He knows your needs and pardons your shortfalls. You are loved. Selah.

PRAYER

Father, thank you for loving me this much. Your love never runs out on me. Amen.

JULY

Day 192

O Lord, you have examined my heart and know everything about me. You know when I sit down or stand up. You know my thoughts even when I'm far away. You see me when I travel and when I rest at home. You know everything I do. You know what I am going to say even before I say it, Lord.
Psalms 139:1-4 NLT

Who testifies about you? Can you confidently say the Lord knows you? Does He know your thoughts and ways? Does He delight in you? Sometimes, it is worth asking yourself these questions to examine your ways. With the help of the Holy Spirit, you will know and judge yourself. For the one who judges himself will not be judged. (1 Corinthians 11:31).

In John 5, Jesus talks about how the Father has entrusted Him with everything, including judgment and life. He said his judgments are true and just. That is why, as you study the Word of God, it is able to discern your thoughts and motives; you can see yourself in the Word, and you can be informed about your true nature through knowledge. Go to the Word today; He will examine you.

PRAYER

Your Word have I hidden in my heart that I may not sin against you, Amen.

JULY

Praise the Lord

JULY

Day 193

Behold, bless ye the Lord, all ye servants of the Lord, which by night stand in the house of the Lord.
Psalm 134:1 KJV

Then a voice came from the throne, saying: "Praise our God, all you who serve Him, and those who fear Him, small and great alike."
Revelations 19:5 NIV

We are commanded to praise and serve Him who sits on the throne. How can you serve Him whom you cannot see with your eyes? You believe because the one who said so can be trusted. He is true to His every word. You obey by presenting your bodies as a living sacrifice, holy and pleasing which is your reasonable act of worship (Romans 12:1). He chose to live with you, and He is holy. You are also to serve others in love, just like serving Christ himself (Deuteronomy 10:8).

Why praise at night? Night represents adversity. It takes the humble God lover and seeker to praise him during adversity and stand on his watch until change comes. But as you keep your watch, soon this will be your confession: *Those who trust in the LORD are like Mount Zion. It cannot be moved; it abides forever. Amen.* (Psalm 125:1)

PRAYER

Psalm 126:1: *When the LORD restored the captives of Zion, we were like dreamers. God has restored you. Amen.*

JULY
Day 194

By the rivers of Babylon, There we sat down, yea, we wept when we remembered Zion. We hung our harps upon the willows in the midst of it. For there those who carried us away captive asked of us a song, And those who plundered us requested mirth, Saying, "Sing us one of the songs of Zion!" How shall we sing the Lord's song in a foreign land?
Psalms 137:1-4 NKJV

Take back your harps, says the Lord! It's so easy to let go of what God has entrusted in your care in the face of adversity and challenges. Hagar couldn't bear to see her child die, so she abandoned the child and wandered afar to cry to God. But it was the child's cry that God heard and sent his angel to give water and His word (Genesis 21:17).

Your instrument in this verse signifies your gift, talent, whatever God has given you to do. That change in your circumstance has made you stop using your gift. Go back, and play in the foreign land. Sing again, oh barren one (Isaiah 54:1). Your song is your deliverance. In your doing or actions lies your salvation. God is closer to the broken. Shalom.

PRAYER

Abba, as I take my harp, let your righteousness reign.
Amen.

Day 195

I will praise You with my whole heart; Before the gods will sing praises to You. I will worship toward Your holy temple, And praise Your name For Your loving kindness and Your truth; For You have magnified Your word above all Your name. In the day when I cried out, you answered me, And made me bold with strength in my soul.
Psalms 138:1-3 NKJV

Praise is a mighty weapon. Praising God with your whole heart before anything else is choosing his magnificence above all else. Your worship takes the burden off you and sets you free from yourself.

In fact, Isaiah 61:3 says, *"To all who mourn in Israel, He will give a crown of beauty for ashes, a joyous blessing instead of mourning, festive praise instead of despair. In their righteousness, they will be like great oaks that the LORD has planted for His own glory."* When you praise, it is for your own well-being.

The name of Jesus is to be lifted up above everything else. When you praise and worship the name of Jesus, you give Him the right to take over.

He is love. His loving kindness endures forever. You can trust and depend on His love. And most of all, He is the truth. There is nothing that can be trusted or tasted to be true like the name of Jesus, His love and His Word. You are anchored!

PRAYER

Thank you, Jesus; I am bold with strength in your name.
Amen.

JULY

Safe in Christ

JULY

Day 196

Though I walk in the midst of trouble, thou wilt revive me: thou shalt stretch forth thine hand against the wrath of mine enemies, and thy right hand shall save me. The Lord will perfect that which concerneth me: thy mercy, O Lord, endureth for ever: forsake not the works of thine own hands.
Psalm 138:7-8 KJV

The TPT translation says, *"By your mighty power I can walk through any devastation and you will keep me alive, reviving me. Your power sets me free from the hatred of my enemies. You keep every promise you've ever made to me! Since your love for me is constant and endless, I ask you, Lord, to finish every good thing that you've begun in me!"* Psalms 138:7-8.

This means that, contrary to man's perspective, the Lord is not late with his promise to return, as some measure lateness. But rather, His "delay" simply reveals his loving patience toward you, because he does not want any to perish but all to come to repentance. (2 Peter 3:9 TPT)

Whatever your need, God is good and faithful to keep His promise. But above everything, your Salvation is His paramount desire—to be with Him eternally.

PRAYER

Father, thank you for saving me through Jesus. Amen.

Day 197

You've gone into my future to prepare the way, and in kindness you follow behind me to spare me from the harm of my past. With your hand of love upon my life, you impart a blessing to me. This is just too wonderful, deep, and incomprehensible! Your understanding of me brings me wonder and strength.
Psalms 139:5-6 TPT

No other god can be called a father. No other religion has the privilege of fellowship with the one they worship. No other God can tell the end of a thing from its beginning.

What a mighty God we serve!

He is the one who goes before your future and prepares it for you. In His kindness He guides and leads you in the path of righteousness for His name sake. Though you will walk through difficult challenges and trails, He is always with you, following behind to spare you from harm. Amen.

His hand of love imparts a blessing on you. This truth of His long-suffering is wonderful and deep. He understands your frame—that you are dust—yet He loves you unconditionally. Praise God. Amen.

PRAYER

Abba, thank you for your unconditional love for me and being precious to me. Amen.

JULY

Day 198

Where could I go from your Spirit? Where could I run and hide from your face? If I go up to heaven, you're there! If I go down to the realm of the dead, you're there too! If I fly with wings into the shining dawn, you're there! If I fly into the radiant sunset, you're there waiting! Wherever I go, your hand will guide me; your strength will empower me.

It's impossible to disappear from you or to ask the darkness to hide me, for your presence is everywhere, bringing light into my night. There is no such thing as darkness with you. The night, to you, is as bright as the day; there's no difference between the two.
Psalms 139:7-12 TPT

You are safe in Jesus because you are hidden in Christ in God. You are seated far above any powers and principalities that want to cause you harm.

Secondly, believe that because you are in Christ you cannot hide from God. He knows you, even your thoughts. You have the Holy Spirit to help you. He can identify with your pain, that is why He asks you to give Him your burdens. Come to Jesus and allow him to help you through the power of the Holy Spirit, Amen.

PRAYER

Spirit of the Living God, I surrender myself to you. Help me through Christ our Lord. Amen.

JULY

Day 199

My soul cleaveth unto the dust: quicken thou me according to thy word. I have declared my ways, and thou heardest me: teach me thy statutes. My soul melteth for heaviness: strengthen thou me according unto thy word.
Psalm 199:25-26, 28 KJV

There are times in our lives our state of affairs makes us cleave to things that can hurt us in future. Sometimes, you feel like you are ready to give up on life so you cling to dust, hoping that death could be better than living.

Hope thou in the Lord. Declare your ways to the Lord and He will hear you. He will quicken you by His Word, The LORD is near you. The Lord is near to those that are broken hearted and hear their prayer. Call on the name of the Lord, He is the Saviour. Amen

PRAYER

Heavenly Father, thank you for being my salvation and my song of deliverance. As I trust in you, I know you will grant me the wisdom to know what to do and strength to go through in Jesus' name. Amen.

JULY

Day 201

Think about Jesus' example. He held on while wicked people were doing evil things to him. So do not get tired and stop trying. You are struggling against sin, but your struggles have not yet caused you to be killed.
Hebrews 12:3-4 NCV

It is easy to say I can do what Jesus did. I can also work miracles, prophesy, and heal the sick, but can you endure? How long can you endure and be patient with wickedness, disrespect, dishonesty, or not being treated fairly?

Today we are all being encouraged not to get tired of doing good and be patient with others. Love suffers long. Shalom.

PRAYER

Lord Jesus, you thought me how to live in this world. To be the salt and light, I pray that you continue to give me the grace I need to live and love like you with the help of your Spirit. Amen.

JULY
Day 201

Keep your lives free from the love of money and be satisfied with what you have. God has said, 'I will never leave you; I will never abandon you.'
Hebrews 13:5-6 NCV

Deuteronomy 31:6: *So we can be sure when we say, "I will not be afraid, because the Lord is my helper. People can't do anything to me."* Psalm 118:6

The Lord is my helper. I keep my focus on Him. The Lord is helping me I shall not be afraid. What can man do to me?

The Lord will not abandon me. He will satisfy me in drought.

The Lord is with me I will not be afraid. God is keeping me through Jesus Christ our Lord, Amen.

PRAYER

I declare I will not be afraid. I will not lack and as surely as I live on this earth, know I will continue to see the goodness of the Lord. Amen.

JULY

Day 202

Love and truth bring forgiveness of sin. By respecting the LORD you will avoid evil. When people live so that they please the LORD, even their enemies will make peace with them.
Proverbs 16:6-7 NCV

Love is kind, forgives, does not keep records of wrongdoing, and is patient. It is amazing that the Scriptures did not say that loving God makes one not sin but that reverence for God makes one avoid evil.

Do you respect God? Selah.

It is easier for anyone to say they love God, whilst that might be true, do you honour Him enough to run from sin?

Remember, if a man's ways please the Lord, He makes even your enemies live at peace with you. Shalom.

PRAYER

LORD, as you are so I am. Teach me to love you and my neighbour as you have loved me. Teach my heart to honour you in all I do. Amen.

Day 203

God, examine me and know my heart; test me and know my anxious thoughts. See if there is any bad thing in me. Lead me on the road to everlasting life.
Psalm 139:23-24 NCV

Once in a while, I believe this is a prayer we should all pray with a sincere heart: Examine me, oh Lord, and know my heart.

Not only my heart but my thoughts, the anxiety and see if there are any evil ways in me. Correct me and lead me on the way to everlasting life.

Bless is the man who knows God's correction because He weighs your heart's motives. When He reveals you to you, would you accept the correction in humility? Selah.

PRAYER

Father, put your light on me and reveal all the things I need to deal with. Guide me Holy Spirit through Christ Amen.

JULY

Day 204

But let everyone who trusts you be happy; let them sing glad songs forever. Protect those who love you and who are happy because of you. LORD, you bless those who do what is right; you protect them like a soldier's shield.
Psalm 5:11-12 NCV

Happiness is based on happenings, but joy is of the Lord. It says no matter what comes my way, I find my strength in God, and I trust Him. Joy is peace and stability, for they are what God gives.

God says I will always give you reasons to trust me, a reason to make melody in your heart. I protect those who love and trust in my name. He blesses and shields you from all evil. Amen.

PRAYER

Thank you, Father, for giving me joy. I know your joy is my strength. Amen.

JULY
Day 205

The counsel of the LORD standeth for ever, the thoughts of his heart to all generations.
Psalm 33:11 KJV

How would you live your life knowing that God's plan for you stands forever? Would you live circumspectly to redeem the time, or would you do whatever you like, thinking that His purpose for you will stand anyway? Think about it.

The more I look intently at this Word, the more I understand why some people unknowingly miss their way, thinking what God has for them is for them.

Brethren, Jesus Himself told us He must work while it is today. What are you doing? Are you in line with His counsel?

PRAYER

Father, thank you giving me your counsel. Help me to discern your voice and obey you through Christ our Lord, Amen.

JULY

Day 206

I exhort therefore, that, first of all, supplications, prayers, intercessions, and giving of thanks, be made for all men; For kings, and for all that are in authority; that we may lead a quiet and peaceable life in all godliness and honesty. For this is good and acceptable in the sight of God our Saviour.
1 Timothy 2:1-3 KJV

God's hope for humanity is that we stay connected and that all men will be saved.

One way of instituting God's agenda on earth is through prayer. When we pray for people in authority, they will do what pleases God.

Remember, God desires that prayer should be made for all men; it is for your benefit.

PRAYER

Heavenly Father, thank you for making me a peacemaker and a soul winner in Jesus' name, Amen.

JULY
Day 207

For he shall give his angels charge over thee, to keep thee in all thy ways.
Psalm 91:11 KJV

Angels are God's messengers. They have ranks and different functions. They are strengthened by obeying the Word of God Almighty. Psalm 103:20 NLT; *Praise the LORD, you angels, you mighty ones who carry out his plans, listening for each of his commands.*

These beings have been charged with your protection and wellbeing. Hallelujah, Amen.

You are not alone. You are not without.

Father God cares for you. The next time you speak His Word, remember that Angels go to work. Amen.

PRAYER

Father, thank you for Angels assigned to me an heir of salvation. Amen.

JULY

Day 208

Now all of us can come to the Father through the same Holy Spirit because of what Christ has done for us. So now you Gentiles are no longer strangers and foreigners. You are citizens along with all of God's holy people. You are members of God's family.
Ephesians 2:18-19 NLT

Being in the spirit is not the end of the relationship with God. What do you do when you gain access into the spirit? Selah.

Through Jesus Christ's redemption, we are part of God's family. Through the spirit, you have access to come to God by the Holy Spirit, who is also the Spirit of God. You are no more a stranger. You are a child of the Kingdom.

Today, I ask you what you will do with such knowledge and access? You are a child of a king with a mandate.

PRAYER

Father, thank you for your Spirit which helps me to know your will for me, Amen.

Day 209

JULY

Love is patient and kind. Love is not jealous or boastful or proud or rude. It does not demand its own way. It is not irritable, and it keeps no record of being wronged. It does not rejoice about injustice but rejoices whenever the truth wins out. Love never gives up, never loses faith, is always hopeful, and endures through every circumstance.
1 Corinthians 13:4-7 NLT

Being jealous, proud, boastful, or rude does not show love. Choose to be patient instead of demanding your own way and being irritating. Instead of keeping a record of wrongs, be kind. Instead of rejoicing in injustice, rejoice over truth.

When you love, you do not give up. You don't lose faith; you are always hopeful enduring through every situation. Because Christ dwells in your heart richly, you are enabled to love. No one can love truly outside of God. God is love. Love abides in you. You can love and you are lovable. Amen.

PRAYER

My Heavenly Father is love; I am love. Amen.

JULY

Day 210

The eyes of all look to you in hope; you give them their food as they need it. When you open your hand, you satisfy the hunger and thirst of every living thing. The LORD is righteous in everything he does; he is filled with kindness.
Psalm 145:15-17 NLT

Jesus revealed that to you has the mysteries of the Kingdom been granted (Matthew 13:11).

What makes God righteous is the fact that all He does is good and right. In Him is no deceit. He is love, and all He does or allows to come to you is done in love. Whatever your hunger is, He can and will satisfy you, only believe, trust and be obedient to His Word.

John 6:28–29 (NKJV): 28 Then they said to Him, "What shall we do, that we may work the works of God? "29 Jesus answered and said to them, "This is the work of God, that you believe in Him whom He sent." Only believe.

The only work God requires of you is that you believe. Do you believe in Jesus? Do you believe He will do whatever He has said He will? Do you believe He loves you and will do the best for you? Only believe. Amen.

PRAYER

Lord, I know as I look to you, I will be radiant for in you I hope. Amen.

JULY

Day 211

Now let your unfailing love comfort me, just as you promised me, your servant. Surround me with your tender mercies so I may live, for your instructions are my delight.
Psalm 119:76-77 NLT

Merciful is an attribute of God. Mercy is leniency, charity, compassion, sympathy, kindness, forgiveness, tolerance, magnanimity, pity, grace etc.

Our God is all that. Whatever kind of His mercy you need. Ask for it and believe you have received it. It is intriguing the Psalmist made us aware that we need His mercies to live. Without His daily mercies, we would be consumed by the enemy. Thank you for your tender mercies, Amen.

PRAYER

LORD, I receive your mercy today and for anything connected to my life. May the knowledge of your unfailing love comfort me, Amen.

JULY

Day 212

May God himself, the God who makes everything holy and whole, make you holy and whole, put you together—spirit, soul, and body—and keep you fit for the coming of our Master, Jesus Christ. The One who called you is completely dependable. If he said it, he'll do it!
1 Thessalonians 5:23-24 MSG

No one can promise to make you holy other than God Almighty. His nature is holiness, so He calls you, and as you believe, He makes you holy to have communion with Him. Without holiness, no one can see God (Hebrews 22:14).

As you keep abiding in Him, He changes you to become more like Him, body, mind, and soul. God is dependable, Do not despise your journey in God. We mature in our journey with Him.

Enjoy every victory. Learn from the struggles. Celebrate your weakness and exchange it for His strength. Strive to learn from His spirit and do His will. He has imparted His holiness unto you.

PRAYER

Heavenly Father, I bless your name for making me holy and whole as you are. Thank you for putting me together spirit, body, soul and mind. Making me fit for the coming our Lord Jesus Christ Amen.

AUGUST

Prayer

AUGUST

Day 213

Never stop praying.
1 Thessalonians 5:17 NLT

You cannot stop breathing and live, so it is with prayer. You cannot stop praying and live spiritually. PRAYER IS THE SPIRITUAL OXYGEN!

I believe in the Bible, that is the only thing the Lord commands us not to stop doing. The Lord is the Lord of spirits. You can only communicate with Him in the spirit. *"Pray in the spirit at all times, with every kind of prayer and petition. To this end, stay alert with all perseverance in your prayers for all the saints."* Ephesians 6:18.

We may have known praying in the spirit as praying in tongues. Does that mean that those who don't pray in tongues don't speak to God or are not praying in the spirit? Praying in the spirit simply means keeping your mind and spirit focused on God. If you have not received the gift of praying in tongues, desire it and ask the Holy Spirit to baptise you with the manifestation of speaking in tongues.

You are a spirit being, and God wants to have access to your being through that medium.

PRAYER

Daddy, thank you for the gift of prayer. A secret place I can relate and speak to you without any hindrance and limit.
Amen.

Day 214

Rejoice evermore. Pray without ceasing. In everything give thanks: for this is the will of God in Christ Jesus concerning you.
1 Thessalonians 5:16-18 KJV

Apostle Paul begins his letter to the Thessalonians admonishing them to be sober in these times. I would also echo what he said, "Be sober and vigilant for you are a child of light, know what the will of the Father is and observe to do it." PRAY WITHOUT CEASING!

We are not in ordinary times; the adversary is roaring. Let our inner man be quickened. We are the army of the LORD. Let us command the will of the Father to be done on earth as it is in heaven. My mandate as a servant of God is to ignite the passion to pray to God in this season.

Rejoice evermore because Jesus has conquered sin and the grave. He has put on you His righteousness. Contend for the promise, and come to the throne room in joy and confidence to obtain mercy. Let us join our hearts to worship, seek the Lord and His strength, and give thanks always. Amen.

PRAYER

Daddy, thank you for your joy. I rejoice in your salvation. I receive the grace to pray today in Jesus' name. Thank you for Your Holy Spirit that is in me to strengthen me in Jesus' name, Amen.

AUGUST

Day 215

Never restrain or put out the fire of the Holy Spirit.
1 Thessalonians 5:19 TPT

KJV says, "Quench not the Spirit". The Easy version writes, "Do not stop the work of God's Spirit". NLT adds "Do not stifle the Holy Spirit. This affirms you are capable of doing any of these without even realising that you have."

Prayer is not only communion with the Godhead but also the opportunity to involve the Trinity in your dealings. The spoken Word, with obedience, activates the Word of God. It allows the Holy Spirit and Angels to go to work based on what the Father says and what He hears (what you said).

But when the truth-giving Spirit comes, he will unveil the reality of every truth within you. He won't speak on his own, but only what he hears from the Father, and he will reveal prophetically to you what is to come. He will glorify me on the earth, for he will receive from me what is mine and reveal it to you. (John 16:13-14 TPT).

The Spirit of Truth will guide you in ALL truth, unveiling any hidden truth to your spirit. He reveals ONLY what He HEARS of the Father, the mind of God concerning you. He will show you what is in Christ and make it available to you. You need prayer to make this a reality in your life. You pray, the Holy Spirit Works. Amen.

PRAYER

Daddy, thank you for the gift of prayer. As I pray, the Holy Spirit, my guide and helper, will reveal prophetically to me what is and is to come. Amen.

AUGUST

Day 216

Embrace the power of salvation's full deliverance, like a helmet to protect your thoughts from lies. And take the mighty razor-sharp Spirit-sword of the spoken Word of God. Pray passionately in the Spirit, as you constantly intercede with every form of prayer at all times. Pray the blessings of God upon all his believers.
Ephesians 6:17-18 TPT

Jesus is the only way to The Father (God), The Truth (the light of the world) and the Life (the sustainer of life). Without Jesus as your saviour, you are a living dead. You are like a wind tossed about, with no foundation. You are not anchored to the rock which is Jesus.

Salvation is a gift from God to man, you do not earn it by doing any work. Yours is to believe and receive the finished work of Jesus Christ. This Salvation has the power to deliver you from any thoughts from the enemy. Thoughts about your sins, past, health etc. Knowing you are saved with the Truth of God, the Word of God (Sword of the Spirit) is a mighty raiser in Prayer.

Pray with the Word, aligning your spirit with the Spirit of God. Be intimate with Him, pray about everything and for believers everywhere. God hears every prayer and will answer. Amen.

PRAYER

Daddy, thank you for Salvation. I am healed in my mind. I decree and declare I have the mind of Christ; this I pray in Jesus Christ our Lord's name, Amen.

AUGUST

Day 217

Be persistent and devoted to prayer, being alert and focused in your prayer life with an attitude of thanksgiving.
Colossians 4:2 AMP

Persistence is a true character trait of a single-minded, purposeful person—the one who knows exactly what he wants and won't change his/her mind easily or relent. To be committed, loyal, and consistent is to be devoted.

You see, Prayer is not just saying a few words to God, and it ends there. It must be a lifestyle of persistence and devotion, where you have made a decision in your mind by faith that until you see and receive God's promise, you won't give up. The Bible says that this is the kind of attitude we should have in prayer (Romans 12:12).

Intimacy with God is built through different channels of communication, yet these traits of our human nature are a determining factor in receiving our answered prayers. Everything we need in life is already given to us, but you receive according to the knowledge of Him you have and the power at work in you (Ephesians 3:20, 2 Peter 1:3).

Remember to be alert and focused in prayer. The enemy's way is a distraction. Be on guard and thankful because God hears.

PRAYER

Thank you, Daddy, that you hear me always in Jesus' name, Amen.

AUGUST

Day 218

Now Jesus was telling the disciples a parable to make the point that at all times they ought to pray and not give up and lose heart.
Luke 18:1 AMP

Today, Jesus is telling you to have a lifestyle of prayer, don't give up and don't lose heart. Prayer is an essential part of our lives. The Lord invites us to talk to Him about everything. Ask for His help when needed and seek His guidance. He loves you that much to want to be ALWAYS intimate in prayer with you. Not some of the time.

He cautions you not to give up in prayer. Human nature tends to give up when we do not see the answers we desire our prayers early on. But don't give up. Do not allow doubt and unbelief to render your prayer ineffective. For a doubtful person cannot receive anything from God (James 1:7).

In the same vein do not lose heart. "Therefore, we do not lose heart. Even though our outward man is perishing, yet the inward man is being renewed day by day. For our light affliction, which is but for a moment, is working for us a far more exceeding and eternal weight of glory." (2 Corinthians 4:16-17 NKJV). Your waiting is working for you an external weight of glory, Amen.

PRAYER

Daddy, thank you for prayer. I will pray continually, not giving up and definitely not losing heart because I know you hear me in Jesus' name, Amen.

AUGUST

Day 219

Now when Daniel knew that the writing was signed, he went into his house; and his windows being open in his chamber toward Jerusalem, he kneeled upon his knees three times a day, and prayed, and gave thanks before his God, as he did afore time.
Daniel 6:10 KJV

The spirit life of prayer is praying at all times, in supplication, and making your request be known unto God (Ephesians 6:18). At least make a conscious effort to commune with the Lord, as Daniel teaches us with his lifestyle of prayer, and like the Apostles in John 21:15-17, three times a day.

He knelt before God, showing us the posture of his heart, that is humility. He chooses to humble himself through the day before God and draw strength from heaven by praying. Praying is a channel of tapping into the gracious mercy and strength of God for your daily journey.

He gave thanks. Always remember to thank God for hearing your prayers and not dealing with you as your sins deserve. Bless Him for His faithfulness, He is a good Daddy.

Daniel never stopped praying when he knew his enemies' plan for him. Don't stop praying when God reveals hidden things to you. Intensify your prayers until you see results. Pray without ceasing.

PRAYER

Thank you, Daddy, for the gift of prayer; in Jesus' name Amen.

AUGUST

Day 220

Know ye that the Lord he is God: it is he that hath made us, and not we ourselves; we are his people, and the sheep of his pasture. Enter into his gates with thanksgiving, and into his courts with praise: be thankful unto him, and bless his name. For the Lord is good; his mercy is everlasting; and his truth endureth to all generations.
Psalm 100:3-5 KJV

In our study of prayer, it is also important to emphasise that you need to know who God is, who you are, what you have access to, and what is readily available to you through our Lord and Saviour, Jesus.

Be confident in this knowledge that the Lord is God! He is the one true God, the only omnipresent, omnipotent, and all-wise God. He made you and has already made everything available for your welfare; you just need to believe.

When you come to Him in prayer, come with Thanksgiving. Enter His dwelling with praise, telling Him how marvellous and excellent He is. He is a good Shepherd, a faithful Father, and a dependable friend who sticks closer than a brother. Be grateful and bless His name.

To Him be all the honour, glory, and power. Your mercy endures through all generations. Amen. That is how you get God's attention. Through the knowledge of who He is and what he can do.

PRAYER

Daddy, may my worship please you alone in Jesus' name, Amen.

AUGUST

Day 221

Are there any believers in your fellowship suffering great hardship and distress? Encourage them to pray! Are there happy, cheerful ones among you? Encourage them to sing out their praises! Are there any sick among you? [...] And the prayer of faith will heal the sick and the Lord will raise them up, and if they have committed sins they will be forgiven.
James (Jacob) 5:13-15 TPT

Hardship and stressful situations are part of our human journey. We encounter these situations in diverse ways as we go about our everyday lives. Apostle James is making us aware that in our fellowship with the brethren when we notice any form of these sufferings, we should encourage them to pray.

Prayer should be the first form of action when you find yourself in any situation, especially the ones that are beyond your capability. You have been bought with a price (1 Corinthians 6:20). You honour God by giving Him control of your affairs. Let Him know you are depending on Him and His provision. It delights His heart when we do that.

When you are happy, remember to praise God, He gives us all things to enjoy (James 1:17). When sick, call the elders or others to stand in prayer for you; the prayer of faith heals. When you lack wisdom ask (James 1:5).

PRAYER

Daddy, thank you that as I pray, you are taking away every affliction, distress, and sickness in Jesus' name. Amen.

AUGUST

Day 222

"And when you pray, you shall not be like the hypocrites. For they love to pray standing in the synagogues and on the corners of the streets, that they may be seen by men. Assuredly, I say to you, they have their reward. But you, when you pray, go into your room, and when you have shut your door, pray to your Father who is in the secret place; and your Father who sees in secret will reward you openly.
Matthew 6:5-6 NKJV

How you pray is important. The verse above does not imply that you should not pray outside, such as on the streets, in the church, in your car, or in any public place. Jesus was making us aware that God sees and hears beyond what we say and do. He weighs the motives of the heart in prayer, as Proverbs 21:2 states.

Why are you praying? Where were you praying? Were you praying that way because you need to, or is it because you want people to see you can pray and maybe applaud you? It is ok to pray when you find yourself in an unusual place and you need to call on your God to come to your aid. When you find yourself in those situations, you may not be mindful of where you are because you're calling on God desperately.

But let us also be mindful of those around us. Jesus showed us that true repentance is of the heart. Prayer is the flow from the heart. God looks past what He hears from the mouth and sees the condition of your heart and your motives.

PRAYER

Father, may my prayers be to you an offering acceptable.
Amen.

AUGUST

Day 223

When you pray, do not say the same words many times. People who do not believe in God do that. They use many words that mean nothing. They think that when they pray like that, their gods will hear them. Do not pray like they do. God your Father already knows what you need. He knows this even before you ask him.
Matthew 6:7-8 EASY

What you say can preserve life or destroy it; so you must accept the consequences of your words (Proverbs 18:21). There is power in your words. More so when you speak the Word of God in faith. When you live as a living sacrifice to please the Lord, sanctified as a vessel of honour, you carry the very presence of God.

Such a life carries God's power, the grace of God rests on you. When you speak things happen in the spirit. Such a dedicated life is a spirit life. You become one with the Lord; you have the mind of Christ. Therefore you speak according to the will of God.

Jesus then is teaching you that when in prayer, God already knows your needs. In fact, He has already made available everything that you would ever need on this earth to fulfil your purpose (2 Peter 1:3). Yours is to believe, ask in faith, and not doubt that He heard (James 1:6).

PRAYER

Daddy, thank you for answering my prayers and providing every need of my heart. in Jesus' name, Amen.

AUGUST

How to Pray

AUGUST

Day 224

After this manner therefore pray ye: Our Father which art in heaven, Hallowed be thy name.
Matthew 6:9-10 KJV

We have learnt through our previous devotionals, the attitude we should have when praying, the posture in prayer and the position when waiting for the manifestation of our answers. Jesus, our example is showing us how to pray. After informing us not to use repetition of words, this is the way we should pray.

We should know and be assured of who we are praying to. He is the Father of our Lord Jesus Christ and our Father also (John 20:17). A Father bears the responsibility of taking care of His children, bringing them up in the way they should go, and teaching them how to live. You don't only pray to ask your Father your needs; in prayer, you listen to Him, too, for His instructions and guidance.

'Which art in heaven' means His abode. He has also made His home in your heart, where you have access through your spirit. Your spirit knows how to communicate with your Father through Jesus, the way to the Father.

'Hallowed be your name.' His name is Holy. His name is who He is. He is who His name is. My LORD. The King of all kings. Holy are you, Lord. Amen.

PRAYER

ABBA, thank you for the privilege of you, in Jesus' name. Amen.

AUGUST

Day 225

Thy kingdom come. Thy will be done in earth, as it is in heaven. Give us this day our daily bread.
Matthew 6:10-11 KJV

The Lord has established His throne in heaven, and His kingdom rules overall.
Psalms 103:19

The Kingdom of God is everywhere, but it does not manifest everywhere, because it is not everyone who has accepted the Lordship of Jesus Christ over their lives. If you have accepted Jesus as your saviour, you will have access to the manifestation of the Kingdom's operations in your life. As you pray, you can ask His kingdom to come and operate in your life, your home, and everything connected to your life.

God gave us our will and will not infringe on it. He comes where He is invited. You need to ask the Lord's will to be done on earth, in your life and space, as it is in heaven. Then He will take charge.

A Father is the provider of the family. That is why God is called Jehovah Jireh, God our Provider. He provides your needs according to His riches in Christ Jesus. And His riches are limitless. There is no need of yours that can bankrupt heaven. ASK!

PRAYER

Jehovah Jireh, my Provider, thank you for establishing Your Kingdom over my life. Let your will be done in me, and thank you for Your constant provision through Jesus Christ our Lord. Amen.

AUGUST

Day 226

And forgive us our debts, as we forgive our debtors.
Matthew 6:12 KJV

The Word of God is revelatory. A duty unfulfilled is a debt unpaid. To forgive means to stop blaming or being resentful of someone, to cancel (a debt) owed.

Unfulfilled debts primarily involve sins of omission (something that has been left out) and sins of commission (something you are instructed to do). Every transgression that goes against law and order involves an unfulfilled debt, meaning you know the right thing to do, yet you do not do it!

Jesus is teaching us that confession of your debt is enough for remission, that is, cancellation of any debt you owe rather than trying to do good work to reduce or partly pay your debt, as some teach. The Lord requires you to love and be grateful. He has forgiven you. Extend the same generosity to others. Forgive others as you have been forgiven (Luke 7:41).

But there is forgiveness with You, That You may be feared and worshipped [with submissive wonder]. (Psalms 130:4 AMP). The love of God leads us to repentance. When we choose the path of forgiving, you are reverend. It takes the brave of hearts to be generous in letting go of debt. You are the wealthier in God's kingdom. Choose to let go today in Jesus' name, Amen. May God grant you the grace to forgive all your debtors. Amen.

PRAYER

Abba, thank you for forgiving all my debts and the grace to forgive my debtors, Amen.

AUGUST

Day 227

And lead us not into temptation, but deliver us from evil: For thine is the kingdom, and the power, and the glory, forever.
Matthew 6:13 KJV

Temptation is part of our life's journey. It is the desire to do something that is wrong or unwise. The Bible says that God does not tempt us with evil (James 1:13). The Bible defines temptation as a trial in which man can decide to be faithful or unfaithful to God. We are tempted by our own desires, BUT God tries us to build and mature us. (James 1:2-3).

Matthew 26:41: *"Watch and pray, that ye enter not into temptation: the spirit indeed is willing, but the flesh is weak. We need the Holy Spirit's help daily to lead us. He guides and teaches us the way we should go so that we will bring glory to the Father. You need the Holy Spirit!"*

Psalm 121:7-8: *"The LORD shall preserve thee from all evil: he shall preserve thy soul. The Lord shall preserve thy going out and thy coming in from this time forth, and even for evermore. The Lord is able to deliver you from any evil. He is the Sovereign God. He is all-knowing, all-powerful, so trust Him."*

Jeremiah 15:21: *"And I will deliver thee out of the hand of the wicked, and I will redeem thee out of the hand of the terrible."*

Psalm 22:28: *"For dominion belongs to the LORD, and He rules over the nations. Amen."*

PRAYER

ABBA, thank you for delivering me from all evil and not leading me into temptation. In Jesus' name, Amen.

AUGUST

Day 228

The eyes of your understanding being enlightened; that ye may know what is the hope of his calling, and what the riches of the glory of his inheritance in the saints.
Ephesians 1:18 KJV

Enlightenment is necessary to know the hope with which God has called you and the riches of His glorious inheritance in the saints. As Psalm 79:1 states, you are God's inheritance. According to His riches in Christ Jesus, you lack nothing and are complete in Him.

The heart relates to the spiritual perception of man. It is the antenna of man. Proverbs 4:23 says, *"Guard your heart above all else, for it determines the course of your life."* The heart can be desperately wicked for out of it flows the issues of life, so it should be guarded with the Word of God (Jeremiah 17:9).

Your heart guards the decisions you make. It has the ability to have knowledge of heavenly things. When it is flooded by the Holy Spirit, He lights up the understanding of your heart to perceive the will of God for your life, the hope of His calling and the riches of His glory in the inheritance of the saints. You are the portion of God on this earth and co-heir with Christ.

PRAYER

Heavenly Father, thank you for enlightening the eyes of my heart to know and seek you. In Jesus' name, Amen.

AUGUST

Pray for Others

AUGUST

Day 229

Pray in the Spirit at all times and on every occasion. Stay alert and be persistent in your prayers for all believers everywhere.
Ephesians 6:18 NLT

I like how the easy version presents this same verse; "As you stand strongly like that, always pray for God's help. Pray about everything as God's Spirit helps you to pray. For this purpose, watch carefully all the time. Also, continue to pray for all God's people everywhere."

It is important for me to emphasise that we have enemies to fight against, a captain to fight for, a banner to fight under, and certain rules of war by which we are to govern ourselves. Ephesians 6 shows us what we have and what we need to do. Praying in the spirit is having your mind focus on God. What happens is, you are creating a consciousness of the reality of His presence around you. That is why God seeks worshippers that will worship Him in spirit and in truth. (John 4:24).

Furthermore, our weapons of warfare are not physical. It is important that you train your mind, heart and align your spirit with the will of God. This will help you effectively use the weapons available to you. In your fight stay alert and persevere for all believers everywhere. The fervent prayer of a righteous man avails much. (James 5:16).

PRAYER

Heavenly Father, thank you for equipping me in the spirit to win all battles in Jesus' name, Amen.

AUGUST

Day 230

I pray for them. I do not pray for the world but for those whom You have given Me, for they are Yours. I do not pray that You should take them out of the world, but that You should keep them from the evil one.
John 17:9, 15 NKJV

The disciples would experience dangers and trials, so Jesus sought the protection and blessing of God on them. His prayer was always answered. The term 'world' here, refers to wicked, rebellious, and vicious men. Jesus prayed for God to bless his disciples. They were not of the world; they had been taken out of the world (chosen), and they belonged unto God.

The petition was not offered for evil, disobedient, rebellious men but for those who were God's friends. Jesus is still making intercession for us, protecting us who are in Him. That is why it is important for you to keep His Word. The Word sanctifies you as it is the truth; it also nourishes and protects you from the evil devices of the enemy. (John 17:17).

John 6:39: *"And this is the will of Him who sent Me, that I shall lose none of those He has given Me, but raise them up at the last day."* As long as you stay humble under God's mighty hand, in faith, through Jesus you are safe. He is able to keep you until the coming of our Lord Jesus.

PRAYER

ABBA, thank you for keeping me in perfect peace, Amen.

AUGUST

Day 231

But I say to you, love your enemies, bless those who curse you, do good to those who hate you, and pray for those who spitefully use you and persecute you, that you may be sons of your Father in heaven; for He makes His sun rise on the evil and on the good, and sends rain on the just and on the unjust.
Matthew 5:44-45 NKJV

Praying for someone who deliberately caused you hurt is not something that comes easily to our natural man, yet God commands us to love our adversaries and even bless those who do not say good things to and about you, whose words and deeds are evil toward you.

It is because you have His nature, you are His likeness and a spirit being. You are not supposed to live your life ordinarily, like those who intentionally persecute and spitefully use you. Live by the spirit and walk in love. Choose to owe no one but to love them (Romans 13:8). Love is the excellent way. Love always wins.

He admonishes us to pray for them too. It is good to receive counsel, but I believe so strongly the Holy Spirit is the best counsellor. As you pray for the one that caused you pain, He works on yourself. Addresses the pain, He chooses the best solution, and also deals with or heals the one that caused the problem. Your Father is the Peacemaker, not only peace for your soul but peace for all men everywhere.

PRAYER

Heavenly Father, thank you for showing me the way of peace. Amen.

AUGUST

Day 232

If you see a fellow believer sinning in a way that does not lead to death, you should pray, and God will give that person life. But there is a sin that leads to death, and I am not saying you should pray for those who commit it. All wicked actions are sin, but not every sin leads to death.
1 John 5:16-17 NLT

There is power in intercession. It is the action of intervening on behalf of another; you mediate between God and the person you are praying for. The Word of God shows us that a person will receive life when we ask God in prayer to forgive their sins. But it is related to sin that does not lead to death.

The sin that leads to death is the one you do not confess and repent. Hebrews 12:16-17: *"Every sin you confess, God is faithful to forgive and clean you up,"* 1 John 1:9. *"Remember the one born of God doesn't continue sinning."*

"But those who brazenly violate the Lord's will, whether native-born Israelites or foreigners, have blasphemed the Lord, and they must be cut off from the community. Since they have treated the Lord's word with contempt and deliberately disobeyed his command, they must be completely cut off and suffer the punishment for their guilt."
Numbers 15:30-31 NLT

Let us be careful how we use the name of the Lord and His Word.

PRAYER

Heavenly Father, thank you for forgiving my sins and transgressions in Jesus' name, Amen.

AUGUST
Day 233

"Then you will take delight in the Almighty and look up to God. You will pray to him, and he will hear you, and you will fulfil your vows to him.

You will succeed in whatever you choose to do, and light will shine on the road ahead of you. If people are in trouble and you say, 'Help them,' God will save them. Even sinners will be rescued; they will be rescued because your hands are pure."
Job 22:26-30 NLT

There is something about praying to God and praying for others that is profound. The above verse shows us we should take delight in God and look up to Him. When we delight in Him, He hears us in prayer. We should honour every vow we have made. Sometimes, in our desperation, we make vows we don't keep after God has heard and delivered us from our storm.

You need to know that honouring your vows not only pleases God, He also blesses you. He makes you succeed in whatever you do. He shines light on your path and leads you in the path of righteousness that honours Him.

Also, when you intervene for others, God listens to your prayer. What an honour. When you pray for those in trouble, He will save them, rescuing the sinner because your hands are pure. Make the Almighty your delight, He will honour you.

PRAYER

Heavenly Father, thank you for honouring me when I pray for others, in Jesus' name, Amen.

AUGUST

Day 234

He will regard the prayer of the destitute, and not despise their prayer.
Psalms 102:17 KJV

God has eyes on the destitute. He will turn his attention to the prayers of those who have been abandoned. He will not despise their prayers. He has compassion for His creation, and He is a Father to those who have accepted Jesus as their Saviour.

Job 36:5: "Indeed God is mighty, but He despises no one; He is mighty in strength of understanding." He made us, as sheep for His pastures. He knows our frame and needs. He understands what we go through. We have a High Priest who can identify with us (Hebrews 4:15).

Psalm 22:24: "For He has not despised or detested the torment of the afflicted. He has not hidden His face from him but has attended to his cry for help."

God will not hide, hate, or dislike what torments you. God is bigger than whatever afflicts you. If you pray to Him, He promises He will not hide His face from you but will attend to you.

Today, as you read His Word, why don't you take time to tell Him those thoughts that are causing you sleepless nights and pain? He is waiting. Shalom.

PRAYER

ABBA, thank you for not turning away from my afflictions. Hear my prayer and answer me in Jesus' name. Amen.

AUGUST

Pray of Victory

AUGUST

Day 235

And at midnight Paul and Silas prayed, and sang praises unto God: and the prisoners heard them. And suddenly there was a great earthquake, so that the foundations of the prison were shaken: and immediately all the doors were opened, and every one's bands were loosed.
Acts 16:25-26 KJV

There is something about praying and worshipping God at midnight. What makes it more powerful is the situation and where they found themselves. Prison. Who would want to praise God after being beaten and put into jail for delivering a girl possessed by a demon? But those who know their God will always exploit (Daniel 11:32).

There are unique situations in our lives that look like prisons. We can't help ourselves, and sometimes you can't figure out how you got in, but God will not forsake the prayer of the destitute (Psalm 102:17). If only you will pray, He will listen and make a way. When you pray, don't forget to exalt His name above the situation you are in. Worship is chosen to lift the name of God above all others. You choose to look above the physical and ordinary to live in the spiritual. For we know everything happens first in the spirit.

Anytime you live above the physical, in spirit and truth, there is a 'suddenly.' Sudden miracles happen when a person believes God to be who He says He is—a Way Maker!

PRAYER

Father, thank you for hearing my prayer and worship. Amen.

AUGUST

Day 236

But each day the Lord pours his unfailing love upon me, and through each night I sing his songs, praying to God who gives me life.
Psalms 42:8 NLT

God is generous and sovereign because He sustains all His creation. The Bible says all creation is sustained by the Word of His power (Hebrews 1:3, Colossians 1:17). The Psalmist sings about his longing for God in verse 1 of this chapter. He further explains that as he longs and spends time in His presence, the Lord pours His unfailing love on him each day. What a wonderful experience.

Like Psalm 91:1, as you dwell in the secret place of the Most High, you shall abide under the shadow of the Almighty. As you dwell in His presence, out of your belly shall flow rivers of living waters, yielding its fruit in season. You will not wither, whatsoever you do will prosper for the Lord is with you (Psalm 1:3).

Worship flows easily from a heart of contentment. You sing the songs of the Lord, making melodies in your heart for Him. After this, prayer becomes a kind of conversation with one you know and not only read about. You understand why you sing even at night. You acknowledge God is mighty, He gives you life. Worship Him in the beauty of holiness. God bless you.

PRAYER

Heavenly Father, thank you for sustaining me, leading me, and guiding me through the path of life. In Jesus' name, Amen.

AUGUST

Day 237

But the end of all things is at hand: be ye therefore sober, and watch unto prayer.
1 Peter 4:7 KJV

The second coming of our Lord Jesus Christ is very near. We are cautioned to be on guard, hold on to our faith, and be sober—that is, not drunk with alcohol but filled with the Holy Spirit. We are to be moderate, clear-headed, and serious in doing what pleases the Lord. The hour has already come for you to wake up from your slumber because our salvation is nearer now than when we first believed (Romans 13:11).

Therefore, prepare your mind for action. Be sober-minded. Set your hope fully on the grace to be given you at the revelation of Jesus Christ (1 Peter 1:13). We live by faith and not by sight. We live by the revelation of our Lord Jesus Christ. You receive Grace when you receive the revelation of Jesus which enables you to act according to the revelation you receive.

As we pray, we are always reminded to be watchful; why? 1 Peter 5:8 tells us; *"Be sober, be vigilant; because your adversary the devil, as a roaring lion, walketh about, seeking whom he may devour: We are not ignorant of the devil's devices, that is why we need to be alert and watchful as we pray. When we are watchful, we will not fall into temptation."*

PRAYER

Father God, thank you for the gift of salvation. I receive grace to be sober and watchful. In Jesus' name, Amen.

AUGUST
Day 238

Truly, I say to you, whatever you bind on earth shall be bound in heaven, and whatever you loose on earth shall be loosed in heaven. Again I say to you, if two of you agree on earth about anything they ask, it will be done for them by my Father in heaven. For where two or three are gathered in my name, there am I in the midst of them."
Matthew 18:18-20 RSV

You are made in the likeness of God to operate like Him on earth. In Genesis 1:26, God said let us make man in our image and likeness to have dominion, and it was so. The Word is teaching us in this verse about the power of agreement, and about our dominion through what we say.

"One of you routs a thousand, because the LORD your God fights for you, just as he promised," Joshua 23:10. This verse shows you what happens when two or more stand together in faith, touching anything on earth. The next time you are in a situation, find one who will agree with you in prayer in Jesus' name.

Leviticus 26:8: *"The addition of God is divinely calculated."*

But remember in all that you do, do it in the name of Jesus. In Him do we have redemption. He is your salvation.

PRAYER

ABBA, thank you for showing me how to draw from grace. Amen.

AUGUST

Day 239

And at midnight Paul and Silas prayed, and sang praises unto God: and the prisoners heard them.
Acts 16:25 KJV

Who is the Silas in your life? Everyone will go through their midnight season. Where you will need someone to bear you up in prayer and intercede on your behalf. The company you keep is very important in your Christian walk. The scriptures say in Job 42:10, *"After Job had prayed for his friends, the LORD restored his fortunes and gave him twice as much as he had before."*

Paul faced numerous imprisonments, challenges, and difficulties, but it wasn't until he was imprisoned with Silas that a dramatic and sudden release occurred. When Silas accompanied him, they prayed together and worshipped. Then suddenly, in verse 26, the prison doors were opened. Not only them but also those around them. This confirms what the scriptures say in Leviticus 26:8; *"Five of you will pursue a hundred, and a hundred of you will pursue ten thousand, and your enemies will fall by the sword before you. The divine calculation is faith discerned."*

In the next phase of your life, distinguish yourself and surround yourself with likeminded people, those that have the same vision as you, who share your belief and fear of God.

PRAYER

ABBA, thank you for surrounding me with friends who please you and who are destined to help me fulfil my purpose. In Jesus' name, Amen.

AUGUST

Day 240

Let us then approach God's throne of grace with confidence, so that we may receive mercy and find grace to help us in our time of need.
Hebrews 4:16 NIV

You have a High Priest who has ascended into heaven and is seated interceding on your behalf. Walk in faith, approach the throne room of grace to obtain mercy and find grace to help you in time of need.

First,, He tells us to be confident and bold. Confidence in what you believe is not pride. Be confident that you are righteous because Jesus has made you holy. Go to your Father in boldness to receive His pardon and find unmerited favour.

And if we know that He hears us – whatever we ask – we know that we have what we asked of him (1 John 5:15). Trust in the Word of God. Believe what He says He will do, and He will do it. He listens to your prayers. Tell Him your needs today.

Mercy and grace await you in His presence. Seek His face. Selah.

PRAYER

Daddy, thank you for giving me access to your throne of grace. I come in the volume of the books of what is written of me. Be it unto me according to your Word in Jesus' name. Amen.

AUGUST

Day 241

To the roots of the mountains I sank down; the earth beneath barred me in forever. But you, Lord my God, brought my life up from the pit. "When my life was ebbing away, I remembered you, Lord, and my prayer rose to you, to your holy temple. "Those who cling to worthless idols turn away from God's love for them.
Jonah 2:6-8 NIV

'I sank down, and the earth barred me in forever. But You Lord my God brought my life up from the pit.' May this confession be yours in Jesus' name, Amen. Wherever you are and whatever you are going through, if you will call on the name of the one true God, your life will be spared like Jonah's. Amen.

Some people worship things that have no value. They do not receive God's love that could be for them. When you choose an idol over God, you forsake the mercies of God. Repent from idolatry.

Lord, you are the person who makes me strong. You are like a city with strong walls - a city that I can hide in. I can hide in you when troubles happen to me. People will come to you from countries all over the earth. [...] This time I will teach them how strong and powerful I am. Then they will know that the Lord is my name.
Jeremiah 16:19-21 Easy

PRAYER

Thank you, Abba, for becoming my strong tower and defence. Amen.

AUGUST

Day 242

In the days of His earthly life, Jesus offered up both [specific] petitions and [urgent] supplications [for that which He needed] with fervent crying and tears to the One who was [always] able to save Him from death, and He was heard because of His reverent submission toward God [His sinlessness and His unfailing determination to do the Father's will]. Although He was a Son [who had never been disobedient to the Father], He learned [active, special] obedience through what He suffered.
Hebrews 5:7-8 AMP

Prayer makes a lot of difference. Through prayer, you are ushered into the throne of grace, and divine empowerment is received. The Lord GOD has opened my ears, and I have not been rebellious, nor have I turned back (Isaiah 50:5). The Lord answers when we pray, it's up to us to be obedient or rebellious.

Jesus had the determination to do His Father's will. That was His focus and drive. What is your focus and drive in your life? Do you desire to please God?

Although He was God's Son, He learnt obedience through the things He suffered. Your light affliction cannot be compared to the joy that awaits you with the Father (2 Corinthians 4:17 Be Encouraged). God is with you. Choose to suffer for His name's sake, that waits for you eternal glory.

PRAYER

ABBA, thank you for your grace and mercy in times of need. Amen.

AUGUST

Day 243

Yet I am confident I will see the LORD's goodness while I am here in the land of the living. Wait patiently for the LORD. Be brave and courageous. Yes, wait patiently for the LORD.
Psalm 27:13-14 NLT

God is the Eternal One; He is not time-bound or limited by human capacity. He is all in all, self-sufficient and Sovereign in all His ways.

Putting your confidence in such a Father should give you a sense of rest, waiting patiently that He is faithful to all His promises.

When you have talked to Him about it, wait on Him. Shalom.

PRAYER

Abba, I declare my confidence in you. My hope in your word is true and steadfast. As wait I know I will continue to see the goodness of the Lord in the land of the living.
Amen.

SEPTEMBER

God's Goodness

SEPTEMBER

Day 244

For since the beginning of the world men have not heard, nor perceived by the ear, neither hath the eye seen, O God, beside thee, what he hath prepared for him that waiteth for him.
Isaiah 64:4 KJV

Our God is extraordinary. He is not in the business of doing mediocre or unremarkable things. He is the Lord Most High, our El Elyon. Our Jehovah Sabaoth, the Lord of Host, Jehovah Nissi, the Lord, our banner, Elohim, the Living God. He is the One and Only true God.

This month, He promises you who believe in His name that as you wait on Him, He will do what no eye has seen, no ear has heard, nor what you cannot even perceive about your life. In Jesus' name, Amen.

How great is your goodness which You have laid up for those who fear You, and bestowed on those who take refuge in You in the sight of the sons of men (Psalm 31:19). If you will only believe, you will testify. As soon as you travail, you'll bring forth because God is the one who will cause you to deliver. You are the blessed of the Lord. Amen. HAPPY NEW MONTH.

PRAYER

ABBA, thank you for mind-blowing testimonies, for surrounding me with songs of deliverance, and for perfecting that which concerns me. In Jesus' name, Amen.

SEPTEMBER

Day 245

How great is the goodness you have stored up for those who fear you. You lavish it on those who come to you for protection, blessing them before the watching world.
Psalms 31:19-NLT

Before you were born all your days were written in His books. God made you with a purpose, He made available all the things you will need to make your life worth living on this earth. He made your Eden before placing you. (Genesis 2:15).

God rained down on both the righteous and unrighteous, but His goodness is for those who fear Him. The benefit of being a child of God is to enjoy His loving kindness, as Psalm 63:3 states. When you experience this kind of kindness, you praise Him for who He is: a loving Father.

"Answer me, O LORD, for Your loving devotion is good; turn to me in keeping with Your great compassion." Psalm 69:16. Remember God blessed you before the watching eye of the world. Hallelujah, sing praises to His name. Amen.

PRAYER

ABBA, thank you for surrounding me with your loving kindness. Amen.

SEPTEMBER
Day 246

It will be said in that day, "Indeed, this is our God for whom we have waited that He would save us. This is the Lord for whom we have waited; Let us shout for joy and rejoice in His salvation."
Isaiah 25:9 AMP

There is something you will say when the Lord visits you. He does this by doing something significant. You will rejoice in His salvation and shout for joy. For indeed it will be by the finger of God.

When you wait on God, He always shows up. It might not be on your time or how you want Him to, but He is always on time, for He holds times and seasons in His hand.

Therefore the LORD longs to be gracious to you; therefore He rises to show you compassion, for the LORD is a just God. Blessed are all who wait for Him (Isaiah 30:18). There is power in waiting on God. Receive the grace to wait on His salvation. The LORD will be gracious to you in Jesus' name. Amen.

PRAYER

Abba, thank you for the grace to wait on you. Be gracious to me and show yourself on my behalf as I wait on you in Jesus' name. Amen.

SEPTEMBER

Day 247

But as it is written: "Eye has not seen, nor ear heard, Nor have entered into the heart of man The things which God has prepared for those who love Him." But God has revealed them to us through His Spirit. For the Spirit searches all things, yes, the deep things of God. For what man knows the things of a man except the spirit of the man which is in him? Even so no one knows the things of God except the Spirit of God. Now we have received, not the spirit of the world, but the Spirit who is from God, that we might know the things that have been freely given to us by God.
I Corinthians 2:9-12 NKJV

What God has for you is hidden in the spirit. Those who love God and wait on Him have received not the spirit of the world but the Spirit who is from God. The purpose is that you will know what God has for you.

The Spirit reveals to your spirit that which is freely given to you by God. It only takes the Spirit of God to reveal the things of God. Be encouraged and build your spirit life in Christ Jesus. His desire for you is to seek Him and His will for you, then He will reveal it to your spirit. Selah.

PRAYER

ABBA, Father, thank you for Your Spirit that reveals and leads me to the knowledge of you in Jesus' name. Amen.

SEPTEMBER

Day 248

Powerful kings and mighty nations will satisfy your every need, as though you were a child nursing at the breast of a queen. You will know at last that I, the Lord, am your Savior and your Redeemer, the Mighty One of Israel.
Isaiah 60:16 NLT

The Lord is the rock, the sure foundation on which we stand. His majesty and dominion are from everlasting to everlasting. He shares His glory with none. He is Sovereign, the Only God, the maker of the universe. The heavens are His throne, the earth is His footstool, yet His dwelling is among men. He is your Father and Provider.

Today, He is reminding you of the kind of people He has ordained to satisfy your every need. Powerful kings and mighty nations. Not just any nation (people are sometimes referred to as nations), but powerful and mighty. Why? Because you are His child! And because HE CAN!

As a nursing child relies on the mother, you just need to wait on Him as your source. Live in this expectation, God is faithful to His Word.

PRAYER

Abba, thank you for causing powerful and mighty nations to serve my every need in Jesus' name, Amen.

SEPTEMBER

Day 249

I will exchange your bronze for gold, your iron for silver, your wood for bronze, and your stones for iron. I will make peace your leader and righteousness your ruler. Violence will disappear from your land; the desolation and destruction of war will end. Salvation will surround you like city walls, and praise will be on the lips of all who enter there.
Isaiah 60:17-18 NLT

Elohim is the only one that can turn your life around just by believing in Him. He blesses and adds no sorrow. *"The blessing of the LORD brings wealth, without painful toil for it,"* Psalm 10:22. Wealth is a crown for the wise; the effort of fools yields only foolishness. (Proverbs 14:24). The fear of the Lord is the beginning of wisdom, but fools despise wisdom and instructions. (Proverbs 1:7). Yours is to follow His lead. Violence will disappear from your dwelling. He will surround you with His salvation and all who come to you will have praise on their lips.

PRAYER

Father, thank you for divine exchange in Jesus' name, Amen.

SEPTEMBER

Day 250

Give us help from trouble: for vain is the help of man. Through God we shall do valiantly: for he it is that shall tread down our enemies.
Psalms 60:11-12 KJV

Deliver me from my troubles oh God. You are mine Salvation. In you alone do I find safety for vain is the help of men. I acknowledge my insufficiency in my ability, what do I have that you did not give? No king is saved by his vast army; no warrior is delivered by his great strength. (Psalm 23:16). Believe that through God you shall do courageously. For it is God that works and fights on your behalf for His glory.

"The LORD is my strength and my shield; my heart trusted in him, and I am helped: therefore my heart greatly rejoiceth; and with my song will I praise him." Psalm 28:7. The Lord delights to win your battles for you. Will you let Him? Trust and listen and He will guide you in all your ways.

PRAYER

Abba, thank you for helping me when I am in trouble. Through your help, I know I will valiantly defeat all my foes and enemies in Jesus' name. Amen.

SEPTEMBER

Day 251

But I will never, no never, lift my faithful love from off their lives. My kindness will prevail and I will never disown them. How could I revoke my covenant of love that I promised David? For I have given him my word, my holy, irrevocable word. How could I lie to my loving servant David?
Psalms 89:33-35 TPT

Has God given you any promise? Has He spoken through His Prophet to you? Then He is reminding you He will always be faithful to His Word. HIS WORD IS IRREVOCABLE!

He said I will not take my love from you. He is love. His banner over your life is love like a seal of ownership that He loves you and will never leave you. Do you believe it? Have faith in God's faithfulness. Because He is the covenant-keeping God. He keeps His covenant to the third and fourth generations.

In every situation you find yourself in, God's kindness will prevail over it. Believe His Word is true, speak it over your life and situation and put on the whole Armour of God and, after everything, stand. (Ephesians 6:10-20).

God bless you. Selah.

PRAYER

Thank you, Abba, for your kindness over me. Amen.

SEPTEMBER

Bless the Lord

SEPTEMBER

Day 252

Because your loving kindness is better than life, my lips shall praise you. Thus I will bless you while I live; I will lift up my hands in your name. My soul shall be satisfied as with marrow and fatness, and my mouth shall praise you with joyful lips.
Psalms 63:3-5 NKJV

Praise is an expression of respect and gratitude, possibly admiration for someone or something. We praise God for He has a name above every other name. We praise Him because of His generosity and faithfulness. You can also have reasons why you praise Him. Today may you count your blessings and give Him the praise due His holy name.

Only the living can praise Him. As long as you breathe, live to praise our King. In praise, not only do you remember Him for what He has done but how He satisfies you always with the choice(best) of the earth. The best things of life, marrow and fatness. He is that good!

His loving kindness is better than life. You know there is nothing better than having the breath of life. Bless is the man that has truly tested the loving kindness of Elohim. It is sweeter than honey on the honeycomb. Selah.

PRAYER

Father, I praise you for everything, now and forever Amen.

SEPTEMBER

Day 253

For You, O God, have tested us; you have refined us as silver is refined. You brought us into the net; you laid affliction on our backs. You have caused men to ride over our heads; we went through fire and through water; But You brought us out to rich fulfilment. I will go into your house with burnt offerings; I will pay you my vows.
Psalms 66:10-13 NKJV

We get tested on what we learn at school in order to show that we understand what has been taught. This also leads to promotion and sometimes rewards. So, it is with our walk with our God. Count it all joy when you fall into diverse trials for then your faith has a chance to grow. (James 1:2-3). God allows certain trials our way. He allows the enemy to test us through our own desires to show what is not right so He can heal us. (James 1:13-14).

But rest assured, after your trials, God will bring you to your wealthy place, a rich fulfilment. So, you can give Him the glory due His name and pay your vows. Amen.

PRAYER

Abba, thank You for Your moulding and blessings. I believe they are all working for my good. In Jesus' name, Amen.

SEPTEMBER

Day 254

Blessed is the man you choose, and cause to approach You, That he may dwell in your courts. We shall be satisfied with the goodness of your house, Of Your holy temple. You crown the year with your goodness, and your paths drip with abundance.
Psalms 65:4, 11 NKJV

It is the Lord that made us, you are not of yourselves least you should boast. But the one who boast should make his boast in the Lord.
Jeremiah 9:24

For what do you have that the Lord did not give you?
1 Corinthians 4:7

You are blessed among men when you are chosen by God.
John 15:16.

And He causes you to approach His court, His dwelling place. What a privilege you have. God declares that He will satisfy you with the goodness from His holy temple.

He will crown your year with goodness, and your path will drip with abundance. You are God's treasured possession, made for his pastures. Have faith in His Word and believe in His faithfulness. He will not fail you.

PRAYER

Heavenly Father, thank you for choosing me and bringing me to your dwelling. I bless you for my path dripping with abundance in Jesus' name. Amen.

SEPTEMBER
Day 255

Oh, bless our God, you peoples! And make the voice of His praise to be heard, Who keeps our soul among the living, And does not allow our feet to be moved.
Psalms 66:8-9 NKJV

Praise is a powerful tool. The scriptures show that if we do not praise the Lord, He will cause the stones to worship Him. (Luke 19:40). He says let everything that has my breath praise me (Psalm 150:6). As long as you are breathing you must offer a sacrifice of praise to the one who made you.

When you praise, He says, let your voice be heard. When you are praising someone for something they have done, you say it to them. So it is to God. Proclaim His faithfulness to all, tell of His wonders and magnify His name. Acknowledge He is good, and His mercies endure forever and ever.

And if you still can't find a reason to praise Him, He reminds you that He is the one who keeps your soul among the living. Hallelujah. He is the one who does not allow your feet to be moved. Always praise Him anyway.

PRAYER

Abba, thank you for keeping my soul and my feet steadfast. My praise is to you alone! Amen.

SEPTEMBER

Day 256

Let the peoples praise You, O God; Let all the peoples praise You. Then the earth shall yield her increase; God, our own God, shall bless us. God shall bless us, And all the ends of the earth shall fear Him.
Psalms 67:5-7 NKJV

Praise is a form of acknowledging what someone has done. We praise God for His acts. We praise His name because He holds all things by the power of His Word.

The scriptures tell us when we praise God, the earth yields its increase. He magnifies Himself above everything and shows Himself strong on our behalf. Leviticus 26:4: *"I will give you rains in their season, and the land will yield its produce, and the trees of the field will bear their fruit."*

Joel 2:26 says of the Lord, you will have plenty to eat, until you are satisfied. You will praise the name of the LORD your God, who has worked wonders for you. My people will never again be put to shame. Amen and Amen.

PRAYER

Heavenly Father, thank you for blessing the earth to yield its fruits for me in Jesus' name, Amen.

SEPTEMBER

Day 257

Blessed be the Lord, Who daily loads us with benefits, The God of our salvation! Selah Our God is the God of salvation; And to God the Lord belong escapes from death.
Psalms 68:19-20 NKJV

It pleases the Lord when He provides your daily needs. It delights His heart when you come to Him believing that He is able to provide everything you need according to His riches in Christ Jesus.

He that comes to God must believe He is a rewarder of those who diligently seek Him. (Hebrews 11:6). Without faith it is impossible to please God. He has loaded your day with benefits. Believe Him to receive it. But it is through Jesus Christ His son. Amen.

He is the God of your salvation. He has redeemed your life from the pit of hell and the grave. He has given eternal life to those who believe in Him and accept Him as their Saviour and Lord. He alone can save you from death. Accept His life today.

PRAYER

Heavenly Father, thank you for being my salvation and daily loading me with your benefits, in Jesus' name, Amen.

SEPTEMBER

Day 258

I will praise your mighty deeds, O Sovereign Lord. I will tell everyone that you alone are just. O God, you have taught me from my earliest childhood, and I constantly tell others about the wonderful things you do. You have allowed me to suffer much hardship, but you will restore me to life again and lift me up from the depths of the earth. You will restore me to even greater honor and comfort me once again.
Psalms 71:16-17, 20-21 NLT

Do not let circumstances decide whether you should praise God or not. Live to praise Him anyway at all costs. Let praise and thanksgiving be your lifestyle.

God writes His Word on the tables of our hearts so that even at a tender age, we can see and relate to Him through nature. Be open to receiving His teachings. When God allows hardships, He will restore and lift you up, and comfort you. Let His praise arise in your heart and trust Him in all your ways.

PRAYER

Abba, thank You for teaching me and restoring me through Jesus Christ our Lord. Amen.

SEPTEMBER

Day 259

Bless the Lord, O my soul; And all that is within me, bless His holy name! Bless the Lord, O my soul, And forget not all His benefits: Who redeems your life from destruction, Who crowns you with loving-kindness and tender mercies, Who satisfies your mouth with good things, So that your youth is renewed like the eagle's. Bless the Lord, all His works, In all places of His dominion. Bless the Lord, O my soul!
Psalms 103:1-2, 4-5, 22 NKJV

The Lord on high is mighty. Jehovah El Elyon is the God most high, yet His dwelling is among men. He chooses to live in your heart. Bless His name, keep praising Him, and forget not His benefits, who daily crown you with loving kindness and tender mercies.

He has redeemed you from destruction, crowning you with His salvation. He has satisfied your mouth with good things and renewed your youth like the eagles in all places of dominion. Bless His name.

PRAYER

Abba, thank You for your loving kindness and tender mercies and for renewing my youth like the eagles. Amen.

SEPTEMBER

Day 260

I will thank you, Lord, with my whole being. I will sing and praise you in front of the gods. I look towards your holy temple, and I bend down to worship you. I thank you for who you are. You love your people and they can always trust you. You are more famous than anyone, because you always do what you promise. When I prayed to you, you answered me. You made me brave and strong. The Lord stands with me to do what he has promised. Yes, Lord, your special love will always continue. You have made us who we are, so do not leave us now!
Psalms 138:1-3, 8 EASY

All that I am says 'thank you' to the Lord. I will tell people about all the great things that you have done. (Psalms 9:1). Out of the abundance of the heart the mouth speaks. (Luke 6:45). When you are grateful to the Lord, let the people know how great your God is.

God is the one that makes you brave and strong in the face of adversity because He is your faithful Shepherd. He keeps His promise and will never leave you.

PRAYER

Heavenly Father, thank you for answering me when I pray and for being my good Shepherd in all my ways. Amen.

SEPTEMBER

God is King

SEPTEMBER

Day 261

May the king be famous forever! May people remember him for as long as the sun continues to shine. May people from all nations use his name when they bless one another. May they all say that God has blessed the king! Praise the Lord, the God of Israel, as he deserves. Only he does such wonderful things.
Psalms 72:17-18 EASY

You who believe there is a God who made the heavens and the earth and all that is in it. You who fear the name of the Lord, may the Son of righteousness rise with healing in His wings over you and yours. (Malachi 4:2).

The King of Kings is famous forever because He made it so. All creation testifies and sings of His glory, His loving kindness and tender mercies. And it will be so as long as the sun continues to shine.

All the people on earth bless one another with God's name for He is the only God that blesses, and no one can alter. Only He does such wondrous things.

PRAYER

Abba, thank You for all the wondrous things you do. I bless your Holy name in Jesus Christ our Lord. Amen.

SEPTEMBER

Day 262

You will guide me with Your counsel, And afterward receive me to glory. Whom have I in heaven but You? And there is none upon earth that I desire besides you. My flesh and my heart fail; But God is the strength of my heart and my portion forever.
Psalms 73:24-26 NKJV

Blessed is the man who has the counsel of the Lord. He is like the tree planted by the living waters, always fresh and always fruitful. The Holy Spirit is your Counselor. He is responsible for guiding you into all the truth of God. As you relate to Him in uprightness, humility, and obedience, He will teach and direct your ways.

Jesus is the high priest over your confession (Hebrews 3:1). Keep your focus on heavenly things, things that are praiseworthy, lovely, be kingdom minded. Seek to please God, love the brethren and God will keep you in peace even among evil men. Let God be your priority. He Himself has promised never to leave you nor forsake you. He is faithful in keeping that promise.

PRAYER

Father, thank you for counselling and comforting me in Jesus' name. Amen.

SEPTEMBER

Day 263

For God is my King from of old, Working salvation in the midst of the earth. You divided the sea by your strength; You broke the heads of the sea serpents in the waters. You broke the heads of Leviathan in pieces, And gave him as food to the people inhabiting the wilderness. You broke open the fountain and the flood; you dried up mighty rivers. The day is yours, the night also is Yours; You have prepared the light and the sun. You have set all the borders of the earth; you have made summer and winter.
Psalms 74:12-17 NKJV

God is the King of old. He is the one who works salvation on the earth because He created it. His mighty works are evident in creation and its operations. He sustains all things by the power of His Word, which is Jesus Christ.

He is the provider and has everything under His control. Whatever you need, He is well able to provide. He is the All Sufficient One. Trust Him.

PRAYER

Father, you are magnificent and gracious in all your doings. Thank you for caring for me; in Jesus' name, Amen.

SEPTEMBER

Day 264

Lord, through all the generations you have been our home! Before the mountains were born, before you gave birth to the earth and the world, from beginning to end, you are God. Teach us to realize the brevity of life, so that we may grow in wisdom.
Psalms 90:1-2, 12 NLT

A dwelling place is a place of residence, safety, refuge, hiding place, or home. God is your dwelling place. It delights His heart to have you in His habitation. As you continue to dwell with Him, He will shield you from the storms of life.

He is not going to be your dwelling place now. He has always been your dwelling, but it depends on you to stay in that abode. He is from everlasting to everlasting; He has not changed. Psalm 71:3 says, *"Be my rock of refuge, where I can always go. Give the command to save me, for You are my rock and my fortress."*

As we dwell with you, Abba, teach us to number our days so we may apply our hearts to wisdom.

PRAYER

Father, thank you for being my dwelling. In Jesus' name, Amen.

SEPTEMBER

Day 265

When you sit enthroned under the shadow of Shaddai, you are hidden in the strength of God Most High. He's the hope that holds you and the Stronghold to shelter you, the only God for you, and your great confidence. He will rescue you from every hidden trap of the enemy, and he will protect you from false accusation and any deadly curse. His massive arms are wrapped around you, protecting you.

You can run under his covering of majesty and hide. His arms of faithfulness are a shield keeping you from harm. Don't fear a thing! Whether by night or by day, demonic danger will not trouble you, nor will the powers of evil launched against you. Even in a time of disaster, with thousands and thousands being killed, you will remain unscathed and unharmed. God sends angels with special orders to protect you wherever you go, defending you from all harm.

If you walk into a trap, they'll be there for you and keep you from stumbling. For here is what the Lord has spoken to me: "Because you have delighted in me as my great lover, I will greatly protect you. I will set you in a high place, safe and secure before my face.
Psalms 91:1-4, 6-7, 11-12, 14 TPT

Today I just want to remind you of what God says about you. God bless you. Selah.

PRAYER

Thank you, Abba, for all you have done for me. Amen.

SEPTEMBER

Day 266

But you, O Lord, will be exalted forever. Your enemies, Lord, will surely perish; all evildoers will be scattered. But you have made me as strong as a wild ox. You have anointed me with the finest oil. My eyes have seen the downfall of my enemies; my ears have heard the defeat of my wicked opponents. But the godly will flourish like palm trees and grow strong like the cedars of Lebanon.
Psalms 92:8-12 NLT

Your enemy is an enemy of God. Workers of iniquity are enemies of God. Although God is merciful He cannot look at sin. Evil doers may look like they are flourishing but the end for them is eternal death and being separated from God forever.

But to you who fear the Lord, He will anoint your head with His finest oil making you strong like the ox. You will witness the downfall of those that persecute your life. You will run and not grow weary, you will walk and not faint, for God will go before you as a cloud by day and fire by night. You will flourish in all you do, strong like the cedars.

PRAYER

Father, thank you for making me strong like the Ox. Amen.

SEPTEMBER

Day 267

Your throne, O Lord, has stood from time immemorial. You yourself are from the everlasting past. The floods have risen up, O Lord. The floods have roared like thunder; the floods have lifted their pounding waves. But mightier than the violent raging of the seas, mightier than the breakers on the shore- the Lord above is mightier than these! Your royal laws cannot be changed. Your reign, O Lord, is holy forever and ever.
Psalms 93:2-5 NLT

God cannot be defined. He is enthroned from everlasting to everlasting. He is unchanging from time immemorial. He is the unchangeable God, immovable. He is trustworthy and His Word is settled. Amen.

Floods are used figuratively in the Bible as a destructive tool both used by God and the enemy. God used the flood in the case of Noah to destroy the earth, yet the same flood was used as a redemptive tool for Noah and His family by obedience to God's Word in building the ark. (Genesis 6:9-17).

Whatever situation you find yourself in, God is able to make it work for your good. You need to faith it into His hands and trust Him. Amen.

PRAYER

Father, I trust you with all my life issues. Amen.

SEPTEMBER

Trust God

SEPTEMBER

Day 268

How lovely is your tabernacle, O Lord of hosts! Blessed is the man whose strength is in You, Whose heart is set on pilgrimage. As they pass through the Valley of Baca, They make it a spring; The rain also covers it with pools. They go from strength to strength; each one appears before God in Zion.
Psalms 84:1, 5-7 NKJV

The dwelling place of God is beautiful. It is where the saints gathered holily to give God what is due Him. God is holy and remember without holiness no man can see God (Hebrews 12:14).

Blessed and greatly favoured is the man who finds strength in God, who has set his heart to seek Him. When they go through difficult challenges, God will make a way. He will provide and guide them as a Shepherd leads his flock.

For the Lord God is a sun and shield; The Lord bestows grace and favour and honour; No good thing will He withhold from those who walk uprightly. (Psalm 84:11).

PRAYER

Father, thank you for being my sun and shield in Jesus' name, Amen.

SEPTEMBER

Day 269

I have found My servant David; With My holy oil I have anointed him, With whom My hand shall be established; Also My arm shall strengthen him. The enemy shall not outwit him, Nor the son of wickedness afflict him. I will beat down his foes before his face, and plague those who hate him. "But My faithfulness and My mercy shall be with him, And in My name his horn shall be exalted. Also I will set his hand over the sea, And his right hand over the rivers. He shall cry to Me, 'You are my Father, My God, and the rock of my salvation.' My mercy I will keep for him forever, and My covenant shall stand firm with him.
Psalms 89:20-26, 28 NKJV

Make these promises your own. Put your name in it and speak it over your life. You also are the chosen of God. God's mercy and faithfulness will not leave you. You are anointed by God for a purpose. Stand in your election, a call to purpose. Thrive to apprehend that which God apprehended your life for. (Philippians 3:12). Forget what is behind and press on (Philippians 3:13).

PRAYER

Father, thank you for finding me. In Jesus' name, Amen.

SEPTEMBER

Day 270

Or what man is there among you who, if his son asks for bread, will give him a stone? Or if he asks for a fish, will he give him a serpent? If you then, being evil, know how to give good gifts to your children, how much more will your Father who is in heaven give good things to those who ask Him!
Matthew 7:9-11 NKJV

If you have accepted Jesus as your Lord and Saviour, you are in the Kingdom of God, which makes God your heavenly Father. Fathers have the responsibility of taking care of their children. God takes His responsibility seriously. God is a good Father.

Through His word, he admonishes you to trust and obey Him and He will take care of you. As a Creator He provides and sustains His creation, raining both on the righteous and unrighteous. If the sinner takes His principles and does them, they get the result thereof. You, as His child, need to obey Him.

Ask Him for your needs in faith. Believe you have received when you pray -Mark 11:24. Your faith in God, believing in what you have asked, is important. But more so ask for forgiveness when you sin (miss the mark), so that nothing can hinder your prayers.

PRAYER

El Shaddai, my all-sufficient one, thank you for being sufficient for me, and all that concerns me. I receive every need you have provided in Jesus' name. Amen.

SEPTEMBER

Day 271

So, do not have trouble in your mind about these things. Do not always say, "What will we eat?", or "What will we drink?", or "What will we wear?" People who do not know God are always thinking about these things. But as for you, your Father in heaven knows that you need them. Instead, always think about the things that are important in the kingdom of heaven. Always do what God shows you is right. Then he will also give you the things that you need each day.
Matthew 6:31-33 EASY

Worrying is a sin and a sign of unbelief in God's providence. We are shown in this verse how to handle life's basic challenges-being Kingdom-minded.

It is natural for one to think about what to eat, drink and wear especially when you do not have the means to provide them. The Word of God is showing us it is not your responsibility to nurse these thoughts. Yours is to ask and thank God for His provision. How it will come by is the evidence of your trust or belief in His Word, and what you have ask from Him

Thank Him and wait for Him. Be sensitive to how the answer will come. Our ways are not his ways. But also, keep your mind on the kingdom agenda whilst you wait. Doing what is pleasing to Him.

PRAYER

Heavenly Father, thank you for providing for my needs. Amen.

SEPTEMBER

Day 272

So, do not have trouble in your mind about these things. Do not always say, "What will we eat?", or "What will we drink?", or "What will we wear?" People who do not know God are always thinking about these things. But as for you, your Father in heaven knows that you need them. Instead, always think about the things that are important in the kingdom of heaven. Always do what God shows you is right. Then he will also give you the things that you need each day.
Matthew 6:31-33 EASY

Worrying is a sin and a sign of unbelief in God's providence. We are shown in this verse how to handle life's basic challenges-being Kingdom-minded.

It is natural for one to think about what to eat, drink and wear especially when you do not have the means to provide them. The Word of God is showing us it is not your responsibility to nurse these thoughts. Yours is to ask and thank God for His provision. How it will come by is the evidence of your trust or belief in His Word, and what you have ask from Him

Thank Him and wait for Him. Be sensitive to how the answer will come. Our ways are not his ways. But also, keep your mind on the kingdom agenda whilst you wait. Doing what is pleasing to Him.

PRAYER

Heavenly Father, thank you for providing for my needs. Amen.

SEPTEMBER

Day 273

So, do not have trouble in your mind about these things. Do not always say, "What will we eat?", or "What will we drink?", or "What will we wear?" People who do not know God are always thinking about these things. But as for you, your Father in heaven knows that you need them. Instead, always think about the things that are important in the kingdom of heaven. Always do what God shows you is right. Then he will also give you the things that you need each day.
Matthew 6:31-33 EASY

Worrying is a sin and a sign of unbelief in God's providence. We are shown in this verse how to handle life's basic challenges-being Kingdom-minded.

It is natural for one to think about what to eat, drink and wear especially when you do not have the means to provide them. The Word of God is showing us it is not your responsibility to nurse these thoughts. Yours is to ask and thank God for His provision. How it will come by is the evidence of your trust or belief in His Word, and what you have ask from Him

Thank Him and wait for Him. Be sensitive to how the answer will come. Our ways are not his ways. But also, keep your mind on the kingdom agenda whilst you wait. Doing what is pleasing to Him.

PRAYER

Heavenly Father, thank you for providing for my needs. Amen.

OCTOBER

Have Faith

OCTOBER

Day 274

For every child of God defeats this evil world, and we achieve this victory through our faith. And who can win this battle against the world? Only those who believe that Jesus is the Son of God. And Jesus Christ was revealed as God's Son by his baptism in water and by shedding his blood on the cross-not by water only, but by water and blood. And the Spirit, who is truth, confirms it with his testimony.
1 John 5:4-6 NLT

The basic standard of a Child of God is that you have defeated this evil world because of Jesus' finished work on the cross. You live in it by faith. Believing in God's son is your qualification to win this battle against the world.

Notice that the Son of God was revealed in baptism by water and by shedding His blood on the cross. You also went through baptism and through the evidence of the Holy Ghost we have been sealed with His promise.

But the cross is also evidence of sonship. Your challenges are all part of the evidence that you are indeed a child of God. The world hates you. Because you are not of this world, it doesn't know you. Despise not your cross. Father, thank you for baptism and the cross. Amen.

PRAYER

Abba, I thank you for Jesus. Because He is my example, I declare I can Amen.

OCTOBER

Day 275

Now faith is confidence in what we hope for and assurance about what we do not see.
Hebrews 11:1 NIV

Faith can be described as a leap into the dark. Yet you are audacious enough to believe God is Who He says He is and able to do what He says He will do.

The whole foundation of what we stand for as a believer in our Lord Jesus Christ is based on faith. What, then, is faith? To me, faith is believing in what you have not seen physically but in what you know from God's Word to be the truth.

Faith comes by hearing and hearing by the Word of God. (Romans 10:17). Faith is developed. Your faith must grow, as certain as your knowledge of the Word of God must grow. It goes hand in hand. (James 1:3).

As you study the Word of God, listening to what is taught by others and the Holy Spirit, your faith grows. Make a conscious effort to nurture your knowledge about what you have believed.

PRAYER

Father, thank you for my life of Faith. Enlarge my capacity to receive you in Jesus' name. Amen.

OCTOBER

Day 276

No one can have faith without hearing the message about Christ.
Romans 10:17 CEV

You cannot have "this kind" of faith without Jesus Christ. Accepting Jesus as your Lord and Saviour places you in the Kingdom of God. It gives you a new nature and identity called a child of God, born again from the kingdom of darkness into the kingdom of our Lord Jesus Christ.

This stature places you in the position of receiving this kind of faith. This standing aids you in growing and maturing through the studying of God's Word, prayer, and all that it entails. As you hear the word, faith is built in you.

The Words you hear are Spirit and Life (John 6:63). They have the power to create and destroy. Jesus Himself is the Word of God. As you continue to hear Him, your spirit bears witness to the Living Word, and they begin to manifest what God has already prepared for those who are called according to His purpose.

PRAYER

Father, build my faith as I listen for your voice every day, in Jesus' name, Amen.

OCTOBER

Day 277

For we walk by faith, not by sight.
2 Corinthians 5:7 NKJV

Walk, from Strong's dictionary, means to live, to deport oneself, to follow as a companion. This helps us understand that you can't live in God's dwelling and not believe that He is Who He says He is and can do what He says He will do.

You cannot walk with who you cannot trust. How can two walk together unless they agree (Amos 3:3). You need to agree and believe in God.

You cannot live as a child of God, and not believe in the invisible attributes of God. They are more real than what you see. For scripture says in Romans 1:20: *"For since the creation of the world His invisible attributes are clearly seen, being understood by the things that are made, even His eternal power and Godhead, so that they are without excuse."* (NKJV)

PRAYER

Father, thank you for giving me this life of faith. With it, I can partake in your invincible presence. In Jesus' name, Amen.

HAVE FAITH.

OCTOBER

Day 278

That your faith should not stand in the wisdom of men, but in the power of God.
1 Corinthians 2:5 KJV

Apostle Paul, in the previous chapters, highlighted how he did not come to them in Corinth in the wisdom of men and excellence of speech but in the demonstration of the Spirit's power in weakness and fear. Remember that God's strength is made perfect in our weaknesses or inadequacies.

God allows that so our boast will be for and in Him. He does that to glorify Himself. God is gracious and kind. 2 Corinthians 4:7 (TPT) tells us we are like common clay jars that carry this glorious treasure within so that the extraordinary overflow of power will be seen as God's, not ours. You are like a pen He wants to use to write.

The mighty power of God in us is at work when you stand in the Word of God and cancel every doubt, hopelessness, and fear of disappointment. Our Father is a good Shepherd who keeps His Word. Have Faith.

PRAYER

Father, thank you for the power of the Holy Ghost. Amen.

OCTOBER

Day 279

I assure you and most solemnly say to you, whoever says to this mountain, 'Be lifted up and thrown into the sea!' and does not doubt in his heart [in God's unlimited power], but believes that what he says is going to take place, it will be done for him [in accordance with God's will]. For this reason I am telling you, whatever things you ask for in prayer [in accordance with God's will], believe [with confident trust] that you have received them, and they will be given to you.
Mark 11:23-24 AMP

The Bible is filled with directions, and assured results. Faith works. Your unwavering belief in the character of God will manifest the Word of His promise.

"True faith rests upon the character of God and asks no further proof than the moral perfections of the One who cannot lie." (A.W. Tozer)

Your part is to take God by His Word, written or spoken, delete every doubt and hold onto Him till you see it manifest. Just believe He will do it!

PRAYER

Father, I believe in You, help my unbelief. Amen.

OCTOBER

Day 280

And Jesus said unto them, Because of your unbelief: for verily I say unto you, If ye have faith as a grain of mustard seed, ye shall say unto this mountain, Remove hence to yonder place; and it shall remove: and nothing shall be impossible unto you.
Matthew 17:20 KJVAAE

Unbelief is a sin! (John 16:9). The next time you are finding reasons to doubt the very existence of God, or what He has done, check the source. You cannot please God if you hold unbelief in your heart.

Come to Him believing that all things are possible. Let this truth be your lifestyle. Grow into Christ's faith nature and be confident of who He says He is.

Grow that little faith with His Word and promises until you can command 'the mountain' (impossible) situations to go, and they will in Jesus' name, Amen. "True faith manifests itself through our actions." (Francis Chan)

PRAYER

Abba, I believe you. Help me to have faith in your finish work all the time in Jesus' name, Amen.

OCTOBER

Day 281

So faith by itself, if it has no works, is dead. But someone will say, "You have faith and I have works." Show me your faith apart from your works, and I by my works will show you my faith. You believe that God is one; you do well. Even the demons believe-and shudder.
James 2:17-19 NRSV

Faith without works is dead. This verse can be used as an example of giving. Lending a helping hand to someone in need when you are able to do so. Proverbs 3:27 says When it is in your power, don't withhold good from the one it belongs to. Meaning you might have that 'thing' now but it belongs to the one who is in need, selah. You are just a custodian.

Faith works best when it is in action. Give to the poor, bless those God has placed in your care, love the brethren, and give alms.

Don't use your faith only in your pursuit of God. Use it in relation to others. As you do for others, you do it unto the Lord, and He will reward you. Faith in God is at work when you believe that God is the rewarder.

PRAYER

Father, thank You for teaching me how to put my faith to work. Amen.

OCTOBER

Day 282

And being not weak in faith, he considered not his own body now dead, when he was about a hundred years old, neither yet the deadness of Sarah's womb: he staggered not at the promise of God through unbelief; but was strong in faith, giving glory to God; and being fully persuaded, that what he had promised, he was able also to perform. And therefore it was imputed to him for righteousness.
Romans 4:19-22 KJVAAE

Faith is a being. (Hebrews 11:1). Faith is living, real and active. You grow your faith through trials, the Word of God, prayer and fasting, as the scriptures also say. Faith without works is dead James 2:26. One of the works of the Holy Spirit is to help grow our faith with the challenges we face. Abraham showed us that each one has their unique discipline with God, where He will bring our way things and situations that will grow our faith. Your ability to trust Him, allows Him to impute His righteousness on you for believing and taking Him at His Word. Just believe.

"A faith that hasn't been tested can't be trusted."
(Adrian Rogers)

PRAYER

Father, I believe you are faithful to your Word, Amen.

OCTOBER

Day 283

Faith opened Noah's heart to receive revelation and warnings from God about what was coming, even things that had never been seen. But he stepped out in reverent obedience to God and built an ark that would save him and his family. By his faith the world was condemned, but Noah received God's gift of righteousness that comes by believing.
Hebrews 11:7 TPT

"When all is said and done, the life of faith is nothing if not an unending struggle of the spirit with every available weapon against the flesh."
(Dietrich Bonhoeffer)

That is what the Scriptures mean when they say, *"No eye has seen, no ear has heard, and no mind has imagined what God has prepared for those who love him."* 1 Corinthians 2:9.

Open your heart to receive what God has for you. It is exceptional but can only be accessed by the vehicle of faith.

Your flesh would always want to see before it believes, but blessed is He who has not seen but believes (John 20:28-29). With God, believe to see. Create your reality with His word.

PRAYER

Heavenly Father, help my unbelief. May your eternal plan for my life be established in Jesus' name, Amen.

OCTOBER

Day 284

For we live by believing and not by seeing.
2 Corinthians 5:7 NLT

Nutrition is to help nourish the body and assist the body in functioning well. When you don't eat well, your body suffers, growth is retarded, and most times, you appear malnourished and unhealthy.

So, it is with your life as a child of God. You have to live by what you believe, not what you see, for your vision is limited. What do you believe? If your life's growth is dependent on the nourishment of your faith, what then do you believe?

Make an intentional choice to believe what God says He is, *"I will be what I will be"* or *"I am that I am"* Exodus 3:14. His promises are all yes, and Amen.

Faith is a being. Grow your faith with His Word, let your faith be active and living. Choose to walk and live this life of faith, your victory on this earth is in that being called FAITH!

PRAYER

Father, thank you for giving me a companion, faith. Amen.

OCTOBER

Day 285

Jesus replied to them, "I assure you and most solemnly say to you, if you have faith [personal trust and confidence in Me] and do not doubt or allow yourself to be drawn in two directions, you will not only do what was done to the fig tree, but even if you say to this mountain, 'Be taken up and thrown into the sea,' it will happen [if God wills it]. And whatever you ask for in prayer, believing, you will receive.
Matthew 21:21-22 AMP

Having personal trust and confidence in the Lord Jesus Christ will enable you to do all things as He strengthens you. (Philippians 4:13). Do not be drawn away by doubt, based on what you see and hear. Your faith's foundation should be the Word of God. When you receive the Word, say it, live it and see it. That is to have a mental picture of God's Word being made manifest. What you see with the eye of the spirit plays an important role in the manifestation of your faith. God always hastens to do what you say and can imagine.

Your confessions and testimonies honour God. Any time you see praise, thanksgiving, or offering, you see the fruit of your lips (Hebrews 13:15, Psalms 119:108, Jeremiah 33:11). Declare your salvation the fruit of your lips.

PRAYER

Father, thank you for giving me the tools of faith to decree and declare Your will on this earth and in my circumstances. In Jesus' name, Amen.

OCTOBER

Day 286

Be on guard; stand firm in your faith [in God, respecting His precepts and keeping your doctrine sound]. Act like [mature] men and be courageous; be strong.
1 Corinthians 16:13 AMP

Be strong, watchful, alert, and act. As men, these are all military metaphors used to describe your positioning. For your enemy roars, looking for someone to devour. You are cautioned to take the position of a soldier skilfully.

This manliness, strength and bravery is a call to live in love. Let everything you do be done in love [motivated and inspired by God's love for us]. (1 Corinthians 16:14).

Your whole duty is to love God with all your heart, mind, and soul. And in doing that, you extend and manifest that love in loving your neighbour as yourself (Luke 10:27). With love, there is no law that is against it. But it takes faith in God's Word, courage, strength, mastery, and the help of the Holy Spirit to love like Christ.

PRAYER

Father, thank you for the call to honour you in love. Amen.

OCTOBER

Day 287

"If you can't?" said Jesus. "Everything is possible for one who believes." Immediately the boy's father exclaimed, "I do believe; help me overcome my unbelief!"
Mark 9:23-24 BOOKS

There is a part of you that believes God is who He says He is. You believe He made all things and even some of the things written in the Bible. You go further to believe Jesus came to die and rose again. But do you believe God is for you? Do you believe He can heal you? Do you believe He can make everything work for your good if you believe it and not doubt it?

It is easy for you to say God is good. He is a good Father and Shepherd. But do you believe it for yourself? Today, I want to challenge the part of you that holds unbelief, the part that whispers God will not do it for you.

God loves you! His love is not the humankind, with limitations. It is enduring and full of mercy. Have faith, for ALL THINGS ARE POSSIBLE WITH GOD!

PRAYER

Father, thank you for reminding me to hope in you. Help me to overcome my unbelief in Jesus' name. Amen.

OCTOBER

New Life

OCTOBER

Day 288

I am crucified with Christ: nevertheless I live; yet not I, but Christ liveth in me: and the life which I now live in the flesh I live by the faith of the Son of God, who loved me, and gave himself for me.
Galatians 2:20 KJV

You are crucified with Christ through your baptism in His name. Baptism signifies death with Christ Jesus; when you come out of the water you are resurrected into your new life. This life is lived by the faith of the Son of God. Again, you are reminded Christ is the originator of this life of faith.

You need to become aware of this new life and live like it. A life in the Spirit is where you reign and rule like Christ on this earth. Because He lives in you, you are hidden in Him from harm. I see you and I see the resurrected Christ. Glory be to God. Amen.

Most times, we are waiting for a glorified body when we die but Christ in you, living through you is the Hope of glory. You are glorified in Christ. Amen.

PRAYER

Lord Jesus, thank You for living through me. Amen.

OCTOBER

Day 289

For by grace you have been saved through faith, and this is not your own doing; it is the gift of God- not the result of works, so that no one may boast. For we are what he has made us, created in Christ Jesus for good works, which God prepared beforehand to be our way of life.
Ephesians 2:8-10 NRSV

God wants you to be conscious you are saved by His unmerited favour through believing in Him. Not because of what you have or will do, but through the finished work of Jesus who is the Christ. This truth puts you in the place of humility and assurance of blessings of God's faithfulness and mercy. You can but only boast on His mercies!

You have been made into good works. God created it in Christ Jesus before He formed you. As you find your way in Him, He will lead you in the path that glorifies Him.

PRAYER

Father, thank you for choosing me before the foundation of the world to glorify you in Jesus. Amen.

OCTOBER

Day 290

For I am not ashamed of the gospel; it is the power of God for salvation to everyone who has faith, to the Jew first and also to the Greek. For in it the righteousness of God is revealed through faith for faith; as it is written, "The one who is righteous will live by faith."
Romans 1:16-17 NRSV

For me, the Gospel is the birth, life, death, and resurrection of our Lord Jesus Christ. Without that, there is no Christianity. His sacrifice has given us a newness of life. It is through Him that we can call God Father. Through Jesus, we can relate to the Holy Spirit.

No one can go to God without Jesus Christ! This is by faith, when you believe that Christ's righteousness is imputed unto you and God is revealed to your spirit. We live by faith because, though you might not see it, you believe and receive it. You live your life in Christ, for in Him there is no lack. Amen.

PRAYER

Father, thank you for giving me the life of Jesus Christ. Amen.

OCTOBER

Day 291

The Father loves the Son and has placed all things in his hands. Whoever believes in the Son has eternal life; whoever disobeys the Son will not see life, but must endure God's wrath.
John 3:35-36 NRSV

The Father loves the Son but gave Him up to die, so as to reconcile the World to Himself. John 3:16 shows us how much God loves us that He gave His only begotten Son. Whosoever believes in Him will have eternal life. Why do you give up what you love? So, you can get what you desire.

When you believe in the Son, you have eternal life. That is why we must be cautious not to judge. Some people might not show it but they believe in our Lord Jesus Christ. Disobedience also has its consequences; in that you will not see life. You will not have eternal life but the wrath of God. Therefore, I beg you by the mercies of God to repent and believe in our Lord Jesus Christ.

PRAYER

Father, thank you for your Son, Jesus. Through Him, I have salvation and access to you. Amen.

OCTOBER

Day 292

Look at the proud; his soul is not straight or right within him, but the [rigidly] just and the [uncompromisingly] righteous man shall live by his faith and in his faithfulness. [Rom. 1:17; Gal. 3:11.]
Habakkuk 2:4 AMPC

God hates pride! Pride focuses on you, your achievements, and your dignity. Me, myself, and I, basically. There is no room in acknowledging God and the fact that whatever you have is from Him.

Scriptures say of a prideful person, his soul is not right within Him. His soul's focus is for his own pleasure and not to please God. James 4:6 tells us God opposes the proud but gives grace to the humble.

A righteous man is one who seeks to do what is right in the sight of God. God says, live in the faith you have. Believe that I am a rewarder of those who seek me. I will bless him and his thousand generations (Exodus 20:6).

PRAYER

Father, thank you for making me right through Jesus Christ, Amen.

OCTOBER

Day 293

"If you obey the commands of the Lord your God and walk in his ways, the Lord will establish you as his holy people as he swore he would do.
Deuteronomy 28:9 NLT

It is the will and pleasure of God to establish you. God honours obedience, and He is a covenant-keeping God. He watches over His Word to fulfilment. Can you remember the number of times you did wrong, but because of His mercies, He kept you safe and provided for you?

This is what you need to grasp in your spirit today. God created everything and rules over all. But He has His chosen people. He cares for all His creation, but He establishes those that obey Him. Isaiah 1:19 says If you are willing and obedient, you will eat the best of the land (BSB).

God is a good God, but a Father to the elect. His holy people. He knows them by name. Seek to know Him through Jesus Christ by faith.

PRAYER

Father, thank you for your Son Jesus; through Him, I can know you. Amen.

OCTOBER

Day 294

Now the God of hope fill you with all joy and peace in believing, that ye may abound in hope, in the power of the Holy Ghost.
Romans 15:13 RV1895

God is the source of hope. Hope does not disappoint. Because God is your hope, He will not fail!

And the hope of God never makes us ashamed because the love of God has been poured out into our hearts through the Holy Spirit, which has been given to us. Romans 5:5 (A Faithful Version).

Now that you know that hope is of God, may He fill you with His hope through Jesus. May you be filled with all joy and peace in believing that He is, and a rewarder of those who diligently seek Him.

This joy and peace live in your heart, which is the work of the Holy Spirit. It is the Power of God that works in the children of obedience. You thrive and flourish in everything you do, for God is your source.

PRAYER

Father, thank you for being the source of my joy and peace in Jesus' name, Amen.

OCTOBER

Day 295

God called us to be holy and does not want us to live in sin. So the person who refuses to obey this teaching is disobeying God, not simply a human teaching. And God is the One who gives us his Holy Spirit.
1 Thessalonians 4:7-8 NCV

God made us holy as He is holy. But through Adam's disobedience, sin entered our lineage, resulting in our sinful nature. Glory be to God, who, through Jesus, has imputed His righteousness to us and called us into sanctification.

It is God's desire that you do not live in sin. When you refuse to obey this message and continue to live in your own way, you are disobeying God, which is a transgression—a deliberate act of going outside the will of God.

For God has not called us to impurity, but to holiness [to be dedicated, and set apart by behaviour that pleases Him, whether in public or in private]. (1 Thessalonians 4:7 AMP). Strive to live for Him through the help of the Holy Spirit in Faith. You are called to be holy!

PRAYER

Father, thank you for calling me unto holiness. Amen.

OCTOBER

Day 296

I can do all things in him that strengtheneth me.
Philippians 4:13 RV1895

You were not created by God without limitations on this earth. He made you complete in Him. You have His abilities through His breath. *Sin limits our capabilities to tap into God's Supernatural abilities.* But bless be our Lord Jesus Christ, who has made it possible for us to triumph over sin.

Through and in Jesus you can do all things, hallelujah, praise God. In Him, you have His infinite abilities. Remember that;

"I know what it means to lack, and I know what it means to experience overwhelming abundance. For I'm trained in the secret of overcoming all things, whether in fullness or in hunger. And I find that the strength of Christ's explosive power infuses me to conquer every difficulty." Philippians 4:12-13 TPT.

May this truth be your reality.

PRAYER

Father, thank you for Jesus. In Him I can do everything for your glory, Amen.

OCTOBER

Day 297

For this reason, all who obey you should pray to you while they still can. When troubles rise like a flood, they will not reach them. You are my hiding place. You protect me from my troubles and fill me with songs of salvation. Selah.
Psalms 32:6-7 NCV

Being in God does not exempt you from troubles. As long as you are in this flesh you will do something that does not, please God. But we have an Advocate, The Helper who helps us in weakness and prompts us to ask for forgiveness.

The Psalmist says the happy one is the one whose sins are forgiven, and wrongs pardoned. Happy are you whom the Lord does not "consider" guilty. Psalm 32:12: *"Wow, that is something worth rejoicing about. That is a position in Jesus in God. Accept Jesus as your Saviour. Salvation is in no other than Jesus."*

He also reminds us that when troubles come your way, God will hide you and show you the way to take and hide. Have faith in God and His Word.

PRAYER

Father, thank You for Jesus in Him I am safe. Amen.

OCTOBER

Day 298

Keep thy heart with all diligence; for out of it are the issues of life. It is difficult for any man to live a flawless life without the Word of God as the standard. His Word is Truth!
Proverbs 4:23 KJV

Proverbs 4:23 NLT tells you to "Guard your heart above all else, for it determines the course of your life."

How can you guard your heart? By storing the Word of Truth in it, using it as a standard for your life, and rejecting anything that is not in line to His Word. Remember that you have the Holy Spirit as your helper. As He guides you in all truth, your work is to believe and obey His voice. He will bring you to your wealthy place. Be diligent in your walk with the Word of God.

PRAYER

Holy Spirit, as I listen for your voice and guidance may I be sensitive to discern you from all others, Amen.

OCTOBER

Day 299

Rejoicing in hope; patient in tribulation; continuing instant in prayer.
Romans 12:12 KJV

Romans 12:12 says: *"Do not forget to rejoice, for hope is always just around the corner. Hold up through the hard times that are coming, and devote yourselves to prayer."* (The Voice).

Hope is to anticipate usually with pleasure. This hope you anticipate can be for good or bad things. Through life, hope is what keeps the soul. God encourages you today to be patient in hope. Not only that but pray also that your faith will stand even through the season of waiting. Patient is the brother of hope. When you keep both, it will not disappoint.

PRAYER

Heavenly Father, as I hope in you, I receive the grace to seek you in prayer and patiently I will wait on you through Christ to receive my Promise Amen.

OCTOBER

Day 300

Let not mercy and truth forsake thee: bind them about thy neck; write them upon the table of thine heart: So shalt thou find favour and good understanding in the sight of God and man.
Proverbs 3:3-4 KJV

Kindness and loyalty are something we all desire to receive when we need it. God reminds us to keep these same kindness and loyalty in our hearts ready to give it to others. In doing that, what you get in return is favour and good understanding with God in the sight of men.

In God, giving in any aspect is not losing but gaining. Stay kind and loyal. God is the rewarder not humans. Humans are but the vehicle God uses to fulfil His purpose.

PRAYER

Lord, may I be the one you use to show mercy and kindness to others in Jesus' name Amen.

OCTOBER

Day 301

For God is the one who provides seed for the farmer and then bread to eat. In the same way, he will provide and increase your resources and then produce a great harvest of generosity in you. Yes, you will be enriched in every way so that you can always be generous. And when we take your gifts to those who need them, they will thank God.
2 Corinthians 9:10-11 NLT

Generosity is the nature of God. It is also in His children.

He blesses you to be a blessing to lead others to give Him glory. When you withhold your seed or giving, you forsake your harvest. And that doesn't glorify God.

"One gives freely, yet gains even more; another withholds what is right, only to become poor. A generous soul will prosper, and he who refreshes others will himself be refreshed. The people will curse the hoarder of grain, but blessing will crown the one who sells it."
Proverbs 11:24-26 BSB

PRAYER

I receive the grace to be more generous in all my ways. Lord, continue to show me ways I can be a blessing to many through Christ our Lord Amen.

OCTOBER

Day 302

But take diligent heed to do the commandment and the law, which Moses the servant of the LORD charged you, to love the LORD your God, and to walk in all his ways, and to keep his commandments, and to cleave unto him, and to serve him with all your heart and with all your soul.
Joshua 22:5 KJV

Being diligent in this context is wholly, vehemently, muchness to keep, guard, observe, and give heed to what God has commanded. In addition, He asks that you cleave to Him and serve as well with everything you have and are.

When you have done your part, He is a faithful Father and friend to keep you in all your ways. God has expectations. Selah

PRAYER

I will be diligent in keeping your Word my Daddy. Thank you, Holy Spirit for helping me, Amen.

OCTOBER
Day 303

Take care, brothers, lest there be in any of you an evil, unbelieving heart, leading you to fall away from the living God. [13] But exhort one another every day, as long as it is called "today," that none of you may be hardened by the deceitfulness of sin.
Hebrews 3:12-13 ESV

Depending on your culture, beliefs, and perceptions, among other things, you cannot use your feelings as a basis for decisions. These affect how you feel and view things. (Think about anything you judge based on your feelings, were you wrong? Can you correct it? Was another involved, will you apologise?).

Unbelief is a sin, and every sin is deceitful. Be encouraged and stand on God's faithfulness to every Word of His promise. God loves you.

PRAYER

Holy Spirit, correct me in judgement. Make me a pacemaker in all I do. Amen.

OCTOBER

Day 304

And because of him you are in Christ Jesus, who became to us wisdom from God, righteousness and sanctification and redemption, so that, as it is written, "Let the one who boasts, boast in the Lord."
1 Corinthians 1:30-31 ESV

God our Father's precision is immaculate. His wisdom is unsearchable, yet He gives us access to search for it.

You cannot on your own become what He desires you to become, so in His wisdom, He gives you a new birth and asks you to trust the helper who will teach you all things. This is the generosity of God so that no one can boost of himself. It is a gift of God, making you to be like Him is the Work of Himself. You believe and trust Him in all your ways, acknowledge Him and He shall direct your path, Amen.

PRAYER

God, thank you for Jesus who is all I need to be all you want me to be. May I be conscious of this truth in all I do, Amen.

NOVEMBER

Pray Always

NOVEMBER

Day 305

Then Abraham prayed to God; and God healed Abimelech, and also healed his wife and female slaves so that they bore children. For the Lord had closed all the wombs of the house of Abimelech because of Sarah, Abraham's wife.
Genesis 20:17-18 RSV

Abraham is the father of faith. But did you know he was also a man of prayer? There were so many instances when he worshipped and prayed to God for change, help, and to intercede for souls. You can't live on earth and not pray. Prayer is the medium through which we interact with God and institute heaven's agenda on earth.

It is good to pray for those who do good to you, but it is more powerful when you pray and intercede for those who hurt you and despitefully use you. God honours such prayers. Matthew 5:44: *"But I say to you, love your enemies and bless the one who curses you, and do what is beautiful to the one who hates you, and pray over those who take you by force and persecute you."* Amen.

Prayer is also a way through which God works in our weakness. Abraham prayed for Abimelech and his family, and God restored him, (Genesis 20:17). As Jesus did in Luke 23:34.

PRAYER

Father God, thank you for the spirit of prayer. Today, I choose to intercede for all those who hate me. Bless them in Jesus's name. Amen.

NOVEMBER

Day 306

Therefore, he who speaks in a tongue should pray for the power to interpret. For if I pray in a tongue, my spirit prays but my mind is unfruitful.
1 Corinthians 14:13-14 RSV

There are different kinds of prayer, as well as different dimensions and realms of prayer. It is also interesting to know that there are different languages in prayer.

Prayer has its dynamics, and effective prayer requires a lifestyle and culture that will provoke the answers from God. Apostle Paul's letter to Corinth teaches us the importance of walking in love in chapter 13. Chapter 14 enlightens us to seek understanding of what we pray, especially when one prays in an unknown tongue called "speaking in tongues", which is a heavenly language. (1 Corinthians 14:2).

It is important to know what the Spirit is interceding for on your behalf. What is your Spirit communicating with the Spirit of God about? This knowledge makes you effective and efficient. It also helps you understand what you have to do.

PRAYER

Father God, thank you for giving me a heavenly language where I can speak with you in mystery, interpreting and understanding what I prayed in Jesus' name. Amen.

NOVEMBER

Day 307

O my God, incline thine ear, and hear; open thine eyes, and behold our desolations, and the city which is called by thy name: for we do not present our supplications before thee for our righteousnesses, but for thy great mercies. O Lord, hear; O Lord, forgive; O Lord, hearken and do; defer not; for thine own sake, O my God, because thy city and thy people are called by thy name.
Daniel 9:18-19 RV1895

God's faithfulness is what makes Him dependable. He is merciful and kind. His loving kindness is better than life. He hears us because He is righteous. He chooses to do what is right.

We choose to pray to God not based on what we have done but on God's righteousness and the finished work of Christ. You are in God's will; seek His counsel, and He will direct your path. God is still on His throne, and we are His people. Don't cease praying.

PRAYER

Father God, thank you for hearing me in your righteousness in Jesus Christ, my Lord. Amen.

NOVEMBER

Day 308

So whenever we are in need, we should come bravely before the throne of our merciful God. There we will be treated with undeserved grace, and we will find help.
Hebrews 4:16 CEV

Isn't it amazing to know you have a safe place in time of need? Where you can obtain mercy when you fault, grace to sustain you and strength to finish.

The passion translation says, 'So now we come freely and boldly to where grace is enthroned, to receive mercy's kiss and discover the grace we urgently need to strengthen us in our time of weakness.'

Love is enthroned where God is. He is love; where love is, there is grace. He is the one who is for the downcast.

"Now that we know what we have—Jesus, this great High Priest with ready access to God—let's not let it slip through our fingers. We don't have a priest who is out of touch with our reality. He's been through weakness and testing, experienced it all—all but the sin. So let's walk right up to him and get what he is so ready to give. Take the mercy, accept the help." Hebrew 4:14-16 MSG. Come boldly to the one who loves you, who will treat you and your need with undeserved grace and help where you need it most.

PRAYER

Abba thank you for giving me a High Priest that I can go to. Amen.

NOVEMBER

Day 309

He will regard the prayer of the destitute and will not despise their prayer. Let this be recorded for a generation to come, so that a people yet unborn may praise the Lord: that he looked down from his holy height, from heaven the Lord looked at the earth, to hear the groans of the prisoners, to set free those who were doomed to die; so that the name of the Lord may be declared in Zion, and his praise in Jerusalem.
Psalms 102:17-21 NRSV

The Lord is your ever-present help in times of need. He has regard, listens, and answers you when you are in need especially to the one who is destitute. A destitute is one who lacks the means to provide for himself, poor, disadvantaged, distressed, and oppressed. You and I find ourselves in that situation one way or another.

God is saying I will hear you when you call on me. I will answer and send you help. He is the I AM, all-sufficient one; He holds all things together. Don't forget to teach your children about God. One generation will praise Him to another generation. Call on Him now. Amen.

PRAYER

Father God, thank you for being there for me always. A shield of comfort and strength. Amen.

NOVEMBER

Day 310

Confess therefore your sins one to another, and pray one for another, that ye may be healed. The supplication of a righteous man availeth much in its working.
James 5:16 RS1895

Confession is a powerful tool in prayer. Forgiveness gives way for the mercies of God to overflow in our hearts. Jesus often in His ministry forgave sins and asks the person healed not to sin again. It is with the same principle that Apostle James, in James 5, tells us to anoint with oil, pray for the sick and the Lord shall forgive if any sin is committed.

Because confession to one another is one of God's tools of forgiveness and restoration, the enemy has attacked it. We do not trust ourselves and those in the church body to confess our faults to them, with the fear that they will tell others and look at us differently.

But God is merciful. If you have anything you know you have done that torments you, pray to God but also find a trustworthy person to confess to. God honours that. Job forgave and prayed for his friends, and God restored them, (Job 42:10). Amen.

PRAYER

Heavenly Father, thank you for the power of confession. I bless you for bringing people my way whom I can confess to. Through Christ our Lord, Amen.

NOVEMBER

Day 311

After walking a little farther away from them, Jesus fell to the ground and prayed, "My Father, if it is possible, do not give me this cup of suffering. But do what you want, not what I want." Then Jesus went back to his followers and found them asleep. He said to Peter, "You men could not stay awake with me for one hour? Stay awake and pray for strength against temptation. The spirit wants to do what is right, but the body is weak."
Matthew 26:39-41 NCV

The position and posture you take in prayer is as important as what you say. God desires you to be honest with how you feel in prayer. Jesus showed us that in His prayer, that if it was possible the cup of suffering should be taken from Him. But He added not what I want, but what you, Father, want is what I desire. May that be your prayer today. Amen.

He further showed us that a man's spirit is willing to do what is right and pleasing to God, but his body is weak—weak to temptation and sin. You overcome temptation by strengthening your spirit through spiritual exercises.

Seek God's will and build your spirit to overcome the desires of the flesh. Help us, God, in Jesus' name. Amen.

PRAYER

Father, I thank you that even in my weakness you are still with me, offering strength and wisdom. Thank you for being a good father. Thank you, Holy Spirit, for strength. Thank you, Jesus, for being my wisdom. Amen.

NOVEMBER

Day 312

And it shall be that everyone who calls upon the name of the Lord [invoking, adoring, and worshipping the Lord Jesus] shall be saved (rescued spiritually).
Acts 2:21 AMP

We are in times so close to the days mentioned by the Apostle Peter in Acts 2:21 and Prophet Joel mentioned in Joel 2:32. Where people will find themselves in a place where all they can do is call on the name of the Lord, and they will be saved.

Salvation is in no other than Jesus Christ. No one can come to God except through His son Jesus. When troubles, trials and tribulations come your way remember God is ever present. He admonishes us to pray to Him through Jesus and He will hear and answer us. The answers don't always come as we expect, but trust His ways. He will give you peace that surpasses understanding and rest for your soul.

"Trouble naturally belongs to God's moral government, and it is one of his invaluable agents in governing the world." By E. M. Bound in his book 'The Essentials of Prayer'. God bless you.

PRAYER

Abba thank you for the name, Jesus. Amen.

NOVEMBER

Day 313

And the LORD turned the captivity of Job, when he prayed for his friends: And the LORD gave Job twice as much as he had before. Then came there unto him all his brethren, and all his sisters, and all they that had been of his acquaintance before, and did eat bread with him in his house: And they bemoaned him, and comforted him concerning all the evil that the LORD had brought upon him: Every man also gave him a piece of money, and everyone a ring of gold.
Job 42:10-11 RV1885

There is something about praying for those who hurt you and despitefully use you that brings healing to your soul and restoration. This act has the ability to turn your captivity around as bitterness scriptures say it defiles you (Hebrews 12:15).

Every heart knows its own bitterness (Proverbs 14:10). But as you make a decision to pray to God about it, He takes it, deals with your heart, heals you and restores to you the joy of salvation.

Notice Job's friends and family came around when God turned His captivity around. Until God sets you free, your adversaries and even friends are not at liberty to come to you. Bitterness, anger, and malice are spiritual barriers. May the Lord deliver us from these in Jesus' name. Amen.

PRAYER

Lord Jesus, I thank you for redeeming me; you have my heart. Help me to live like you every day. Amen.

NOVEMBER

Day 314

Yes, the Almighty will be your gold And your precious silver; For then you will have your delight in the Almighty, And lift up your face to God. You will make your prayer to Him, He will hear you, And you will pay your vows. You will also declare a thing, And it will be established for you; So light will shine on your ways.
Job 22:25-28 NKJV

God has given everything to us freely, but I have also come to know that for it to work in your life, conditions must be attached to its manifestation.

Eliphaz, one of Jobs' three friends, draws our attention to the truth that if you want to declare a thing and for it to be established, you have to make the Almighty your gold and precious silver. Your delight should be God and all that concerns Him.

He also added, after you have made Elohim your all-in-all, lift up your face to Him in prayer and supplication, make your request known to Him, and He will hear you and answer you. Then pay your vows. Offer a sacrifice of Thanksgiving. It honours God. When you do that, God will always establish you. Amen.

PRAYER

Abba, thank you for teaching me the ways to everlasting contentment, joy, and life Amen.

NOVEMBER

Day 315

Jesus replied, "Let the faith of God be in you! Listen to the truth I speak to you: If someone says to this mountain with great faith and having no doubt, 'Mountain, be lifted up and thrown into the midst of the sea,' and believes that what he says will happen, it will be done. This is the reason I urge you to boldly believe for whatever you ask for in prayer-be convinced that you have received it and it will be yours.
Mark 11:22-24 TPT

Let the "faith of God" be in you. What does that mean? It is the belief of the righteousness of Christ imputed to you so that the life you now live and have is Christ's life, the Anointed one.

Jesus is showing you how to live like Him, how you can see the manifestations of your words, how you need to envision what you say, and how you must believe that it is happening, and it shall. That is the faith of God, that He is who He says He is and will do whatever He says He will. So, you are in Christ.

In prayer, God gives us access through Jesus to come boldly to obtain mercy and to ask of Him our needs. Believe in God, have no doubt, and see with your Spirit's eyes what you have asked, and it has happened. Amen.

PRAYER

Father, thank you for the eyes of faith. I believe, and I receive it through Christ our Lord. Amen.

NOVEMBER

Day 316

I write this letter to you who believe in the Son of God so you will know you have eternal life. And this is the boldness we have in God's presence: that if we ask God for anything that agrees with what he wants, he hears us. If we know he hears us every time we ask him, we know we have what we ask from him.
1 John 5:13-15 NCV

I have often used verse 14 as I pray, but as I studied this verse, the Holy Spirit opened my eyes to see that the one who has boldness in God's presence is the one who believes in the Son of God. Believing in the Son of God gives you eternal life and access to God's presence. You see, no one can come to the Father except through the Son Jesus Christ; John 14:6 affirms this.

"And He tells you, because you are in the Son, anything you ask in accord with His will for you He hears you. And remember all His plans for you are good to bring you to an expected end." Jeremiah 29:11.

He then assures you that if He hears you every time you ask, then you will have what you ask for. Hallelujah, God be praised. Keep asking in Jesus' name; you will receive it. Amen.

PRAYER

Abba, thank you for the grace to believe in Jesus. I believe, so I say I have all I need, Amen.

NOVEMBER

Day 317

Lord, I call to you. Come quickly. Listen to me when I call to you. Let my prayer be like incense placed before you, and my praise like the evening sacrifice. Lord, help me control my tongue; help me be careful about what I say. Take away my desire to do evil or to join others in doing wrong. Don't let me eat tasty food with those who do evil.
Psalms 141:1-4 NCV

In prayer, you seek God's attention. When in need, you desire to see Him come to your aid quickly. You acquaint yourself with the tradition of how to get to His presence. But in doing all this, do you get to see the results or answers you desire?

The Psalmist is showing you some keys in and after prayer. He desires that his prayers please God. It might be your need, your desire but does it please God? Is it His will for you? Does that sacrifice please Him?

He then shows you the need to control your tongue and the words you speak. Your words have to align with what God is saying about you, not your circumstances. Finally, he asks that God help him have the right desires. May God help us. Amen.

PRAYER

My Father, may my desires be aligned with your will for me in Jesus's name. Amen.

NOVEMBER

Day 318

The Lord is kind and shows mercy. He does not become angry quickly but is full of love. The Lord is good to everyone; he is merciful to all he has made. Lord, everything you have made will praise you; those who belong to you will bless you. They will tell about the glory of your kingdom and will speak about your power. Then everyone will know the mighty things you do and the glory and majesty of your kingdom.
Psalms 145:8-12 NCV

The Lord is a responsible creator. He is good to everyone; The Psalmist tells us He is merciful to all He has made. That includes those who do not believe and worship Him.

Creation manifests the glory of the Lord. The skies demonstrate His awesome power; day and night, they do not cease to praise God. But it's those that belong to God that will bless Him. Telling others of the glory of the kingdom of God shows you belong to Him. Speak of His power to your children and grandchildren (Psalm 145:4).

Unless you proclaim the mighty works and miracles of God, He can cause the stones (unbelievers) to take your place. Luke 19:40: *"Let the name of the Lord he magnified."*

PRAYER

Lord, I will not keep silent for the stones to give you glory. I choose to bless you in all I do, Amen.

NOVEMBER

Day 319

Answer me when I pray to you, my God who does what is right. Make things easier for me when I am in trouble. Have mercy on me and hear my prayer. You know that the Lord has chosen for himself those who are loyal to him. The Lord listens when I pray to him. But you have made me very happy, happier than they are, even with all their grain and new wine. I go to bed and sleep in peace, because, Lord, only you keep me safe.
Psalms 4:1, 3, 7-8 NCV

Prayer is a safe place where you can pour out your soul to God. It is a place where you can tell God all the things that do not make sense to the human mind. God delights in you trusting Him with your emotions.

God always does what is right! Psalm 145:17: *"He takes care of His own, making sure they are safe, provided for, and protected. He shows you mercy by hearing your prayers."*

The Lord's chosen are loyal to Him. He hears them when they pray and makes them happy—happier and more peaceful than the one who trusts in his riches. God also gives you His peace and rest. Selah.

God bless you.

PRAYER

Abba, thank you. I am grateful for you being my all-sufficient one. Amen.

NOVEMBER

Day 320

The Lord is far from the wicked [and distances Himself from them], But He hears the prayer of the [consistently] righteous [that is, those with spiritual integrity and moral courage].
Proverbs 15:29 AMP

The Lord detests the prayer of the wicked! He hears every prayer, even the unspoken ones but He is far from the wicked. The Lord is Holy, he cannot behold evil. That is why He encourages you to take falsehood from you, (Ephesians 4:25).

But God is close to the righteous—the one who remains in the posture of what Christ has imputed on him—his righteousness. You are right before God because of Jesus and His finished work on the cross. Stand in that truth.

The scriptures say it is spiritual integrity and moral courage. Know who you are and be confident of that truth, then stand in it. Live it and experience the presence of God in that position. You are in Christ in God. You are a son, an heir, and God hears your prayers. He is close. Believe this truth! Pray to Him and trust He will answer in Jesus' name. Amen.

PRAYER

Holy Spirit, I know you are with me. Help me to be conscious of you always, Amen.

NOVEMBER

Day 321

Pray like this: 'Our Father, dwelling in the heavenly realms, may the glory of your name be the center on which our lives turn.
Matthew 6:9 TPT

Our Father, what a privilege to be called a child of God. Jesus showed and created awareness to you on this earth in that you can call God a Father.

When you are praying, be conscious of who you are and talking to – your Father. There is a confidence in knowing that the one you are talking to is not outside of you but the very one who made you and knows you. You are from Him. But His abode is in heaven and in your heart.

The glory of God is that He provides for you according to His riches in glory in Christ Jesus. He is delighted in you calling Him a Father. He enjoys providing for your needs. Trust Him with your needs, not only physical but emotional and psychological issues. God loves you.

PRAYER

Heavenly Father, I am grateful for your desire for me to prosper me in all I do for your glory. Amen.

NOVEMBER

Day 322

Ask, and God will give to you. Search, and you will find. Knock, and the door will open for you. Yes, everyone who asks will receive. Everyone who searches will find. And everyone who knocks will have the door opened.
Matthew 7:7-8 NCV

The scriptures encourage you to pray, with all prayers and supplication with thanksgiving let your request be made known to God -Philippians 4: 6. Jesus explained in the gospel of Matthew to ask because God will give to you. Don't be weary in your asking. for your heavenly Father wants to know you tell Him what you need.

Search, He added, and you will find. Remember, God's kingdom is a seeking Kingdom. The more you seek, the more knowledge is added unto you.

To knock means someone has to give you access or open for you to enter. You cannot enter through some doors unless they are open for you. Jesus is the door. (John 10:9). Unless you accept Jesus and be found in Him, there is something you can only see and hear of, but you will not be a part of it. Selah.

PRAYER

Lord, my heart searches and longs for you. May I never be weary of seeking you and your ways. Amen.

NOVEMBER

Day 323

May your kingdom come and what you want be done, here on earth as it is in heaven. Give us the food we need for each day.
Matthew 6:10-11 NCV

Our King has a kingdom, the Lord of host is His name, Jehovah Sabaoth (Isaiah 47:4), our Redeemer. He rules in the affairs of men yet is so loving to give you your will of choice. Will you let His kingdom come, and His will be done in your life? Selah.

The kingdom of God is in your heart as a child of God. When you accept Jesus to be your Saviour, He comes to live in you; He makes His abode in you. That is why the scriptures say, for we have these treasures in earthen vessels that the Excellency of power may be of God and not us. (1 Corinthians 4:7). Your Excellency is of God.

Like Jesus said, not my will but yours be done. Let that be your prayer today. And as you seek His rulership in your life, He will guide and lead you in the way everlasting to the glory of His name.

You will want nothing, for He will provide daily, your needs. He is a good Father.

God bless you.

PRAYER

Abba, I know I will never lack as I continue to trust and seek your ways, Amen.

NOVEMBER

Day 324

Forgive us the wrongs we have done as we ourselves release forgiveness to those who have wronged us Amen.
Matthew 6:12 TPT

The KJV says, "Forgive our debt as we forgive our debtors." Why is sin a debt? Romans 6:23 tells us the wages of sin are death, but the gift of God is eternal life. It implies that when you decide to let sin rule over you, he becomes your master, and the wage he gives you is death.

Christ is the only life-giver—eternal life. If you desire to have His life, He encourages you to choose to let go of your sinful nature and have the mind of Christ (Philippians 2:5). Ask Him to forgive your wrongs, and He will.

He also tells you, His follower, that *"if I have laid my life for you, then you also represent me by forgiving others of their wrongs. By this they will know you are my disciple."* James 13:35.

Forgiving doesn't come easily; if you struggle, ask the Holy Spirit to help you. As you remember how much He forgave you, it will be easy to forgive others. Shalom.

PRAYER

Father, thank you for forgiving me and giving me the grace to forgive in Jesus' name, Amen.

NOVEMBER

Day 325

Lord, I call to you. Come quickly. Listen to me when I call to you. Let my prayer be like incense placed before you, and my praise like the evening sacrifice.
Psalms 141:1-2 NCV

King David was the man after God's heart. His earnest desire was to please God, to be found in Him and to do what He asked. God showed His love to David by the abundance of victories He gave him. And David responded by heeding His voice.

Because of their intimacy, King David often called on God to respond to him quickly, and God did. God deals with you in the measure you respond to His Word. Do you have any urgency in your Spirit when you hear God's word? Do you act quickly?

He continues to ask that His prayers be like incense in the presence of God, implying that his prayers will be established in God's presence. Your praise is a sacrifice in His presence. Keep praying and praising; it is building a memorial in God's presence in Jesus' name. Amen.

PRAYER

Father, let my life be unto you a living sacrifice, pleasing to you my audience of one. Amen.

NOVEMBER

Day 326

The Lord is close to all who call on him, yes, to all who call on him in truth. He grants the desires of those who fear him; he hears their cries for help and rescues them. The Lord protects all those who love him, but he destroys the wicked.
Psalms 145:18-20 NLT

The Lord is your ever-present help in times of need. He knows those who are His and cares for them. The God of the heavens and earth, the maker of the universe, says I am close to ALL who call on me. To everyone who calls me in sincerity, truth, and honesty, I am close.

Notice that He is committed to you coming close when you call because He created you and is responsible. The second verse tells you that He grants the desires of those who fear Him. Your fear of God will qualify you to receive your heart's desire.

Not only that, but He is also sensitive to their cry for help and rescues them. He is Jehovah Sabaoth (Psalm 18:2), the Lord our protector. To those who love Him, He protects but destroys the wicked. The Lord is generous and kind to those who honour Him. Selah.

PRAYER

Father God, keep me close in your shelter, for as I dwell in the shadow of your wings, I will fear no evil and will receive the desires of my heart. Amen.

NOVEMBER

Day 327

You ask [God for something] and do not receive it, because you ask with wrong motives [out of selfishness or with an unrighteous agenda], so that [when you get what you want] you may spend it on your [hedonistic] desires.
James 4:3 AMP

When you cannot provide what you need, it is normal to search or ask from the one you know is capable of providing. You ask because you believe you will receive your desire.

God encourages you to ask Him for your needs. In this passage of scripture, He is showing you why you don't receive what you ask. It's because your motive for asking is wrong. Verse one of James 4 tells us that we fight because of our selfish desires, which are at war within.

These desires are what give birth to your wrong motives, and you act on them. God weighs the motives of the heart (Proverbs 21:2), so He says I will not satisfy that pleasure because it does not glorify me. Neither will it bring any good to you.

PRAYER

Father, create in me a clean heart with the right motives for your glory through Jesus Christ our Lord, Amen.

NOVEMBER

Day 328

First of all, then, I urge that supplications, prayers, intercessions, and thanksgivings be made for everyone, for kings and all who are in high positions, so that we may lead a quiet and peaceable life in all godliness and dignity. This is right and is acceptable in the sight of God our Savior, who desires everyone to be saved and to come to the knowledge of the truth.
1 Timothy 2:1-4 NRSV

The love of God is expressed through you in how you love others. Paul urges us to pray for all men and for people in authority because God desires that everyone be saved.

Not only is salvation important but that we may have a peaceful and quiet life. In prayer, we ask that the will of God be done as it is in heaven, and until someone prays, nothing changes.

For even with people in authority who does not believe in God, God through your prayers can use him/her to do His will and for the good of the people. God is encouraging you to seek Him in prayer not only for yourself but for leaders as well. He will listen and answer. God bless you as you pray.

PRAYER

Father, as I seek you in prayer, may your will be done on earth as it is in heaven. Amen.

NOVEMBER

Worship God

NOVEMBER

Day 329

Lift up a great shout of joy to the Lord! Go ahead and do it- everyone, everywhere! As you serve him, be glad and worship him. Sing your way into his presence with joy! And realize what this really means- we have the privilege of worshipping the Lord our God. For he is our Creator and we belong to him. We are the people of his pleasure. You can pass through his open gates with the password of praise. Come right into his presence with thanksgiving. Come bring your thank offering to him and affectionately bless his beautiful name! For the Lord is always good and ready to receive you. He's so loving that it will amaze you - so kind that it will astound you! And he is famous for his faithfulness toward all. Everyone knows our God can be trusted, for he keeps his promises to every generation!
Psalms 100:1-5 TPT

Sometimes, all you can really and have to do is worship and thank God for everything. Shout with the voice of triumph, make melodies in your heart to the Lord, for He is good, and His mercies endure forever.

What are you thankful for today? What will you praise Him for? What will you worship Him for? He is worthy of it all. Shalom.

PRAYER

My adoration belongs to you alone. Thank you, God.

NOVEMBER

Day 330

I will praise you, Lord, because you rescued me. You did not let my enemies laugh at me. Lord, my God, I prayed to you, and you healed me. You lifted me out of the grave; you spared me from going down to the place of the dead. Sing praises to the Lord, you who belong to him; praise his holy name.
Psalms 30:1-4 NCV

We praise 'because'. In other words, praise is motivated by something. It is easy to praise God when you receive answers to your prayers, when you are healed, or when there is a tangible miracle by the hand of the Lord.

King David tells us why he is praising the Lord. He said it was because the Lord did not allow his enemies to have their way with him. God did not let the enemy triumph or rejoice over him. What has the Lord delivered you from? Have you given Him the praise due Him?

The Lord spared your life from going under the grave. Sing His praise, you who belong to Him. To those the Lamb has redeemed your life from death, praise Him, Shalom.

PRAYER

Abba, I thank you for the past and its victories. I praise you now for what you are doing, and I am grateful for my future, for I know you are taking care of me through Christ our Lord. Amen.

NOVEMBER

Day 331

Give thanks to the Lord and pray to him. Tell the nations what he has done. Sing to him; sing praises to him. Tell about all his miracles. Be glad that you are his; let those who seek the Lord be happy. Depend on the Lord and his strength; always go to him for help. Remember the miracles he has done, his wonders, and his decisions.
1 Chronicles 16:8-12 NCV

It is right and just to give thanks to the Lord my Father and your Father and to pray to Him. To sing His praise for His loving kindness and tender mercies. Who forgives all your transgressions and blots your sins away? Give thanks to the Lord our God.

It is righteous to tell of God's kindness and miracles, to let others know He is a faithful Father. Make your boast in the Lord, be glad you are His, the sheep of His pastures.

Depend on the Lord and the strength, He provides. Lean not on your own understanding. In all your ways as you acknowledge Him. He shall direct your path for His glory in Christ. Remember the Lord's kindness and put Him also in remembrance in all you do. Amen.

PRAYER

Heavenly Father, I am eternally grateful for you being mindful of me and everything that concerns me, Amen.

NOVEMBER

Day 332

So brothers and sisters, since God has shown us great mercy, I beg you to offer your lives as a living sacrifice to him. Your offering must be only for God and pleasing to him, which is the spiritual way for you to worship. Do not be shaped by this world; instead be changed within by a new way of thinking. Then you will be able to decide what God wants for you; you will know what is good and pleasing to him and what is perfect.
Romans 12:1-2 NCV

God's mercies stir us into repentance (Romans 2:3-4). When you accept Him, He desires for you to live for Him. That your life will be a living sacrifice, which you will offer daily to Him. Your life should be an offering, you must be willing to give it to Him, only for Him and pleasing. In that, He calls it your spiritual act of worship.

He shows you the most excellent way. Do not be shaped by the world but instead change the way you think. When you renew your mind with the Word of God, you will be able to decide what God wants from you. You will know what is good, pleasing, and perfect to Him. God wants the best for you; if you align your will under Him, He will keep and manifest all His promises to you. Selah!

PRAYER

Lord, through the help of your Spirit, let me live every aspect of my life for the glory and praise of your name, Amen.

NOVEMBER
Day 333

For the LORD giveth wisdom: out of his mouth cometh knowledge and understanding. He layeth up sound wisdom for the righteous: he is a buckler to them that walk uprightly.
Proverbs 2:6-7 KJV

Wisdom is the right application of knowledge. It is a skill in the art of war, shrewdness (outwitting the enemy. God gives it. He also teaches you knowledge and helps you understand situations.

His wisdom is stored for the upright, those who fear Him. The fear of God is not regarding punishment but respect. When you respect God, paying attention and willing to do as He commands, He becomes your shield and salvation. selah (pause and meditate). Amen.

As a child learns to listen and obey his father's instructions, so His counsel increases with provision and protection. The Lord will never withhold from the upright.

PRAYER

Father, thank you for everything that you have given me that pertain to life and goodliness. Amen.

NOVEMBER

Day 334

Pursue peace with all people, and holiness, without which no one will see the Lord: looking carefully lest anyone fall short of the grace of God; lest any root of bitterness springing up cause trouble, and by this many become defiled.
Hebrews 12:14-15 NKJV

Follow, pursue, seek after eagerly after peace. You cannot be at peace with other people if you do not have peace within you. In other words, you cannot give what you don't have.

Jesus is the peace giver. He is the only one called the Prince of Peace. As we follow Him, we will not only see good things but also live at peace with others. Remember, blessed are the peacemakers, for they will be called children of God (Matthew 5:9).

PRAYER

As you are so I am. Thank you Jesus for being my peace and making me a peace giver Amen.

DECEMBER

God Remembers

DECEMBER

Day 335

But God remembered Noah and all the wild and tame animals with him in the boat. He made a wind blow over the earth, and the water went down. The underground springs stopped flowing, and the clouds in the sky stopped pouring down rain.
Genesis 8:1-2 NCV

Sometimes, pain and uncertainty make you forget how kind and merciful God has been to you. Remember, God is good. He wants you to be reminded that He has remembered you, just like He remembered Noah in the days of the flood. He is eager to cease every raging storm and cause His face to shine on you.

Jeremiah 29:11 says, "For I know the plans I have for you, declares the Lord, plans for welfare and not for evil, to give you a future and a hope." The Manufacturer of a thing has the use of the product in view before he made it. You are not just any product but a being made in God's image and likeness, to function on this earth as a god. He knows when to let the rain, the storm to pass and make road in the desert. Be steadfast in your thanksgiving, change is coming.

PRAYER

My Father, I have confidence in you. Amen.

DECEMBER

Day 336

The Lord has made known his victory, he has revealed his vindication in the sight of the nations. He has remembered his steadfast love and faithfulness to the house of Israel. All the ends of the earth have seen the victory of our God.
Psalms 98:2-3 RSV

The Lord has made known His victory. How? Salvation is of no other than through Jesus Christ. Through the finished work of Christ, we know we are victorious; no matter what comes our way, Jesus has overcome. As He is, so are we on this earth. (1 John 4:17.

This is why it is important to identify and enforce the victories won in Christ in your everyday life, through your confessions of faith and prayer. He remembers His love and faithfulness to His covenant and makes manifest His promises. Every victory in your life is a testament that God can be trusted with keeping His Word. It depends on you to keep your faith in Christ and keep your hope alive. You are remembered. Believe it and thank God for His steadfast love. Amen.

PRAYER

Father, I trust in all your promises. I believe and I receive in Jesus' name. Amen.

DECEMBER

Day 337

It is he who remembered us in our low estate, for his steadfast love endures forever; and rescued us from our foes, for his steadfast love endures forever; he who gives food to all flesh, for his steadfast love endures forever.
Psalms 136:23-25 RSV

Your help is in the name of the Lord. He is the one who remembers you in your weakness. Because His love endures forever, He will remember you. Amen.

The Lord remembers His covenant of love and rescues you from your foes. He will not allow your enemies to triumph over you, for His name's sake. Be courageous and have faith in His Word. He is your provider; Jehovah Jireh is His name. Trust in His providence. Ask Him for your needs, and He will hear and
answer you. You have not recieved because you have not asked. Moreover, if you have asked and have not recieved be certain your motives are right James 4.

PRAYER

Father God, thank you for remembering me in this season. With you leading me, I am more than a conqueror, in Jesus' name. Amen.

DECEMBER

Be Thankful

DECEMBER

Day 338

Then on that day David first appointed that thanksgiving be sung to the Lord by Asaph and his brethren. O give thanks to the Lord, call on his name, make known his deeds among the peoples! Sing to him, sing praises to him, tell of all his wonderful works! Glory in his holy name; let the hearts of those who seek the Lord rejoice! Seek the Lord and his strength, seek his presence continually! Remember the wonderful works that he has done, the wonders he wrought, the judgments he uttered.
1 Chronicles 16:7-12 RSV

When you remember God's goodness, your heart moves peculiarly. King David reminded us to intentionally give thanks to the Lord first in everything.

I encourage you to cultivate a habit of gratitude towards God, praise and make melodies in your heart to Him. God always dwells in the praises of His people, tap into His strength, and praise Him,

PRAYER

Father, I recall the victories and blessings you have brought my way. In this, I give you all glory and honour.
Amen.

DECEMBER

Day 339

Be thankful in all circumstances. This is what God wants from you in your life in union with Christ Jesus.
1 Thessalonians 5:18 GNT

God is a good Father to His children. He is generous and kind. His desire for you is to keep you in perfect peace even in the mist of the storms of life. He is able to use every situation to benefit you as you trust Him with your heart and have faith in His Word.

His Word shows you in this letter to the Thessalonians, who were "appointed to tribulations" (1 Thessalonians 3:3) to give thanks to God in every circumstance. Why? Because unless the Lord allows it concerning His child, it won't happen. And if it does, remember He can work it out in your favour. Isn't that amazing?

Your attitude in every circumstance is as important as how you come out. Have a posture of thanksgiving, God is working on your behalf. This, too, shall pass. Hallelujah, praise God Amen.

PRAYER

Abba, if you gave Jesus up for me. I know you will not let my enemies trump over me. Thank you. Amen.

DECEMBER

Day 340

I will praise the name of God with a song; I will magnify him with thanksgiving. This will please the Lord more than an ox or a bull with horns and hoofs.
Psalms 69:30-31 RSV

The word 'praise' comes from the Latin 'pretium,' meaning price or value, and may be defined generally as an ascription of value or worth. King David, the man after God's heart, reveals to us what pleases God more than sacrifice is praise.

Praising the Lord's name means valuing who He is to you, acknowledging His sovereignty, and agreeing with His Word. This act pleases God.

You have a will, not like angels who are always in His presence and adoring Him. When you choose to praise and magnify Him, it honours Him. He desires your praise more than a sacrifice. Put on your garment of praise and thanksgiving, and let's give Him the glory due His name.

PRAYER

Abba, let my praises rise like a sweet perfume to you. You are worthy of my praise. Hallowed be your name Amen.

DECEMBER
Day 341

The peace that Christ gives is to guide you in the decisions you make; for it is to this peace that God has called you together in the one body. And be thankful. Christ's message in all its richness must live in your hearts. Teach and instruct one another with all wisdom. Sing psalms, hymns, and sacred songs; sing to God with thanksgiving in your hearts. Everything you do or say, then, should be done in the name of the Lord Jesus, as you give thanks through him to God the Father.
Colossians 3:15-17 GNT

Being thankful is a choice which becomes a lifestyle. Show me a grateful person and I will show you a contented person. When you live your life with a thankful attitude, God blesses everything you do and have. He cares for you.

The richness of Christ's message should be alive in our hearts and cause you to be grateful for being a partaker of such grace.

Sing and make melodies in your heart to Him. Also, in everything you say or do, do it in the name of the Lord and as unto Him. Be thankful. Be intentional about being grateful for everything and watch how God turns things around for you.

PRAYER

I cannot name all my blessings, nor can I count them. For everything you have done for me, knowingly and unknowingly, thank you, Abba.

DECEMBER

Day 342

Know that the Lord is God! It is he that made us, and we are his; we are his people, and the sheep of his pasture. Enter his gates with thanksgiving, and his courts with praise! Give thanks to him, bless his name!
Psalms 100:3-4 RSV

Thanksgiving makes way for you to receive God's goodness and provision. As a parent I have a responsibility towards my children. They do not need to ask for things which I know I need to provide. I do so willingly and happily. You are the sheep of God's pastures; His provision is for your benefit. Selah.

The Psalmist understands God's provision so well that he shows you how to tap into His abundance. Enter His gates with Thanksgiving and His presence with praise. Today, why don't you try that? Eliminate all doubts and complaints, and let's give God some praise and thanksgiving. Be intentional with gratitude, focus on how good He is. How He came through for you and I know you would have a lot to be thankful about.

PRAYER

With my hands lifted up, my mouth filled with praise, and a heart of thanksgiving, I will bless you, oh Lord. Thank you, Daddy. I love you, Lord.

DECEMBER
Day 343

The Lord is my strength and my shield; in him my heart trusts; so I am helped, and my heart exults, and with my song I give thanks to him.
Psalms 28:7 RSV

Who strengthens you? Where do you derive your source of strength? Who protects you? In whom does your heart trust? Do you offer Thanksgiving after the help?

It is easy for anyone to say God, but the shocking truth is that our strength and trust is from ourselves. We seek what we can do for ourselves when we need to trust God. There is a vast difference between saying it and truly believing He is your strength.

The Psalmist testifies that the Lord is his strength and his shield. He has learnt to trust and depend on His strength and protection. With this assurance, he admits the Lord helps him, he is happy and thanks the Lord. This should be your attitude, total trust in the help and provision of God, and He will help you. Shalom.

PRAYER

With the Lord help I can do all things. He enables me to thrive in all my ways. Thank you, Lord, for being the strength of my life. Amen.

DECEMBER

Day 344

Make a joyful noise to the Lord, all the lands! Serve the Lord with gladness! Come into his presence with singing! Know that the Lord is God! It is he that made us, and we are his; we are his people, and the sheep of his pasture. Enter his gates with thanksgiving, and his courts with praise! Give thanks to him, bless his name! For the Lord is good; his steadfast love endures forever, and his faithfulness to all generations.
Psalms 100:1-5 RSV

Be intentional about thanking God for His goodness, mercy, kindness, love, and provision. Thank you, Father.

There is nothing He will withhold from those who are grateful to him. May God answer you as you praise and thank Him. Amen.

Celebrate the truth about His nature, that He is faithful and true. A present help. A sustainer and steadfast.

PRAYER

Anytime I felt I could not come true, you always proved to be faithful. Thank you for your steadfast love and faithfulness. Amen.

DECEMBER

Day 345

But thanks be to God! For in union with Christ we are always led by God as prisoners in Christ's victory procession. God uses us to make the knowledge about Christ spread everywhere like a sweet fragrance.
2 Corinthians 2:14 GNT

You are not made by God to live in isolation from Him. He calls you His body and gave you a part to play through the gifts He gave. You are to serve one another in love. Your victory in this life is assured with your union with Christ.

Like a prisoner, you trust the leading of the Holy Spirit to lead you in the path that glorifies God. He will use the knowledge of Christ to be a sweet fragrance everywhere for your benefit. In your union with Christ, you are always led. *"Both riches and honor come from You, and You are the ruler over all. Power and might are in Your hand..."* 1 Chronicles 29:12.

What a priviledge to be a child of God, having riches and honour following you, power and might at your disposal halleluyah, God be praised. you are the blessed of the Lord.

PRAYER

Thank you Father God, for making me part of Christ and giving me an inheritance among the saints. Thank you for always leading me. Amen.

DECEMBER

Day 346

How wonderful are the good things you keep for those who honor you! Everyone knows how good you are, how securely you protect those who trust you. You hide them in the safety of your presence from the plots of others; in a safe shelter you hide them from the insults of their enemies.
Psalm 31:19-20 GNT

The Lord's secret is with those who fear him (Psalm 25:15). With them, He reveals who He is. He keeps wonderful things for them. He satisfies their lives with goodness, their paths drip with fatness. The TPT translation calls it a treasure chest. Honour the Lord; He will not withhold excellency from you.

"The Lord is a jealous God," Exodus 34:14. He securely protects His own. As you trust Him and His leading, though the enemy will come like a flood. His Spirit will raise a standard against it. You are His redeemed. Bought by the blood of the lamb.

But His safety is in His presence. Psalm 91 tells us that those who dwell in the secret place of God shall abide under the shadow of the Almighty. As you dwell with Him, you are safe under His wings. Selah.

PRAYER

There is safety with you that you may be feared. Thank you for being everything to me Amen.

DECEMBER

Day 347

Then it came to pass that when the trumpeters and singers joined as one to extol and praise Adonai, and when the sound of the trumpets, cymbals and musical instruments and the praise of Adonai –"For He is good, for His mercy endures forever"-grew louder, the Temple, the House of Adonai, was filled with a cloud. The kohanim could not stand to minister because of the cloud, for the glory of Adonai filled the House of God.
2 Chronicles 5:13-14 TLV

There is something about the glory of God. When it is in a place you cannot delay it. It is the manifestation of the presence of Adonai in a place. Worship brings the glory of the Lord. God inhabits in the praises of His people. (Psalm 22:3).

Scriptures say in Hebrews 4:11, *"Let us labour to enter His rest."* The presence of God is the rest of God. As you worship the I Am and give Him the praise due to His name, He magnifies Himself in anything that concerns you. The verse says the priest could not continue to minister because of the cloud. When His glory comes, your struggles will disappear. Labour to enter His rest. Selah.

PRAYER

As I enter into your presence, I enter into your rest Lord. I am confident you inhabit in my praise, Amen.

DECEMBER

Day 348

Praise the Lord, my soul! All my being, praise his holy name! Praise the Lord, my soul, and do not forget how kind he is. He forgives all my sins and heals all my diseases. He keeps me from the grave and blesses me with love and mercy. He fills my life with good things, so that I stay young and strong like an eagle.
Psalm 103:1-5 GNT

The mouth speaks out of the abundance of the heart. What is in a person's heart is what comes out. When you think and meditate on God's kindness, you will not cease to praise Him. His love, forgiveness, and long-suffering lead us to repentance.

He heals you of all your diseases. Praise Him. He keeps your soul from going astray. Praise Him, for He is kind and merciful.

He blesses you with love and mercy and fills your life with good things. He makes you strong like the eagle. Praise the name of the Lord. Hallelujah, Amen.

PRAYER

When I think about your goodness and faithfulness each day, my heart is swallowed up in gratitude. Amen.

DECEMBER

Day 349

The Lord saved me from death; he stopped my tears and kept me from defeat. And so I walk in the presence of the Lord in the world of the living. I kept on believing, even when I said, "I am completely crushed," even when I was afraid and said, "No one can be trusted." What can I offer the Lord for all his goodness to me?
Psalm 116:8-12 GNT

The Lord's salvation is available to all. Accept Jesus Christ as your Lord and Savior. He is the only one who can deliver your soul from death and give you eternal life, peace, and joy in the Holy Ghost. Amen.

When the Lord saves you, He cleans you up and keeps you from defeat. Yours is to renew your mind with the Word of the Lord and walk in His presence. He makes all things beautiful in their time. (Ecclesiastes 3:11).

The Lord has saved you to bring you into His kingdom, reconciling you back to Himself as He originally intended. Give Him thanks and praise for His mercy. You were once afar off, but through Jesus, you are near. Amen.

PRAYER

Thank you, Father, for Jesus. Because of Him, I live a life of favour. Amen.

DECEMBER

Day 350

Give thanks to the Lord, because he is good, and his love is eternal. In my distress I called to the Lord; he answered me and set me free. The Lord is with me; I will not be afraid; what can anyone do to me? It is the Lord who helps me, and I will see my enemies defeated. It is better to trust in the Lord than to depend on people. It is better to trust in the Lord than to depend on human leaders. Many enemies were around me; but I destroyed them by the power of the Lord!
Psalm 118:1, 5-10 GNT

God is from everlasting to everlasting. You can depend on Him. His love for you is eternal. He is good and kind. Giving thanks to God gives you access to the dimensions of Him. A grateful person will receive gracious abundance from God. He is that good.

When you know and believe that the Lord is with you, you will not be afraid. He is your mighty man in battle. He has already defeated His enemies. Yours is to believe in Him and walk in His council.

You are on the Lord's side. Walk in victory Amen.

PRAYER

I praise you Lord, because you are sovereign, faithful, and true. I trust in your unfailing love and strength. Amen.

DECEMBER

Day 351

Protect me, O God; I trust in you for safety. I say to the Lord, "You are my Lord; all the good things I have come from you." How excellent are the Lord's faithful people! My greatest pleasure is to be with them. Those who rush to other gods bring many troubles on themselves. I will not take part in their sacrifices; I will not worship their gods. You, Lord, are all I have, and you give me all I need; my future is in your hands. How wonderful are your gifts to me; how good they are! Psalm 16:1-6 GNT

During seasons like this, who do you trust for your safety? Who do you believe to provide your provision and sustenance? How excellent is the Lord's faithfulness to all who are His? If He provides for the birds of the air, He shall surely provide for you. Those who worship other gods forsake their own mercy Jonah 2:8.

Only God is good, (Mark 10:18 . He gives wonderful gifts, most importantly eternal life. Accept Jesus as your Lord and
His gift of salvation and if you already have Him, always remember to seek His will in all your ways for as you acknowledge Him in all your ways, He shall direct your path.
Amen.

PRAYER

I will worship no other foreign god or treasure. My heart desires to worship you, the one true God. Amen.

DECEMBER

Day 352

Praise the Lord, for the Lord is good; sing to his name, for he is gracious! For I know that the Lord is great, and that our Lord is above all gods. Whatever the Lord pleases he does, in heaven and on earth, in the seas and all deeps. He it is who makes the clouds rise at the end of the earth, who makes lightning for the rain and brings forth the wind from his storehouses.
Psalms 135:3, 5-7 GNT

Praise is a powerful tool of warfare. Remembrance empowers thanksgiving. It is one of the streams through which praise flows. When you praise you magnify the presence of God in your circumstances. Put your praise on and watch God conquer your challenges.

The Lord controls the heavens and the earth, but He has given us the authority to represent Him. As we lift Him up high, He draws men to Himself and rearranges things for your favour.

God is sovereign and in charge, remember His past victories for you and know He is able to keep you in perfect peace. Praise Him. Selah.

PRAYER

Lord, I remember the victories you gave me. I have done valiantly through you. My praise will continually be to you.
Amen.

DECEMBER

Day 353

We give thanks to you, O God, we give thanks to you! We proclaim how great you are and tell of the wonderful things you have done. "I have set a time for judgment," says God, "and I will judge with fairness. Though every living creature tremble and the earth itself be shaken, I will keep its foundations firm. I tell the wicked not to be arrogant; I tell them to stop their boasting." Judgment does not come from the East or from the West, from the North or from the South; it is God who is the judge, condemning some and acquitting others. The Lord holds a cup in his hand, filled with the strong wine of his anger. He pours it out, and all the wicked drink it; they drink it down to the last drop. But I will never stop speaking of the God of Jacob or singing praises to him. He will break the power of the wicked, but the power of the righteous will be increased.
Psalm 75:1-10 GNT

Sometimes, it is important and relevant to listen to what God is saying now. Can you hear His heart? He is the judge, and He has set a time for judgment. Jesus is coming back soon.

Give thanks and praise to His name. He increases the power of the righteous but breaks the power of the wicked. Selah. May He teach your hearts to seek Him daily, humbling yourselves under His mighty hands.

PRAYER

As I prepare for your coming again, Lord Jesus, help me to live for your glory. Amen.

DECEMBER

Seek God

DECEMBER

Day 354

As a deer longs for a stream of cool water, so I long for you, O God. I thirst for you, the living God. When can I go and worship in your presence? Day and night I cry, and tears are my only food; all the time my enemies ask me, "Where is your God?" My heart breaks when I remember the past, when I went with the crowds to the house of God and led them as they walked along, a happy crowd, singing and shouting praise to God. Why am I so sad? Why am I so troubled? I will put my hope in God, and once again I will praise him, my savior and my God. May the Lord show his constant love during the day, so that I may have a song at night, a prayer to the God of my life.
Psalm 42:1-5, 8 GNT

Why are you sad oh my soul? I shall yet hope in the Lord my salvation. If He did it before, He will do it again. The same God yesterday, today and forever is my God. A present help in time of need. Some trust in their war chariots and others in their horses, but we trust in the power of the LORD our God. (Psalm 20:7 GNT).

The uncertainties of life is what gives you the measure of what is certain. The rain is what makes you appreciate joy. Hunger makes you want to be filled. Without the bad, the good can never be known and appreciated, without darkness light can never shine brighter. Tell your soul hope thou in the Lord.

PRAYER

I trust you, oh Lord, my strength and salvation. You did it before; I know you will do it again. Amen.

DECEMBER

Day 355

And as they ministered to the Lord, and fasted, the Holy Ghost said, separate me Barnabas and Saul for the work whereunto I have called them. Then, when they had fasted and prayed and laid their hands on them, they sent them away. So they, being sent forth by the Holy Ghost, went down to Seleucia; and from thence they sailed to Cyprus. And when they were at Salamis, they proclaimed the word of God in the synagogues of the Jews: and they had also John as their attendant.
Acts 13:2-5 RV1895

Nobody goes to the real presence of God and comes back the same. The Book of Revelations tells us that the glory and splendour of the Lord are such that you can only worship and bow yourself as the twenty-four elders do with the angels and host of heaven. When you encounter the glory of God, there is direction and grace that equips you.

God is the speaking God. Train your spirit with the word of God to know His voice. He doesn't speak outside of His written word. After He gives you direction, He empowers you to act and release grace that equips you for the provision. You are not without. Amen.

PRAYER

Father God, yours is the kingdom, power and glory. With you, I will lack nothing. Amen.

DECEMBER
Day 356

I will tell of the decree of the Lord: He said to me, "You are my son, today I have begotten you. Ask of me, and I will make the nations your heritage, and the ends of the earth your possession.
Psalms 2:7-8 RSV

But to all who did receive Him, to those who believed in His name, He gave the right to become children of God (John 1:2). Romans 8:14: *"For all who are led by the Spirit of God are sons of God."*

Romans 8:16: "The Spirit Himself testifies with our spirit that we are God's children." Galatians 3:26 adds, "You are all sons of God through faith in Christ Jesus."

Are you a son of God? Have you received Him? Do you believe in His name? Are you led by the Spirit of God? Does His Spirit testify with your Spirit?

If you can answer these yes, then the Word of God says, ask of me and I will make the nations your inheritance and the ends of the earth your possession. Hallelujah, praise God Amen.

PRAYER

Heavenly Father, you are a good God. As I ask (your request) in Jesus' name, I know I have received what I asked for. Amen.

DECEMBER

Christ Came

DECEMBER
Day 357

A child is born to us! A son is given to us! And he will be our ruler. He will be called, "Wonderful Counselor," "Mighty God," "Eternal Father," "Prince of Peace." His royal power will continue to grow; his kingdom will always be at peace. He will rule as King David's successor, basing his power on right and justice, from now until the end of time. The Lord Almighty is determined to do all this.
Isaiah 9:6-7 GNT

Many years ago, God fulfilled His Word by sending His Son to be born of a woman on earth. The child Jesus was no ordinary man; He was the Son of Adonai, the one who was from the beginning. He was the one through Whom the world was created. John 1 says He is the Word of God.

He is a wonderful counsellor, Mighty God, Eternal Father, Prince of Peace. He is God. When you see Him, Jesus, you see the Father (John 14:9). This is why we celebrate Christmas, the birth of a fulfilled promise. It gives us hope for the future in a God you can trust.

Whatever He has promised you, keep faith alive, if He didn't spare His Son but gave Him for you, He will not withhold any good from you. Merry Christmas.

PRAYER

Thank you, Father, for giving us your son Jesus. I am eternally grateful. Amen.

DECEMBER

Day 358

An angel of the Lord appeared to them, and the glory of the Lord shone over them. They were terribly afraid, but the angel said to them, "Don't be afraid! I am here with good news for you, which will bring great joy to all the people. This very day in David's town your Savior was born-Christ the Lord! And this is what will prove it to you: you will find a baby wrapped in cloths and lying in a manger." Suddenly a great army of heaven's angels appeared with the angel, singing praises to God: "Glory to God in the highest heaven, and peace on earth to those with whom he is pleased!" Luke 2:9-14 GNT

The Angels announced the birth of our Saviour. When the Word of the Lord comes, it executes the angels to action. They manifest with the glory of the Lord. Don't be afraid. Emmanuel, God is with you.

When Jesus comes into every situation it is good news. His presence brings peace. He is the Saviour of the world. He is our prince of peace. Invite Him into your life and well-being, He will see you through. Christ is Lord. Jesus is the reason for this season.

Psalm 103:20-21, Angels excel in strength as they do the will of God, you also are blessed as you do His will. Angels are willing and obedient waiting to act. Understand and believe Emmanuel (meaning God is with us) is with you, Amen.

PRAYER

When I call on Jesus, all things are possible. For unto me, a child was born. His name is Emmanuel; God with me. Amen.

DECEMBER
Day 359

And it came to pass, while they were there, the days were fulfilled that she should be delivered. And she brought forth her firstborn son; and she wrapped him in swaddling clothes, and laid him in a manger, because there was no room for them in the inn.
Luke 2:6-7 RV1885

And it came to pass. What did? The fullness of time, God's Word, the prophecy of a virgin birth, the promise of Messiah. Every word of God's spoken to you will come to pass. While you live, your day will be fulfilled.

Mary's first child was born in a foreign land in a manger. The place of promise does not always look promising or anything like the end God shows you. But as you trust and obey, you will see the manifestation of His word.

God provides for His vision and purpose. Don't worry about what you eat or put on. Seek Him and His direction; He will sustain you and your purpose. Shalom.

PRAYER

I might not look like my promise, but I serve a God who does marvellous things. Thank you, Father, for Jesus. All your promises are true, Amen.

DECEMBER

Day 360

This was how the birth of Jesus Christ took place. His mother Mary was engaged to Joseph, but before they were married, she found out that she was going to have a baby by the Holy Spirit. Joseph was a man who always did what was right, but he did not want to disgrace Mary publicly; so he made plans to break the engagement privately.
Matthew 1:18-19 GNT

One of the most complicated challenges surrounding a birth happened to Jesus. The period from the time the Angel announced the favour on Mary to when she gave birth to the Savior to His death was memorable.

Sometimes, when you feel your life is full of ups and downs, read the stories about Jesus's life and be encouraged.

The Holy One, the Son of God, was not excused from the complications of life on earth. But with God, He will work all for your good for His glory.

When the situation is challenging, position yourself under the mighty hand of God, have faith in Him and SURRENDER your will. He will turn it around. Shalom.

PRAYER

To the one who sustains the universe by the Word of His power, I trust you with my life. Amen.

DECEMBER
Day 361

But when he thought on these things, behold, an angel of the Lord appeared unto him in a dream, saying, Joseph, thou son of David, fear not to take unto thee Mary thy wife: for that which is conceived in her is of the Holy Ghost. And she shall bring forth a son; and thou shalt call his name JESUS; for it is he that shall save his people from their sins.
Matthew 1:20-21 RV1895

It is our thought process that distinguishes us as human beings. The ability to know right from wrong, the capability to communicate spiritually and download heavenly communications like dreams.

God is interested in your thoughts because your thoughts define your actions. In the coming year I pray that you will allow the Holy Spirit to lead and guide your decisions in Jesus' name, Amen.

Plan according to the word of God. Faith will arise in you as the Holy Spirit empowers you. He will cause you to act. He is the wind beneath God's Word. He will bring His word alive in your natural situation.

PRAYER

Holy Spirit, promise of the Father, be my helper and leader, guide me in the way that pleases the Father, and help me to obey you always. Amen.

DECEMBER

Day 362

All this took place to fulfil what the Lord had spoken by the prophet: "Behold, a virgin shall conceive and bear a son, and his name shall be called Emmanu-el" (which means, God with us). When Joseph woke from sleep, he did as the angel of the Lord commanded him; he took his wife, but knew her not until she had borne a son; and he called his name Jesus.
Matthew 1:22-25 RSV

God works in seasons and times. He works in time but is not bound by time. From everlasting to everlasting, He is the one true God. He was, is and is to come. His Words and promises are yes and Amen in Christ Jesus. Selah.

God watches over His word to manifest it, as long as you live in obedience to His word. Deuteronomy 30:19 tells you God has set life and death before you, as you choose to obey Him you shall eat the good of the land.

Jesus is our Lord, His life is a picture of the life God has designed for us to live, a victorious life. If His birth was prophesied years before fulfilment, yours will come to pass in Jesus' name Amen. Have faith and be patient. Patients builds your stature like Christ and refines you to be the vessel worthy of the blessing.

PRAYER

Lord, I receive of you patient endurance for your promise over my life in Jesus name, Amen.

DECEMBER

Day 363

"Where is he who has been born king of the Jews? For we have seen his star in the East, and have come to worship him." When they had heard the king they went their way; and lo, the star which they had seen in the East went before them, till it came to rest over the place where the child was. When they saw the star, they rejoiced exceedingly with great joy; and going into the house they saw the child with Mary his mother, and they fell down and worshiped him. Then, opening their treasures, they offered him gifts, gold and frankincense and myrrh.
Matthew 2:2-11 RSV

You have a star. That star in the spirit collated with your purpose and gift God has divinely put in you. Your star is designed to attract and lead seekers of your gift to you. A man's gift will make room for him and bring him before great men Psalm 18:16. You are no exception.

Jesus is our example. The things you desire are in your ability to use the gifts and talents God has given you. That will cause men to seek after your star and bless you.

In the new year, seek above all to walk with the Holy Spirit. Wait on Him, He will cloth you with power to do the will of God. You can only please God through obedience.

PRAYER

Father, thank you for the spirit of obedience to use what you have given me so that you can increase my capacity for more in Jesus' name, Amen.

DECEMBER

Day 364

"Keep alert and pray. Otherwise temptation will overpower you. For the spirit indeed is willing, but how weak the body is!"
Matthew 26:40-41 TLB

Mark 14:38 NLT says "Keep watch and pray, so that you will not give in to temptation. For the spirit is willing, but the body is weak." Luke 21:36 also tells us to watch and pray so that we don't enter into temptation.

When you pray, one of the things that is released against the spirit of prayer is the spirit of temptation and distraction. It comes in different forms. Be discerning. Jesus prayed and fasted 40 days, after He was led to be tempted of the devil. What prayer does is revealing self-motives and anything that can hinder the move of God in your life. Be sensitive to what happens around you after you have prayed. Be alert. most times we fall into

temptation not because the enemy is stronger but becuase we fail to understand the potency of what we are asking God for. What you need is already available, the enemy only needs to disqualify and discourage you from recieving

PRAYER

Holy Spirit, increase my awareness in the things I need to deal with as I pray in Jesus' name Amen.

DECEMBER

Day 365

O LORD my God, you have performed many wonders for us. Your plans for us are too numerous to list. You have no equal. If I tried to recite all your wonderful deeds, I would never come to the end of them.
Psalm 40:5 NLT

As the year comes to an end, I encourage you to take time and reflect on the kindness, goodness, and miracles God has done in your life. Count your blessings and if you can name them, I believe you will be so surprised by how good God has been to you and all that concerns you. His kindness always outweighs our sins.

Not only has He been generous in the past, but He is also reminding you that He has great plans for your future. Would you trust Him? His ways are not your ways; He makes all things beautiful in their time. Keep hope alive, and your heart set on Him, only believe. Never stop having a grateful heart. choose to see the good in everything, choose to be the one to bring and make peace , choose to be the god people see. Amen.

PRAYER

Thank you LORD my Father for giving me Jesus and Your Holy Spirit. Thank you for the countless testimonies. I am grateful. Thank you for Angels around me always Amen.

About the Author

Rhoda Obiri Yeboah is the founder of Reel Of Hope Ministry. A God lover, wife, mother and a minister. Rhoda's love and fellowship with the Lord is felt in her writings and her ability to relate it to our everyday life.

She has certificates in BA (Hons), Human Resources. Studied Health and Social Care, Business Administration, Mental health, Counselling, Innovation and enterprise, IAG and Bible College at International Bible Institute of London (IBIOL). Her ministry and resources have transformed many across the globe. Her first book, *Into the Deep*, transformed people's perspective of how God delights in His children. Her depth and understanding of the Word of God are ardent and deep-seated. She is a must-read.

Printed in Great Britain
by Amazon